Is This Working?

Is This Working?

The Jobs We Do, Told by the
People Who Do Them

Charlie Colenutt

PICADOR

First published 2025 by Picador
an imprint of Pan Macmillan
The Smithson, 6 Briset Street, London EC1M 5NR
EU representative: Macmillan Publishers Ireland Ltd, 1st Floor,
The Liffey Trust Centre, 117–126 Sheriff Street Upper,
Dublin 1, D01 YC43
Associated companies throughout the world
www.panmacmillan.com

ISBN 978-1-0350-1504-7 HB

9 8 7 6 5 4 3 2 1

A CIP catalogue record for this book is available from the British Library.

Typeset in Warnock Pro by Palimpsest Book Production Limited, Falkirk, Stirlingshire
Printed and bound by CPI Group (UK) Ltd, Croydon, CR0 4YY

Visit **www.picador.com** to read more about all our books
and to buy them. You will also find features, author interviews and
news of any author events, and you can sign up for e-newsletters
so that you're always first to hear about our new releases.

To Annie and Iris, whom I love.

Contents

Introduction

Between 2021 and 2023, I talked to a hundred strangers, from all walks of life, about their jobs. They talked to me in coffee shops and chain pubs and kitchens and front rooms, on the phone and by video call. We spoke about what work meant to them: *What did they do for a living? Why did they do it? And did they like it?* The stories in this book are taken from those conversations.

Sometimes the person sitting opposite me spoke with a candour that turned a Wetherspoons' corner booth into a confessional. At other times – as was their right – the interviewees were reserved, protecting their true feelings about work through reliable deflections. They would speak to me as if they were in a job interview, hiding their memories beneath corporate jargon, that language of *challenges faced* and *solutions found*. Or they would tell me funny anecdotes instead of talking about themselves. Toolboxes screwed into floors; students caught with bongs made out of barrels.

In finding people to talk to, I tried to pick interviewees who would together resemble a scale model of the British population – fairly typical in the jobs that they did, fairly typical in the places that they lived, in their age, their gender, their immigration status and ethnicity. But, as is so often the case, the scale model never looks quite the same as the real thing: when you miniaturize, you sacrifice detail, you take short-cuts. It is no different here. In the selection of sixty-eight interviews that I have included, demographics and jobs are, by turns, over-represented and under-represented. Take comfort from the fact that this book is not a work of social science. There is no empiricism to be found here. It's just people talking about their jobs.

Nor is this book a piece of journalism. I have no real idea about the truth of what my interviewees tell me. These are unconfirmed reports from unreliable sources. To ask someone – as I often did – to *'Tell me the story of your working life'*, is to give that person freedom to choose a version of their life's work to tell. That freedom is double-edged. It makes the subject more relaxed, but it also leaves interview transcripts understandably marked by self-presentation and myth. Instead, if there is any firm truth to be found in these pages, it is in the way that these accounts of working life chime with the reader's own experiences of work.

Before the strangers begin to talk, perhaps we should take a moment and put the conversations into context. What can we say, in general terms, about work in Britain? What does the scale model look like?

There are things that we already know. We know, for instance, that the UK is a post-industrial society. The statistics say so: in 1970, some 8.6 million people, from a population of fifty-five million, were employed in the production sector (manufacturing, resource extraction, and utilities). By 2016, this had fallen to three million, out of a population of sixty-five million.[1]

The recent histories of once-powerful British manufacturing interests say so: in 1984, Imperial Chemical Industries (ICI) was the first British company to turn a profit of over £1 billion. At that time, it employed 130,000 people in the production of fertilizers, drugs, synthetic fabrics, solvents, plastics, paints, explosives, and just about every other industrial chemical that you can imagine (and many that

1 'Changes in the economy since the 1970s', *Office for National Statistics* (last modified 2 September 2019), https://www.ons.gov.uk/economy/econo-micoutputandproductivity/output/articles/changesintheeconomysincethe1970s/2019–09–02, accessed 3 September 2024.

you can't). Out of ICI's laboratories came Perspex, beta-blockers, and tens of thousands of other patents.

However, by the mid-2000s, everything had changed. ICI had sold off its pharmaceuticals arm, many of its industrial chemical divisions, and its prized intellectual property. It used the proceeds of these sales to reposition itself as a fashionable maker of paints and perfumes. This did not work. In 2008, the conglomerate was broken up and sold, principally to AkzoNobel, a Dutch chemicals group. Factory closures and thousands of redundancies followed.

ICI's death, and the twenty years of chemical asset sales that preceded it, caused no great consternation or political crisis. By 2008, the selling off and winding down of British industry had come to be accepted as a natural part of life, like the death of a distant and elderly relative – something to be met with only a passing sadness. Little has changed since then. Britain has de-industrialized in fact and in spirit. And so, it won't surprise you to hear that there is very little of the old industrial world in the interviews that follow. The people I spoke to were not miners and factory workers, but their sons, daughters and grandchildren. And where do they work? They work, of course, in what economists call *the services economy*.

Eighty-five per cent of us now work in services, along with most of the interviewees in this book. If goods are tangible, services are not, and so *services work* refers to those jobs that produce intangible products: the teacher, the nurse, and the sales representative; the supermarket colleague, the therapist, and the call centre worker; the nursery worker, the childminder, and the HR business partner; the carer, the security guard, and the data analyst; the accountant, the lawyer, and the cam girl. It is a broad and vague category.

The breadth of the concept obscures our view. When we sweep so many jobs into a single category, we understate the differences between them. There are, for instance, differences in pay and status. Consider the trader in an investment bank and the call centre worker. Both spend their days looking at a screen and talking on the phone, all the while feeling stressed, but in return for their efforts, the trader gets a lot more back in money and status than the call centre worker.

The tasks involved in different services jobs also vary significantly. To some, the idea of the *services economy* brings to mind the knowledge economy of London – an economy of finance, consultancy, law, software, and advertising. In fact, millions of the services jobs that people do in this country are physical ones, where the body is an equal partner to the head and the hands. The carer who hoists a patient six times a day is providing services under his agency contract. So too are the delivery riders charging about the cities, and the workers in a children's home, who might spend several hours of a night shift restraining children ('*One of the kids we looked after, the psychologist said that they needed a minimum of two hours of restraint*'). This is work far removed from the laptop.

And yet, for all its distracting vagueness, the sweeping idea of the *services economy* contains at least one good insight. It captures something of the growing sameness of modern work. The more I spoke to people, the more I heard, again and again, the same refrain: too much of the working day is taken up by a kind of administrative shadow work.

The paperwork has got so much stickier over the years.
– Childminder

It's another hat that teachers wear I suppose: we're administrators. – Secondary school teacher

An awful lot of ministry today is like being an administrator, a pastoral administrator. – Minister

I feel like a box ticker. – Job Centre work coach

In this way, jobs that once looked very different are coming to resemble one another. Yes, some tasks might be different, but the several hours a day of email-writing, note-taking, policy-checking, and data-entry are the same. And it is this that binds together the services concept.

At this point, I should declare my interests. I was brought up to be a creature of London's knowledge economy. I studied history and then law. The pandemic arrived at the end of my studies and at the beginning of my legal career. I spent a year doing pupillage in a lockdown-emptied barristers' chambers. The work involved reading long PDFs and writing long Word documents. Sometimes I would stare at these documents in a South London flat. Sometimes I would stare at them in a mostly empty office. And sometimes I would stare at these documents in my dreams. I became very unhappy – lonely, probably.

I came to feel that the pandemic had poured acid onto my job. It had stripped away the layers of paint and decoration – the status, the sense of apprenticeship and camaraderie, the many rituals of office life – leaving only the bare metal structure of work underneath. When faced with this stripped reality, I could not cope, and I decided to leave law.

A few years before, I had read a book by Studs Terkel, the great American broadcaster and oral historian, called *Working: People Talk About What They Do All Day and How They Feel About What They Do* (1974). In it, Terkel gathered over a hundred monologues of Americans talking about their jobs. They are a window into a different, industrial world. You hear the voices of steelworkers ('*Strictly muscle work*'), deep miners and strip miners ('*I don't dig coal. I take the dirt off coal*') and welders on car production lines ('*I bet there's men who have lived and died out there, and never seen the end of that line*').

When I first read Terkel's interviews, I thought that someone should repeat his experiment in today's changed world. Leaving law reanimated the idea. After a time, I realized that I could be the one to do it. Why not? I had no job, no mortgage, no children, some savings from working as a lawyer, and a background in history. It might even be helpful for getting on in my career, whatever that was going to be.

What if I spoke to someone who showed me what I should be doing with my life? Strung along by such happy delusions, I went for it. I moved out of London. I bought a tape recorder and a van. And I began driving up and down the country, to and from interviews.

As I write this introduction, it is two-and-a-half years since my first interview, an afternoon spent talking to a postman in a seaside town. In that time, the reasons for repeating Terkel's experiment have become more persuasive.

Terkel conducted his interviews in the early 1970s, just as a series of shocks had begun to upend the economies of the industrialized west. The unspooling of Bretton Woods and the international monetary system, the Yom Kippur war, spiking oil prices, spiralling inflation, high interest rates, state retrenchment, de-industrialization. Fifteen years of shock after shock after shock. And, at the end of it all, the world in which Terkel's interviewees once worked had come to look very different; less industrial, more concerned with consumption; a world of shopping centres, not factories.

Fifty years on and it is hard to escape the feeling that the world is once again on the turn. A new wave of shocks has hit the global economy. Some – war and inflation – are similar to those of the 1970s. Others are different: a pandemic, a new politics of climate change, and the emergence of artificial intelligence (AI) systems that are said to threaten hundreds of millions of jobs. We cannot yet know what long-term effect these shocks will have on the British economy. But if – like the US economy of the early 1970s – everything is about to change, then it is surely worth pausing for a moment; pausing to listen, and to attempt to record what it was like to live and work in the early 2020s.

For my part, since that first conversation, it has been two-and-a-half years of interviewing and transcribing and editing, partially interrupted by other work – in a software company and on building sites – and joyfully interrupted by the arrival of my daughter. Today, reading back through the interviews, I can see how much I have learned from them. The strange details come rushing back. The number of birds killed a day in a poultry factory. The order in which patients are woken up in care homes. The reasons why you shouldn't smile when you are shown your bonus in an investment bank. The jokes told in warehouses and on building sites. The many filing cabinets filled with paperwork in the childminder's attic. In all these details, the interviews have taught me about life, and the ways in which our work can at once diminish us and magnify us. But perhaps that is putting it too strongly. After all, it's just people talking about their jobs.

CHAPTER ONE **BODYWORK**

Panel beater

warehouse worker

sex worker

security guard

Panel beater

30s

I don't want my kids to be where I am. I'll be dead at fifty because of what I inhale. You see the dust when the sun shines in. You can have all the extractor fans you want, but you're breathing that in. Even when I go on holiday, I sit there wheezing. I'm thirty-five years old. The sooner I get out of it the better. But people are put on this planet for a reason and I think mine is panel beating. I don't think anything else would have given me the opportunities that I've got doing this job . . .

I was at an inner-city school, a shithole. I got expelled for putting potassium in a fish tank. It was stupid, really. I was showing off.

They had a tropical fish tank in the science building. Potassium and water. It was the only bit of science I knew. I threw some potassium in the tank and it went off [he makes a roaring sound].

I thought, *I'm done for.* The teacher's gonna come back. *Please fish, don't die.*

Twenty seconds later, all the fish sank to the bottom. They didn't float to the top.

I thought, *no no no.*

I'm not proud of this.

After I left school, I didn't have any idea what I wanted to do. I had no grades. My friends didn't have anything about them. They were getting into crimes and whatnot. I wanted to be a chav or to go in the army or something. I didn't have any idea. I knew I didn't want to go to prison.

At sixteen I got a bit of a break. I applied for a panel beating job and I lied, '*Oh yes, I've got these grades*.'

And the boss, my old boss, saw something in me. He gave me an opportunity and thank God he did because I don't know what I'd be doing now otherwise.

I was surprised I got the job but I suppose the majority in this trade are deadbeats from school. Nobody leaves school thinking, *I'm going to be a panel beater*.

When I was seventeen, eighteen, I was coming into work late, I was coming in hungover, I was coming in half-cut sometimes.

One day I got arrested and I was walking back home down a dual carriageway. My boss caught me up and I got in his car. He looked at me and he didn't say a word to me. He just dropped me home. It killed me.

He sat me down later and said, '*You're at a crossroads. Carry on up this road and you'll end up in jail. Turn a corner now and you've got something, you can make something of your life*.'

It always sticks with me. It flipped a switch in me. I got my head down. He gave me a pay rise and the opportunity to earn a bonus and I kept on working and working and working.

I do things methodically.

I do things right. I'm quite passionate about that.

I used to watch how people did stuff on YouTube. I became obsessed with the job. *I'm gonna try doing it this way and I won't tell anyone*. It would pay off. I'd do a job and think, *this is all right, innit?* I was nineteen years old, and I was better than the guys teaching me.

One day my boss said, '*I'm going to enter you into a panel beating competition*.'

I said no because my ex-girlfriend was very controlling, and I knew it would cause issue after issue. He entered me anyway. It was a national panel beating competition.

The judges turned up and watched me work.

I ended up going down to a Toyota factory to do an examination. First, we had to make a sill panel, show our welds on it, do a metal finish with no body filler – all with people watching over everything you're doing.

Then we had to do some jig work for chassis that are bent. That's the kind of work I loved, the big stuff.

At the end they said, '*Third place . . . second place . .*'

I thought, *ach I've not even placed here.*

Then they said my name for first place. *What?* I was over the moon. It was probably one of the proudest moments of my life.

I flew first-class to Japan, and they had a massive ceremony at the Toyota City factory.

It was how they made you feel – like I'd made something of my life. The people I met in Japan, pride in their work radiated from them. It made me think, *I want to go back home and do what they've done there.*

With Toyota, they'd show you why you were doing things, the benefits of doing them, and the consequences of not doing them. At other places they'd say, '*Do this*' or '*Do that*', and I'd think, *but why are you doing that?*

There's not enough of us in this industry, in this country, that are like that. I don't think people understand the consequences of getting things wrong. Even if the car you're working on is a shithole, that could be someone's mum in there. Think about it like that.

But people don't and it absolutely infuriates me. '*That'll do*', they say, or '*I'll just leave that weld off because it's already been painted*.'

After getting back from Japan, I went back to where I lived, and it was like a time warp. Everyone's still the same, walking round in tracksuit bottoms and smoking weed. I've never felt so lucky in my life to have been given an opportunity like that.

It's got a stigma, the motor trade, of grease monkeys under the arches, of cars getting bunged together – and to be fair I've seen a lot of cowboys.

At one of the garages I worked in, you had people that weren't doing the job properly. They had eight panel beaters, and they couldn't cut any more corners if they tried.

I watched a lad throw a spare wheel into the back of a vehicle he'd repaired and one of his welds pinged off. He got the welder out and just tacked it again. If that car got hit, I wouldn't like to know what'd happen. It was an eye-opener.

There was a bonus system at this garage. People would cut corners to earn more money. The insurance estimate would give you ten hours to change a panel on a car. If you did it in five, you'd get your normal wage and earn five hours' bonus. Your bonus would vary but mine was £18 an hour. People were earning crazy money.

I was sat there thinking, I'm doing a nice job here and they're cutting every corner and getting rewarded for it.

I told my boss that I was leaving. He said, *'Don't leave. We're getting bought out and things'll change.'*

The garage was then bought out by a PLC company, everything went above board.

One day we came into the garage, sat down and the manager went round the cowboys in the room. *'Gone . . . gone . . . gone . . . gone . . . gone.'* It was like Christmas.

Now, my colleagues are all genuinely all right lads. My employer appreciates me, and I get paid very well.

I make a conscious effort when I get home to try with the kids. But sometimes I've got no patience. I come home covered in crap. I put my boots on at half six in the morning and they're not getting off until half six at night.

I went to a bonfire with the kids the other weekend. I'd worked Saturday until four o'clock, and I had no patience with them.

I'm aching everywhere all the time.

But that's part of the job, innit? You know what you're getting into. It's like being a firefighter and moaning about having to put a fire out.

My plan is to work my absolute backside off now and give it 'til I'm forty.

I'm still thinking about pieces of work constantly. I've got a job tomorrow and I know it's going to be a naughty job, so I'll go home tomorrow, and I'll be watching TV or bathing my son, or I'll be in bed at night, and I'll be thinking about it. *Shall I try this or that?* And I'll still be thinking about the job as I'm doing it, as I'm preparing the panel, filing it, rasping it.

But I think that's normal.

What else would I be thinking about?

Warehouse worker

20s

In most warehouses throughout the United Kingdom, the pattern is a 6 a.m. to 2 p.m. morning shift, 2 p.m. to 10 p.m. afternoon shift, and 10 p.m. to 6 a.m. night shift.

At the moment, I'm working afternoon shifts at a warehouse for a glasses supplier, so I start my job at 2 p.m.

I wake up between 7 a.m. and 9 a.m.

I do my meditations, prayers, and reading. I tidy up, go shopping, or go to church.

I then prepare for my shift by packing my food, juice, sparkling water, and working tools (a pen, a marker, a knife). I put on some old jeans, safety boots, my coat, and that's how I go to work.

I try to be at least five minutes early to the shift.

The first thing I do is take my scanner gun. If you get a bad scanner, you'll have issues for the rest of your shift. I then put my high vis on, and I go into the waiting area for pickers.

My job is to put away stock on the shelf. My supervisor indicates the pallets where we're supposed to take the stock from. We check that the stock is booked on the system, because if it isn't, we can't put it on the shelves. I then take the stock to the location where you're supposed to unload.

As I unload, I scan both the stock and the shelf where I'm putting the stock. It's not very difficult. But we have to type the codes in manually for some of the boxes. A pattern of ten digits and letters.

It's quite annoying if you have a couple of hundred items in the box that you have to type in manually.

There are three breaks a day of fifteen minutes: 4.15 p.m., 6.15 p.m., 8.15 p.m. A lot of these places don't pay for your breaks.

At the end of the day, we cut down the cardboard boxes and put them in a special cage. We hand in our scanner. Yesterday, I handed it in at about 9.35 p.m.

The job slows down my mind. It gives me time to process and rethink my thoughts.

– *What kind of thoughts?*

About my life. I've had quite a few adventures. Some things didn't work out the way I wanted, others worked out better than I could ever imagine.

But sometimes I speak to people at work. We tell jokes, fool around, laugh and laugh.

We do things like making pyramids in the warehouse with cardboard boxes.

In the supermarket warehouses I've heard that people will tell the handyman, '*There are two leaks in the warehouse.*' The handyman goes to check and finds a box with two leeks inside.

We had one Polish forklift driver who smiled a lot. He'd worked in a factory on a production line before, and compared to that, he loved the warehouse work.

We used to laugh and ask him, '*Is this the dream job? Do you pinch yourself to check it's not a dream?*'

It's a broad spectrum of people who work in the warehouse. Usually, it's up to a third of the crew who are English, a third from Eastern Europe and EU countries, and a third the Commonwealth.

I've met teachers, an ex-soldier, people who had mental health issues.

Quite a few of them are not very well educated. They do not have broader interests. But there are exceptions. There was a guy in the warehouse with us who was an engineer from Mongolia who had studied in Russia for four years. And during the pandemic a lot of people with higher education worked in warehouses, lots of musicians.

When I started working in British warehouses in 2014, I guessed that the system must be logical, because if better ways of organization existed then they would have been implemented.

But I was very naive.

I worked in one warehouse that had an obsolete data system, which made picking more difficult, but managers would still shout at pickers who didn't reach their targets.

They would say, '*If you drop below 60 per cent of the target, you will be sent home*.'

At this warehouse, I saw someone who almost died. A guy was picking in a very narrow aisle. The forklifts were not allowed to drive down this aisle because it was against health and safety regulations. The target culture made people break these rules.

Someone drove down the aisle with his forks up, carrying glass shower doors on a pallet. The wood on the pallet turned out to be rotten and seconds after this forklift had driven past the man picking, the pallet and the shower doors smashed onto the floor. He was seconds from death.

Of course, I do not deny my own responsibility. I should have reported it to the local authorities, but I did not do so, because I needed money, and I was scared of the consequences.

I've also worked in big e-commerce warehouses. In these places there's no time to talk whatsoever.

The stock is brought to you on these towers.

You climb to the top of a small ladder.

You take the item from the tower.

You scan the item and place it on a shelf behind you.

You press the screen to confirm that you've put the item on the shelf.

That's it.

That's what we did for the entire day. There were two half-hour breaks. One was unpaid. So we did ten-and-a-half hour shifts and we were paid only for ten hours.

I had to get the bus to this warehouse. It meant that I would arrive an hour before the shift, and I'd have to wait forty-five minutes after the shift to get home.

I spent thirteen hours outside the house, and I slept for eight hours. It was a real waste of time.

As a picker, the target was three-hundred-and-ten units per hour. If you had large items to pick it was impossible to reach the target, but if you had books, it was easy.

The managers check on you every minute. Their computers are on rolling desks so they can move around the warehouse. On their screens they have information about what you're doing.

There were no windows. We worked in unnatural light in front of the screens for the entire day.

There's writing on the walls of these warehouses.

Things like, '*Show backbone and speak out!*'

But there's no connection between this writing and the practice of the company. If I spoke to my manager about how badly the place was run, I'd get into difficulty straight away.

Some of these e-commerce warehouses are like gulags. HR and administration are the guards. The warehouse team leaders are the prisoners with privileged positions. And then there's the rest of us who do the most menial of jobs.

Yes we were not starved, yes we didn't have to work in minus forty degrees, yes we were free to leave whenever we wanted, but the structure of the company – its rigidity – is like a gulag.

Not all of the e-commerce warehouses are like this. It takes a lot of time, effort and money to build a warehouse with such a degree of automation. Most e-commerce warehouses still rely on the normal labour of walking from one location to another. But I hated the fact we couldn't move. It drove me insane.

I wanted to leave after two weeks. I only stayed because they offered a £500 sign-on bonus if you stayed for a certain period of time. It was £10.40 an hour when I worked there. You also got a 10 per cent discount on the company's own-brand stock.

I remember years ago the company gave the best picker of the shift a £20 voucher. Later on, they rewarded people by letting them choose the music for the shift, but that was scrapped because some people in HR or management didn't like the fact that some of the songs were not sung in English.

The design of the entire company had a complete disregard for the human psyche.

When it comes to the body, there was such a long time between the breaks that my back would hurt, and my hip would hurt.

But the main problem was that the work was a mentally excruciating exercise.

Every hour on this bloody screen, your work would stop, and the screen would let you choose whether to have thirty seconds of mental exercises or thirty seconds of physical exercises.

For the physical exercises, it would tell you to do movements with your arms and hips.

For the mental exercises, sometimes the screen would say, '*Think about something nice*', and I would think, *leaving this place, leaving this place*.

There were times at the e-commerce warehouses when I was extremely depressed. Extremely depressed. I was broken. *In what direction is my life going? Why is my life like this?*

But whenever I have these thoughts, I think of my grandparents who survived the war. I think about my parents who survived the transformation in 1989, when the Polish economy was in really bad shape. We are not now sent to die in trenches. So, in many senses we may be a lost generation but it's not that bad. It could get much worse.

My career has gotten stuck, but I know that I still have time.

Saint Ignatius of Loyola, the founder of the Jesuit order, was thirty-three when he began to study.

Hobbes was sixty-three when he wrote *Leviathan*.

Dostoyevsky published his most important works after he was forty.

And let us also remember that for a time Solzhenitsyn and Shalamov were lost in the gulag, deprived of prospects and literature.

Sex worker

20s

I do Only Fans and I cam model.[2] I need the money. My student maintenance loan only covers three-quarters of my rent.

Before I started, I was having to rely on food banks at the local churches.

The Only Fans is passive income really. It's only about £100 a month. I have to take pictures and videos for my cam site profile anyway, so I post them on Only Fans as well.

I make a lot more money on the cam-site. I found the cam modelling agency online. It's run by models, and they've been very supportive.

The agency has very clear boundaries. For example, none of us do escort, we're purely online. If we're uncomfortable with any of the customers – or if we're losing our mojo – someone from the agency is always there to talk to you. Once I was struggling to manage university and the sex work, so I spoke to one of the agency admins and she helped me make a rota.

Tuesdays, I tend to have Uni during the day, and then 7 p.m. until 10 p.m. I do camming. If I feel like I can do more, then I do.

Wednesdays, Thursdays, and Sundays, I tend to focus on my Uni work.

Fridays and Saturdays are the busiest days on the site.

---

2 OnlyFans is an online content-sharing platform. Content creators, predominantly sex workers, use the platform to share pornographic videos and photos with an audience of paying subscribers.

On Fridays, I'll work the morning shift on the cam-site, which is 5 a.m. until 9 a.m. This is quite busy. For some reason men want to log-on and pay people before they go to work. Who knows why?

Dominatrixes are the most popular characters for cam models.

So whenever I'm modelling, even though I dress the same as I do in normal life, I'm mentally playing quite a dominant character.

To create her, I went on a random name generator and chose from a list.

I have Twitter and Instagram profiles for the character, which are how I reach the international customers who access my Only Fans. On the cam-site, all my customers are from the UK because the site filters them by location.

Before I have a session with a client, I'll ask, '*What are your boundaries? What sort of things are you into? What software do you prefer to use?*'

I have a few regulars on the cam-site. Some of them keep asking me to meet them in person, which I don't do.

You come to expect creepy behaviour. Over time you get better at changing the topic. You could kick the client from the call but then you'd lose their money, so it's all about manipulating the conversation away from the creepy stuff.

A lot of it is manipulation to be honest.

On the site, clients have the option of either the *girlfriend experience* or the *pornstar experience*.

Some clients just want to talk to a woman, to feel like they have an emotional connection. Some clients are more transactional, '*I'm paying for your services, so you need to give me this and this.*'

Most of my regulars want the girlfriend experience. It tends to be one-on-one cam sessions.

When the girlfriend experience session begins, I ask them things like,

'*How are you?*'

'*How was work today?*'

And I pretend to care about their emotional state. But obviously the only reason I pretend to be interested in these men is for their money.

My regulars will book phone calls with me. The calls come through the agency number. They don't get my real number and I don't get theirs.

Sometimes, I'll be going about my day and the phone will ring and I'll go to the bathroom and talk to these men.

The most common calls I'm doing at the moment are humiliation calls. The clients say, '*Oh my God, yell at me.*'

Those are very easy because they're not face-to-face.

I've written out scripts for different types of calls, so I have something to refer to if I ever get stuck. It's all about dragging out the call as long as possible to get the most amount of money.

I'd struggle to maintain my composure if it was face-to-face, because the whole thing is so stupid.

No aspect of this is real. Everything's fake. Take water sports, for example, that's a popular one on camera. But you literally just use a water balloon and hold it behind you. The clients love it and they'll pay extra for it.

Or if you want to drag out a session for as long as possible, you say, '*Do you want to see my other outfits?*', and you'll go off camera and change but you make sure that you change slowly.

I have one client who's into financial domination. Before our sessions he tells me what he earns, what his outgoings are, and what his budget for the call is, so I know exactly what he's got to spend. Part of my interaction with him is belittling him for not tipping me enough. If he sends me some money, I'll say, '*Come on, you can do better than that.*'

It's the easiest call I do.

The public perception of sex work is that it takes place in a dark alley at the back of a building, your stereotypical prostitute in a red-light district.

Don't get me wrong, there are still dark aspects to the industry with people being exploited, but there isn't that darkness to my sort of sex work.

It's quite freeing.

– Has it changed your view of men?

I don't know. I don't like men. I tend to deal with older men in my sex work, fifty-year-old men with wives, families and kids. It's this secret part of their life.

But it's funny. I want to work in the corporate world one day and when I talk to all these men who are all quite high up in companies it's like I'm building connections in that world. You have to be high up to earn enough to pay for these sessions because each one costs about £2 a minute.

It's been good for my confidence too. I'm on dating apps like any normal person is in this day and age. If anyone gives me attitude on those apps, I think, *screw you, people pay me for my sex work.*

My partners do struggle with my work. I'm very up front with them that I do sex work and I'm not going to stop but it's jealousy, I guess. *'Other men have seen your body. Blah, blah, blah.'*

The clients think they're using me, but in reality, I'm the one that's financially gaining from the relationship.

It's using misogyny for my benefit, really.

Security guard

(20s)

In college, I was studying music technology and sound engineering. My life was music-making, music-producing, music-engineering, DJing workshops, mixing workshops, rap workshops.

I was also riding for one of the food delivery apps. I could do it in my own time. It was good for me because I have to care for my father.

Fast forward and Covid hits. Devastating news and devastating situations for a lot of people. The workshops I was attending were redundant, shut down.

I began looking for a job, which was difficult at the time.

My cousin said, *'Why don't you do security?'*

Never in my life would I have thought about doing a security job, but I said to myself, *I need to work, I need to work.*

I applied to a security firm, and I began work as a steward because I didn't have the security licence. My plan was to work towards getting the badge.

I ended up doing a lot of the Covid testing sites across my city. Twelve-hour shifts, back-to-back, at a Nightingale hospital. It was pretty much a twenty-four-hour shift with a thirty-minute rest in between. It was bad, so bad.

Standing there in one spot.

Not allowing your body to move.

You start to feel a lot more crooked.

You're stagnant.

Joint pains.

Issues with your feet.

Two hours can feel like five hours.

And three hours can feel like eight hours.

At the moment, I work security at a bar-restaurant. It's an evening job. It's mostly me on a one-man door, six or seven hours a day.

I'm a black man and I've had cases where a black man has approached me trying to get into a bar. I can see he's intox, on certain drugs. I'm refusing him entry.

He will say, '*All right, you're not gonna support your fellow black man? Is that how it is, yeah?*'

I'll try and explain it.

I'll say, '*Bro, I want to respect you, but you're disrespecting me.*'

But it's a hard situation. It makes me uncomfortable.

You also get a few regulars who've been to other bars but want to come to their favourite bar at the end of the night. If I get one that's drunk out of his face, I give him a pep talk, let him know the rules and what my job is.

I say, '*Hey hey hey I'm gonna stop you right there.*'

'*Why?*'

'*You look out of it. You've had way too many drinks, my guy. Way too many for today. I'm gonna say "No" for tonight. You look like you've had so much fun today. But it's time to rest.*'

They get it. I cool them down.

The *kill 'em with kindness* thing helps. Approach the customer like '*No. Can't come in.*' and they'll react aggressively, '*Whadya mean I can't come in?*'

That can cause a lot of commotion.

If they feel like you're having fun, then it makes the situation a lot easier. And one way to have fun is to smile. I don't want to ruin their night with a sulk on my face.

You see a lot of characters, man. When customers are heavily intox and having fun they're not their usual selves, they're just characters.

I don't want to get too deep into it, but I used to be bullied a lot when I was a kid. I was just the kid at school who nobody wanted to play with *cos you're weird*. So I don't like hurting people. I don't. I don't want people to feel like how I've been treated in the past. I love the purity of being kind and respectful to one another. If I could pass that on to someone else, then I've done my job as a human being.

I remember a time working with a colleague who was too big for his boots. I've often seen security guards like him, who act like they have the power to do whatever they want because they have the badge. I totally disagree with that. *Totally*. Yes, you do have the badge but that doesn't allow you to be a bit of a . . . I don't want to cuss . . . but he was a *d-head*.

I was asking a guy for his ID and this customer says in a jokey way, '*Mate, I'm twenty-seven!*'

My colleague snaps and goes off, '*That doesn't matter. We still have to see your ID. I've seen people who are sixteen and they look about twenty-one.*'

I check the ID and the customers go in.

We then hear them at the bar saying, '*That security guard is a dickhead.*'

My colleague then starts badmouthing them. I asked him if he felt the need to go and grab them from the bar.

He was like, '*Yeah yeah yeah and I have the power to grab them. I can probably say they were intox.*'

I said, '*No way am I letting you do that.*'

He wasn't respecting the job. If customers are chatting back, there's no need to retaliate. He could've got into a serious fight for no reason.

And he's adding to that severe stigma about security guards, that we have a bad demeanour. I wanna rebuke that stigma. I'm not big-built or hench or the going-to-the-gym type. I'm pretty much the friendliest security guard you probably ever found. And I don't say that, the customers do.

Recently, a colleague and I had to remove a gentleman in his forties, who'd apparently sexually assaulted a twenty-one-year-old girl.

We approached him, '*Listen, there's been this report. You need to come straight out.*'

He's denying it. He's intox. I feel a tiny bit hesitant because it's not my style to put my hands on somebody aggressively. And you can tell that he could pick me up and put me on my neck. At the same time, I have the trust of my colleague that what I'm doing is morally correct.

I took over my fears.

We ended up fighting him, dragging him out of the premises.

It's like a flow state.

Get him out, get him out, get him out.

And here's another person who wants to fight.

And here's someone else screaming at the top of her lungs, '*Get off him!*'

And the bar manager sees you grabbing this person. He says, '*What's going on?*'

But he doesn't know what's happening.

All you have in your mind is *let me just get this person out, please . . .*

I'm not going to lie to you, I don't like being in that mind state. It makes me very uncomfortable.

But if it's a chilled shift, I don't have to think about work as vigorously as I usually do. So when I'm standing there I'll always be wondering, *what will the next melody be? What will the next drum pattern be? Who am I going to work with next?*

I have a dream in mind, to be one of the top producers or sound engineers in my city. When I finish my shift, I sit down at my laptop and go for what I'm after.

I also have to care for my dad when I get home from work. I have to make sure that he's getting up the stairs safely, that he's in bed.

A lot of people ask me, '*Do you ever have time for yourself?*'

I say, '*No, not really.*'

Those people say, '*Why are you smiling? You have no reason to smile. Your life is miserable!*'

But I'm smiling. No matter how much of a struggle life is, I'm smiling.

CHAPTER TWO **TALKWORK**

Call centre worker

estate agent

therapist and business owner

trade union organizer

Call centre worker

(40s)

I ended up in this job due to needing a remote job quickly. I couldn't leave my son here by himself because my ex-husband isn't the nicest individual. He's turned up at the door and I don't want my son to have to deal with it alone.

I work for a call centre company that outsources its call centre to different companies. At the moment, we're outsourced to a building materials company. It could be anyone on the phone, from builders to farmers to a pensioner ordering a bag of fertilizer.

I'm on annual leave at the moment, but my next two shifts are Friday and Saturday, 8 a.m. to 4.30 p.m.

The first thing I do in the morning is to sign-in as quickly as possible. If you're a minute late, you're marked as AWOL and you have to work back your time, or you have to go to your manager and say, '*I was a minute late because the system didn't work properly.*'

Then I get started on my calls. It's call after call after call after call. I've a thousand things to do on a call.

First, GDPR.

Then order number or account number.

Then we have to make sure that we're speaking to the right person or that we have permission to speak to the person we're speaking to. Say, Mr John Doe was on file for that account but Mrs John Doe calls us and there's no authorization for her on file. She'll say, '*It's my husband*', but without his authorization, I can't proceed.

This is when you get a lot of obscenities thrown at you. They'll say,

'*No other company works like this.*' But we have to be careful, because we get pulled up on this by our managers.

At the same time as they're speaking to us, we fill out a call profiler form, which is the *customer's name, address, what they're calling about*.

If, say, the courier hasn't arrived, we then have to chase the courier companies by filling a form out with them. Or you might have to email one of the building company's stores via our customer support software.

All the while, you're adding notes to the call profiler form saying what's happened.

You write, '*The customer is very unhappy*.'

You don't write, '*The customer is a pain in the arse.*'

Sometimes you can't get all of these tasks done during the call – sometimes the customer will just bark orders and hang up – so you're left with these forms to fill out. You put yourself on hold to do all this after the customer's gone, but putting yourself on hold means you're not taking the next call, and this hold time shows up on your stats as '*rap time*'.

You're in no-man's land, in between calls.

I've often said to people I work with, '*Give us some time each day to check back with the tickets we've raised and the emails we've sent, and then we can respond to customers.*'

When they want you to take call after call after call, there's no time for you to check your emails, to check responses from couriers, for instance. Customers come back to us furious because nobody's contacted them to tell them anything.

We don't have the freedom to solve customers' problems. We don't have freedom because we don't have the time to chase responses or even tell the customer what's happened. Sometimes you end up getting up early on your personal time to chase things, so customers won't come back and make a complaint.

Generally, the customers aren't ringing to say, '*You're doing a great job.*'

They're ringing to shout at you. For instance, they're angry that their courier didn't come, and they want you to fix it right there and then. You try to remain calm, to keep your composure, but it can be difficult sometimes.

All the calls are monitored. I have to be careful what I say. You could take a bad call from somebody who's terribly abusive and frightening, and on the next call you might be a little bit subdued because you've just had somebody screaming at you, but that next call might be the call that your managers listen to in order to see how you interact with customers. They'll say, *'You weren't very nice to that customer. You weren't very friendly.'*

At the end of the week, you get your stats. You try your best, but the managers will say, *'You haven't taken enough calls in an hour. Your rap time is too long.'*

The stats are on a spreadsheet. Everyone can see everybody else's. I'm always pretty much the worst because I'll engage with people. They'll talk to me. I've heard everything from people telling about their cancer diagnosis, to a domestic violence incident where I stayed on the phone with the caller.

Some people are just ringing to talk. You can always tell. You might be the only person they've spoken to that day. But while you're expected to have empathy and compassion for the customer, you're not supposed to be on the phone for ten minutes.

I started out in a group of fourteen. I'm the only one still there. Nearly everyone was gone in the first two or three months.

Customers tend to treat us badly because they think we're paid to sit there and listen to them. *The Customer is Always Right.* It's that mentality. But I would never speak to anybody in customer service the way I have been spoken to.

One day I took a call from a man who was raging because he couldn't return a tool to a particular store. He had to return it to a different store.

He was on the phone to me in his car and he threatened to kill himself. For fourteen minutes, I had to speak to this man while he travelled from one store to another store, all the while threatening repeatedly to kill himself and the woman he'd just dealt with in the first store.

I was writing everything down because I was scared for her safety. I alerted my managers, and they were feeding me things to say. He was aggressive, so aggressive, and I was afraid he was going to kill that woman, kill himself, or kill his family. I didn't sleep that night because I was so worried he was going to go back to the shop and kill them all.

I thought, *I'm not equipped to deal with this*. But I also know how to calm down angry men. I'm good with my voice. I spoke softly, calmly . . . *calm, calm, calm*.

When he'd got to this other store to get the refund – which was like £40 by the way – I was still on the phone to him. I heard him speak to the woman behind the counter. I wasn't sure what was going to happen. I thought, *is he going to do something to her?* But he was so polite to her, *'I just want to return this'.*

After I'd been screamed at, after he'd told me he was going to kill himself and his family and that it was all my fault, after all that for fourteen minutes, he exchanged the tool and that was it.

I'm shaking now just talking about it.

It's weird. I've got his phone number. I've got his email address, his address. I know his name. But he still spoke to me like that . . .

I got the next day off as paid leave. The managers had to sit and listen to the call that night. I'd hoped that the police would have been informed. I discovered weeks later that nobody was informed.

People's mental health takes a real hit doing this job. Time doesn't pass fast enough. I could be an hour in, and I'll be thinking, *how am I going to make it?*

A lot of days my body hurts even though I've only been sitting in a chair.

Mentally, every bit of empathy has been sucked out of me. I'm drained, just drained.

It's a lot of women from all walks of life working in this job. The company wants our empathy. I think that's why we're hired. But because we're empathetic, the job affects us emotionally. They'd be better off hiring people for whom all the abuse was like water off a duck's back, but then I don't think you'd get the same level of sincerity.

There's got to be a better way of doing it.

I wish computers could take over dealing with customer complaints. Our company does web chat customer service as well and I've had messages from colleagues that have been moved onto that. They say, 'Thank God, I only have to type to people. My life is amazing.'

When the crash was happening in 2007, I worked in a job handling calls for a pension company. People who'd paid into their pensions for years would call to find out their pension was worth nothing. But, even though they'd lost seventy grand, I don't remember those people being as rude as some guy the other week who didn't get a bucket delivered.

A few years ago, I got back into film photography. I'd done it in college, but I couldn't remember how to process film. God, I wasted roll after roll of film, but I started to do candid street photography. I'd walk up to people and say, 'Hi, can I take your picture?'

I had a couple of exhibitions. I always loved how they shot street photography in the 1960s, 70s, 80s. It was fearless, the finding of the extraordinary in the ordinary. With film, you can't take two hundred shots of the same thing. Everything has to align for that split second, and that's the magic.

I actually sold my camera last week. I don't have that any more. I had to sell it because my car broke down and I'm a single parent earning minimum wage. I needed a car so that my son and I could have a little bit of freedom.

I think a lot of people get stuck in this kind of job. It can numb you. I feel like I'm already bad at this job, so when I look at other jobs from time to time, I talk myself out of applying. It's silly. I have to change my thinking, but when you get your stats each week and you're down near the bottom, it's very easy to sink into that abyss. *This is all I'm going to be.*

I'm sorry to be over emotional.

I think it's the thought of going back to work later this week. I was awake at four o'clock this morning worrying about it.

I was thinking, *oh God, two more days and I'll be back there.*

Estate agent

(20s)

I watch inspirational YouTube videos. I watched one – I can't remember what it was called off the top of my head – it was a guy saying that the main thing in life is to be happy in your job. He'd done twelve jobs in one year before he found a job he liked. He went into IT, which is pretty cool.

I always take little bits of advice from these videos. He also said, '*It's not all about the money*' and '*Work to live, not live to work.*'

These are key things.

'*The world's your oyster*', they also say that.

I'm twenty-six now. And from when I was in primary school, my dad worked hard. My parents and grandparents are from India. They came here when my dad was ten years old. They worked hard in bakeries. My granddad then started his own.

I remember my granddad saying that the first house he bought was like five grand. It's crazy, because the same house now is like two-hundred-and-fifty grand.

My dad realized that property could be a good thing. He started buying and selling houses. He built up enough capital to buy a nice house. He then picked up a few buy-to-lets. My dad would take me to all the properties he was buying.

He'd say, '*This needs doing, that needs doing.*'

In 2008, interest rates went down, and he got a lot of properties cheap on interest-only mortgages. The rent he was getting on them was very good. I felt inspired.

– When you were younger, did you know what you wanted to do in your life?

No, not really. I knew I really wanted to make money. I've always been business-minded. I've always loved iPhones, Apple and Steve Jobs.

I studied business management.

I've also done a little bit of stocks and shares investing. I made a little money, and I lost a bit of money. I didn't really know what I was getting into . . .

I'm not gonna lie. I got scammed. You get these Instagram messages.

One guy told me to download these investing apps and he made an account for me, which I found a bit odd. You put the money in there and then you never see the money again. They're very clever in how they do it. When it happened, I felt ashamed, like a bit of a mug.

The only thing I'd invest in now is in property.

Someone said to me, *'You can never go wrong with bricks and mortar.'*

But I also went through a stage of gambling a lot, because I was trying to get the money back from being scammed.

I lost a lot of money gambling. I don't know why I went to the casino.

I'd go at lunchtime from work, just pop in.

Four-hundred pounds on roulette for no reason.

You transfer money from account to account.

And when you're chasing the money, you could be in the casino for six, seven hours. I've been in the casino at 4 a.m. and it's not a nice feeling. I have won money, hundreds of pounds, but I've lost two grand as well. *'The house always wins.'*

I do think Covid ruined my life. I started doing online gambling. I started drinking. I bought cans from the petrol station, and I'd go home and drink them. I was drinking five, six times a week. There was nothing else you could do.

With the gambling, I went to get a coffee one day when I was on furlough and I thought, *I need to be a man and ban myself from these sites.*

I've also had some support with my drinking, I still have a beer, but I'm not really much of a big drinker.

These days, I get to the office for 8.30 a.m. I turn my laptop on and say good morning to everyone. I check my emails and organize my whole day in my calendar.

From 9 a.m. until 11 a.m., I start calling clients, reminding them of viewings that they've got in the afternoon, dealing with maintenance issues, or calling leads – the people who've said they're interested in a property on Rightmove or Zoopla.

From 12 p.m. until 1 p.m., I do a forty-minute workout, or a swim and sauna.

I met a guy yesterday in the sauna and he was like, *'I've been dating this girl for six months and I've paid for every date.'*

I said, *'If that was me I'd halve each bill, even if you've got a lot of money, because we're all humans.'*

In the afternoon, it's viewings for sales or lettings. It's quite full-on. This afternoon, for instance, I had six letting viewings with clients. With the lets viewings, I try to stay humble. I've seen a lot of people talk themselves out of a deal. They'll talk a lot, promise a lot.

They'll say, *'The sofas will be gone. This'll be gone. The landlord's gonna do this for you, that for you.'*

But the landlords sometimes don't do a lot, so I don't promise much, because at the end of the day it's not my property.

At 3 p.m., I head back to the office and tie some deals up by putting offers forward. The main thing is getting the deals done. It's a good feeling when you close a deal, but I'm so used to it now. The hype fades and you think, *what else is there? What else can I do?*

If you sell a house for three-hundred grand, then the estate agent probably gets 1 per cent and then I might get £250. Even a letting, if I let a property I get £80.

My income is about half and half commission and salary. The basic salary is £22,000 and I can do thirty in commission.

I also own an investment property. It's got three flats and a commercial shop downstairs. My dad had really good contacts in the area. You can get some good deals with contacts.

My goal is to carry on working and try to build up more and more money, and more and more connections.

Some commercial shops might then become available and the seller will say, *'Do you want to buy this off market?'*

That's the best way to get good deals.

– Your future is based on property prices rising. Do you ever worry about that?

I don't worry. With tenants, your rental income is going to be there for ever, because some people will never be able to afford a house. Property is one of the best investments ever, the safest and the best. I won't worry about house prices going down, because they always go back up.

Therapist and business owner

(50s)

There's nothing more intriguing to me than the human brain. I see my job as being a detective. Someone comes in. They're experiencing a certain feeling that manifests in different ways. And my job is then to try to work out why they are as they are. Not putting a plaster on, but digging deeper to work out where these behaviours are coming from.

It's satisfying.

Originally, I practised as a CBT therapist in the NHS. I left eight or nine years ago. I had so many ideas, but I felt quite restricted in what I was allowed to do.

Also, to be truthful, I'd been there for so long that I wasn't getting any pay rises. I didn't have a lot of hope that things would get any better for me financially.

I took the leap of trying to work in private practice, and because I'm not very good with company politics, I set up my own business.

We've got twenty self-employed associate therapists working for us now, but I still work clinically.

In my practice today, at the beginning of the treatment, I'll ask the patient, '*What would it look like if you felt a lot better?*'

They might say, '*I might be able to go shopping on my own twice a week without a panic attack.*'

And you can then use that as a measure to see whether someone's improving. You can also just tell when someone's making progress.

Sometimes, physically, you can see them change in their mannerisms and body language.

I do a lot of Eye Movement Desensitization and Reprocessing (EMDR). Sometimes people will feel a bit worse because you're opening Pandora's box. They'll push you away.

But then afterwards they'll say, '*I've noticed that when I encounter the thing that usually triggers me, I don't feel the same about it.*'

They have an *aha* moment.

'*Why have I been beating myself up about this. It was never my fault.*'

You can see a physical shift in their feelings. That's when I feel really good. I love it then.

Another good indicator that someone's getting better is when they're able to start reducing the amount of drugs or alcohol that they're consuming, or when someone's loved ones tell them that they're looking better.

People often have a lot of shame about how they're feeling. They might have intrusive thoughts, horrible thoughts, about things that they've never told anybody.

After I've managed to coax what's happening out of them, I'll say, '*Oh that's really common.*'

They'll say, '*Really?*'

They think they're the only person who thinks these things. Knowing that there's nothing strange or abnormal about them can help people feel a lot better.

I tend to really like my clients. You might think, *there's got to be people that you don't like!*

But it's very rare that I get anybody that I don't like. I'm always saying in our anonymous clinical supervisions, '*Oh, they're so lovely.*'

I think it's because I can see why people are struggling. And I can see that even if they're behaving in ways that are unlike anything you'd ever do.

I try not to judge.

* * *

When Covid first hit, I'd just had spinal surgery, so I wasn't working clinically. I'd also just spent a lot of money renting an office and doing it up. I had a four-year contract. We moved in over Christmas 2019.

When March 2020 came, I was just devastated.

A lot of my associates started focusing on their NHS jobs. And I went from having twenty-eight clients to four. At that point, nobody used Zoom.

I thought, *we'll wait, we'll just wait.*

I had a few meltdowns.

But I'd done some work in the past with some schools. One of the academies contacted me and asked if I'd do some workshops with the staff who were struggling being out of school. These workshops kept my business afloat until people realized that Covid was going to go on and on.

At that point people said, '*Oh go on then, I'll do therapy over Zoom.*'

I saw a lot of people during Covid who were struggling with OCD, triggered by the government advice about germs being on everything.

I did think that there'd be something lost by delivering therapy over Zoom, but I now don't think there is. I've seen people on Zoom who I only ever see on Zoom, and they still have the same results as the in-person therapies.

But during Covid, I did find work very isolating.

I was at work, and it felt like everybody was out sunbathing and having a right nice summer and I was shut in a room, miserable, working every weekend, keeping the business going.

It can be a lonely job. Even though you're talking all day, you're focusing on the other person the entire time. It can be quite draining.

When the bounce back loans came out, I got one to convert my garage into an office. Then, after a lot of pain, I managed to get out of the contract with the office we were renting.

I decided from then on that I'd just stay at home. And that's what I did. It's worked out really well, because I don't have any rent to pay now.

Covid feels like a distant dream. It's weird.

Have I recovered? I don't know. I feel mentally fine, but I also feel tired . . . There's no chance to catch your breath. Sometimes I've thought, *ah it'd be great to work on a supermarket checkout, scanning things, rather than someone's life relying on what you do*.

It can feel like that sometimes. But I do absolutely love my job. And I think when I don't feel enthusiastic about it any more, that's when I should stop. If I can't be enthusiastic and give people hope, or make them feel *this is really hard, but we're going to get through it*, then I should stop.

I don't want to see a therapist that's like '*Hmm.*'

You want someone that's like, '*Right, this is what we're gonna do. We've got a plan.*'

When I say things like that, I can see people relax. They've got a guide.

Trade union organizer

(30s)

I'm from a single parent family. My mum went from job to job over the years, cleaning, hotel work, and now she works as a site manager.

My dad wasn't really around when I was growing up.

From a very young age, I've been volunteering. I'd help out with a community engagement charity that ran a credit union and what we'd now call a food bank.

I also took a real interest in politics. I looked at the Labour Party and I knew that *that* was my party. I believed in the values of it, you know, fairness, justice, respect. There was a councillor who took an interest in mentoring me and at thirteen I started campaigning locally.

When you grow up in a one-parent family, and when you're from a black and ethnic minority background, opportunity doesn't come knocking as much as it would in a more affluent area. I grasped that early on. I wanted to be more.

During uni I worked in a care home. I think everyone should have to do it, working twelve-hour shifts for minimum wage, night and day, short-staffed, with no fixed team because it's all agency staff coming in. On my first shift, the nurse said to me, '*You've got a floor to yourself.*'

I'd never done care work before. It shocked me. I just started going to each patient one by one, doing the best I could.

There was a patient who had lost his mind. He used to wipe his own shit with his hands, and he'd walk around with shit on his hands. Can you imagine being eighteen or nineteen and seeing that? I'd never seen anything like it, and I froze. You have to calmly take him into a room and shower him.

When I graduated from university, I got a job in a trade union as a community co-ordinator. The job involved creating community groups to fight things like the cutting of rural bus routes, or doctors' surgeries being closed down.

I'm now a regional organizer for the same union.

On a Monday, I'm up at 5.30 a.m.

I might be doing a talk to some new drivers at a transport company. The recognition agreement that we have with their employer means we're allowed to go and speak to them at their training school.

I'll be on stage from about 6.30 a.m., and I'll be talking to them about why they should pay their £16 a month into the union. I'll tell them that it's not just about the benefits of legal advice if you have an injury at work, but it's also about the union members who came before, who won all these benefits that they now receive.

I'll say, *'We've got to continue that legacy.'*

I'll then take questions and we'll get people to fill-in the sign-up forms.

I'm back in the office for about 10 a.m., then we'll have a meeting to go through the priorities for the week. *What campaigns are getting results? Where are we in the ballot processes? What fires need putting out?* There's ten of us in our team.

From about 1 p.m., I'm following up on missed calls and I'm checking data to make sure that people's details and memberships are up to date.

If we post a ballot and it doesn't reach the worker because of an incorrect address, then that ballot is lost. Because of that lost ballot we might not reach the 50 per cent plus one turnout that we need under the Trade Union Act. And if we fail at that late stage, it'll ruin all the work we've put in.

To wrap the day up, I'll usually go to a garage or a depot or a factory somewhere. I'll meet with union reps, and I'll speak to members.

Doing this job has affected me in the sense that I'm probably a workaholic. Checking your phone on a date is not a good look, but to me it's normal behaviour. I'm not pressured by hours or targets; I'm pressured by the causes.

We do all this training on *'learning how to switch off'* and I just can't do it. I can't. Part of it's selfishness, because I don't want to think that I'm missing something, so I have a quick look at my phone . . .

When I say to my friends things like, *'Okay, great, We've got a plan now. Let's reconvene next week.'*

They'll often say to me, *'You're in fucking work mode, you are.'*

When there's a ballot going on, it's the most tense time. You feel like saying to the workers, *'Just return the ballot. It's not hard!'*

You want the best for these people, but democracy will only play its part if members vote, whether they vote for or against a deal.

If the members vote against a pay deal, it's kind of exciting. *Right, we're taking them on. We're off to the lawyers.*

I remember one fight with a bus company. If the drivers gave back the wrong change, the bus company were deducting the loss from the drivers' wages – even if it was 50p.

If you're driving a busy bus, then of course you're going to make mistakes taking money. It's illegal to deduct this loss from wages but the workers were signing documents agreeing to this policy, because they thought it was normal.

When we heard about this, we took on the company. Grievances went in. The company got their lawyers to send letters to the union saying that what we were doing was defamation. But all we were saying was that they were abusing their workers and that they needed a better system in place.

We went out to the company gates, flags flying. It's really exciting.

We got the drivers the money back and we went straight into pay negotiations and got them a decent deal.

But after that, you're always looking to the next thing. If you start negotiations for a pay deal in January, you won't settle the deal until October, November. So it's never really a celebration, because you've only got a month or two before you start prepping the representatives for the next negotiation.

People will say it's pure greed from us and that you should give the companies breathing space, but we can't allow our members to fall behind.

And it takes so long to negotiate because most companies will only have ad hoc meetings with union officials.

We do deal with a car company that books out a conference room and no one leaves for seven days until the negotiations are done. I like that. It focuses minds.

Companies make a mistake when they think, *we must be private and hide things from the union*. Sometimes, when you have a decent conversation with a company, when they're transparent and they show you the books, we'll ask them, '*What can you afford?*'

We're not going to go back to our members to ask for a 5 per cent pay deal when the company is near enough on the way out. That's living in la la land.

We mentioned my dad earlier. We did start talking later in life. He was troubled in many ways, and I'll be honest with you it has had an effect on me over time. It's made me question things.

Mums are great and they can do a certain job of playing both mum and dad, but it's never enough. You learn coping mechanisms, because there's only so many times you can lie when kids ask at sports days and Father's Day, '*Where's your dad?*'

It can go one of three ways.

You have a kid yourself and you don't take responsibility for them, and the cycle begins again.

You don't have a kid, but you give up and lose faith in life because you've been let down.

Or you make something of yourself and say, *I'm not going to let that experience make me a lesser person*. I'm determined because I don't want other people to have the experience I had.

CHAPTER THREE **CRAFTWORK**

Baker

software developer

mechanical engineer

chef

joiner

Baker

(30s)

Breads, we do white, granary, oat, muesli, mixed-seed, wholemeal, teacakes, ciabatta, focaccia, olive. Then things like quiche, sausage rolls with the pork mince from the butchers round the corner. Everything's fresh, all locally sourced.

I worked at a supermarket for ten years. One of the managers offered me a baker's position.

He said, '*Do you want it?*'

I said, '*Yeah.*'

But I had a thing where I cringed when I touched flour. After I accepted the job I thought, *shit, I'm going to have to work with flour.* I got over that when I was sent down to the Midlands for a full-day crash course in supermarket baking.

I was then a baker at the supermarket for three years before I applied for a job at a proper bakery. I didn't get it because they went for someone with more experience, but he left after six months.

The owner called me up and said, '*Job's there if you want it.*'

I've been working there on and off ever since. I'm unofficially the head baker, but the owner hasn't announced it because she'd have to give me a pay rise [he laughs]. It's still the best wage I've had, as much as I'd like it to be more. Twenty-six-and-a-half a year.

At the supermarket, it was cheating in a way because it was packet mixes. *A bag of red stuff goes in there. A bag of blue in there.* Whereas at my bakery, you have to weigh your sugar out, you weigh your salt out. It's proper baking.

There was one bloke at the supermarket who didn't give a shit what the bread looked like or how it was done. When it was on the shelves, I'd look at it and think, *come on, really?*

He'd been doing it for years and getting away with it for years. Nobody told him. You could just tell he didn't want to be there.

Now, if something looks shit, I'll make it again. Because if you get a bad loaf, then you'll start losing customers. I want to take care in what I do.

It's a little production line. You've got me mixing the dough. Another guy chops it, moulds it. I'll jump in and mould the dough as well and another guy proves it and bakes it. Each day, we get through four or five 16kg bags of flour, Monday to Thursday. But on a Friday night we'll put out hundreds – nearly thousands – of teacakes. Five hundred loaves. We don't have a break.

Everyone says, '*Ah, you'll be used to the hours now.*' Not really. You don't get used to it, you just cope with it. Come six o'clock on a Saturday night, I'm out like a light.

I try not to go to bed 'til 9 p.m. during the week.

Sometimes I'll have a little nap when I get home but I don't want to sleep my life away. I want to make the most of my time with my missus, my dog, my friends, my family. It's hard at times. I'm constantly tired. I'm probably still catching up on sleep from a year ago.

One time when I was working at the supermarket, I fell asleep standing up and I woke up three inches away from the oven.

I even quit the bakery once because my Fridays were a complete write-off. I'd start one shift at 2 a.m. Friday morning, and I'd be back in for another shift at 10 p.m. Friday night.

Going to work, I'd drive through the city centre and see people out and getting drunk.

I'd think, *I'm twenty-six, that should be me*, and so I left to work in sales, selling tracking systems for agricultural machinery. It was awful. I just couldn't speak. When I spoke to customers, my words came out like mush. You have to have a certain way about you to persuade someone to buy something, and I couldn't do it.

I was bullied at school, just for being fat. And if you're a fat kid, you've just got to take it. It made me quite subdued. Recently I saw one of the people who'd been shitty to me in the pub.

He said, '*How you doing?*'

I said, '*Don't speak to me. You were a twat to me at school.*' Then he was buying me pints all night. Sometimes, you've got to stand up for yourself.

I am a bit louder now. I went to Kavos one year and I came back a totally different person. I enjoyed myself and I felt like I could be me, and that's who I am today.

I feel like baking is what I'm here to do. When you see all the bread on the shelves, all looking nice, you think, *I've done that.* There's a sense of achievement.

It's the same feeling when you make something, and it sells out. You think, *well, I'm doing something right.*

Or when my grandad, who loves his Eccles cakes, has one and says, '*Oh, this is brilliant.*'

– *What do you think about when you're working?*

There's not a lot that goes through my head when I'm baking. I like my mind being somewhere else. We've all been doing it so long that we're on autopilot and the time just flies. But it's not like being a robot. No, the four of us are so close to each other that we'll just chat shit and have a laugh. We've all been there at least two years. We talk about literally anything.

The oven guy, Rob, he's set in his ways and he's a little bit autistic. We call him that because we think he is, and I think his wife thinks he's autistic as well. He comes out with these one-liners, and I can't even remember them but it'll be the funniest shit you've ever heard. We'll be crying with laughter. He's also got his routine and if you break it, he'll have a break-down. Sam'll do something like hide his rolling pin to try to get a reaction.

Sam is a Jack the Lad type, who won't think twice about punching someone. He was a chef before he became a baker. We often say to him, *'Cooking is an art, baking is a science'.* But he's still got his chef hat on, and he'll throw little bits of this and that into the mix. It upsets the balance of the dough and sometimes it doesn't prove right. You try to tell him, but he doesn't listen. The boss knows all this, but she loves him.

People stay working here a long time because the boss is decent. If you've got any money worries, she'll do her best to help you out. We get to go an hour early, take cake, things like that.

And as much as we scream and shout at each other we do all get on, like a dysfunctional little family.

The girl I'm with now she works in the shop, so I've got to be a bit reserved at work. If she heard some of the stuff that was said in the kitchen, shit'd fly.

It's just letting our hair down a bit. It's a lad thing, innit? We don't mean anything by it.

There was one bloke at the bakery called Paul, who was a stereo-typical grumpy little old man. He was good, very good. Everything he did was perfect.

Him and Sam clashed because Sam wanted to do it his own way. I'd stand next to Paul and listen and just watch him work. When you'd do something wrong, he'd point it out.

There were quite a few harsh words in there, *'You cunt, do it like this.'*

He wasn't very complimentary but if you did a good job he'd say, *'Yeah that's all right.'*

Before he retired, he pulled me to one side and said, *'I don't want to say this in front of everyone, because I don't want them thinking I'm being nice. But you're the only one good enough to fill my shoes.'*

For that to come from him, that was everything to me. I told my mum, everyone.

Hopefully I'll be here for however many years and some young'un will come in. I'll start off grumpy and one day say, *'Ah you're all right'.*

Software developer

(20s)

I did a coding boot camp, a nine-week intensive course that takes you from knowing pretty much nothing about software engineering through to being able to get a job as a software developer.

My current company is a digital incubator for a large consulting company. We take clients' ideas from a Post-it note all the way through to launching a digital business for them.

If I think about my company at the moment, it's one-hundred people, twenty of whom are software engineers and then the rest are designers, product managers, venture architects, people like that, all of whom support the building of these digital businesses.

Most days, when I'm in a good mood, I'm like, *it's so nice that we work as a team to build companies.* When I'm in a bad mood, I think, *wait, if you think about what the final product is, the software engineers built that.*

Your value to the thing that you're building is obvious. You're the one building the thing. And you prove that you're worth keeping in your job by coding.

If you join a law firm, then you're signing up for long hours and for a very corporate hierarchical structure. Whereas it doesn't make sense for a software developer to be sitting at their desk at two in the morning if they don't have anything to do. If they're not writing code, then why are they there?

Being a software engineer is an honest job in some ways. You write code and the code either works or doesn't work. There's no bullshit.

But it does mean that when you're then invited to meetings and you have to talk, it's like, *okay, this is getting in the way of me doing my job.*

But for other functions – let's say you're a consultant – a big part of your job is running those meetings, so the incentive is higher for you to speak more.

The other day I was reading something to do with the distraction cycle of humans. Most people can only concentrate for ninety minutes and then they have to take a break for half an hour. And the only exception to that is if you're working with your hands and building something. There's something that's appealing to humans about creating things. And that is part of the reason I enjoy coding.

Of course you're on a keyboard so it's different to building something out of wood.

But you go from nothing and then you have something.

Mechanical engineer

(20s)

My grandad was into all sorts of stuff – building houses, building cars, fixing cars – a real craftsman in everything he did. My dad's the same. He liked his BMWs, so we used to go to scrapyards during the weekend, looking for upgrades, new headlights, seats. We'd go after we'd done the shopping. I used to come out of the scrapyard with my trousers falling down because of the all bits I'd stolen and bought.

Academically, I wasn't anything to shout about. I was very average. I wasn't really a maths person. Bs, Cs, and Ds. But I wanted to become an engineer.

School were like, '*Ah, stick to your photography or product design. You're good at that sort of stuff.*'

I thought that they were probably right, maybe engineering wasn't for me.

So I did photography A level. I have to give my teacher a lot of credit. When he taught photography, it was one of those things where the more you put in, the more you got out.

He had an old Lotus that he tinkered with. I used to photograph the car at events. And at those events, you'd see all these old engineers running cars that they'd built. I thought, *I want to be like them*.

By the end of school, I was pretty advanced at photo manipulation, and I ended up with an A* at A level. I had known nothing about photography before I started the A level, but that photography course made me realize that I was capable of learning new stuff, that I could do what I wanted if I put my mind to it.

I thought, *I've got to do something to do with machines – cars, spaceships, anything.* So I did a foundation course in engineering, then I stayed on to do the degree, then I stayed on to the master's.

My mum was quite disappointed when I told her that I'd been accepted to do a mechanical engineering degree. She said, *'You're going to uni to fix cars?'*

I said *'Yes'* and walked off. It took her a few years to realize that the point was to try and make the cars, but then she said, *'You can't do that. You're not that clever!'* [he laughs].

I did a placement year during my degree. I went to an auto engineering company. I was working with incredibly experienced engineers. They thought I was a graduate, so their expectations of me were quite high. I would ask senior engineers mechanical questions and they'd say, *'Are you joking?'*

'No, I really don't know!'

It took me half a year or so to really get in among the guys. There were some bizarre fellas. One of them would go straight from work to his house, which was a construction site. He was mad about his thermal properties. He wanted to reduce all of the heat leaving his house, so he was insulating the outside of his house.

He'd finish on his house at 10 p.m., have dinner, go to bed, and come into work the next day. He was never in the best of moods, but he was stupidly clever. I've never met a guy like him. If you asked him a question, and you had him stumped, then you had a good question.

I did my final year project on his area of expertise. I sent him an email with my report, three-hundred pages long, *'What do you think of this?'*

He sent a nice email back, *'If I was looking for research and I came across this, it'd be a good tool.'*

For him to say the word *good*, that was enough for me. I thought, *maybe I can get to a good level in this job.*

At the moment, I'm working at a big construction vehicle manufacturer, working on a hydrogen engine.

It's a five-mile cycle to the site. I get in at about 7.50 a.m., have a shower, and start at 8 a.m. Cup of tea. Check my emails. *What needs to be urgently done?* Yesterday, I had to calculate the press fit force for a part of the engine. I vaguely remembered how to do this. I looked at a book, then Google, then spent a couple of hours putting some numbers through the equation.

We then had a meeting 9 a.m. 'til 10 a.m. It was an engine durability meeting, we'd been running the engine for about ninety hours, so we stopped it and had a look at all the components. Everything is arranged on a table in a very white, very clean room.

I'm responsible for the cylinder block and bed plate. It's a fancy bracket. Everybody else's system just bolts onto mine.

I grew up wanting to design race cars, but the person who designs a race car usually makes one guy happy, but there's thousands of builders and tradesmen out there who work bloody hard, and this vehicle can make them happy.

Just before we spoke, I was tinkering with my road bike.

It's weird because time goes really quickly when you're floating around on a project. A few weeks ago, I started taking the bike apart and six hours passed without me eating anything. *Oh I'll just quickly do that job, I'll just tweak that, I'll clean that bit up.* And the time just goes. It's almost like you're not there.

I never get that feeling at work, which is weird because it's engineering, and I get paid to do it.

I think it's the beauty of working on your own thing. You feel like you've achieved something even if you haven't. At work, there's a lot to deliver and it's probably not the engineering I really want to do . . .

I really like push bikes. Everything I do to the bike, I feel a benefit. When I clean the parts, it runs quicker, I can push my body harder, and the faster I go, the more distance I can do.

Whereas at work, it's little tweaks on a CAD screen. I'm doing a lot of bolts at the moment. Trying to make sure our bolted joints are okay, but there's only so much interest that bolts can hold.

It's great to work with a hundred other engineers on the same project. But if I could develop the whole engine myself, like a modern-day Brunel, I would. Everyone wants that ownership.

Chef

(40s)

Since leaving school, I worked a couple of places that were easier to get to because I didn't have transport. Once I gained my NVQ Level 2 and passed my driving test, I started in the higher ends, one rosette, two rosette, the finer dining. I did that for five years to *chef de partie* level, but after that I'd had enough of the hours, of not being paid well, of working Christmas, bank holidays, birthdays, of not being able to attend any social events.

I left and I did building for four, five years.

You're just in a vicious cycle with cheffing. Even if you put your family aside, you'd still be doing sixty hours a week.

If you're lucky enough to get two days off, the first day off you're burnt-out because of the hours. Next day off, you want to go to the pub or go out. Then you go back into work hanging. You feel rundown immediately. You're not rested.

You'd have five hours sleep a night if you were lucky. If you went out, you'd have even less. This is why the ones that work in London, at the real higher end places, they're all coke addicts, because they need it get them through, to function.

What a lot of people outside the trade don't realize is that I'd say 85 per cent of chefs or either alcoholics, drug addicts, or have a gambling problem. Chefs never let you down because they need the money.

It's a funny old game.

It's a funny old mix of people.

Most chefs are slightly off their head.

A real funny industry.

Even when I'd had enough and I left, cheffing drew me back in. It's just one thing that I've always been quite good at and able to do. And it's always been fun in the kitchen.

I've seen people crashing in and having fights, in the walk-in fridge, or outside.

Head chefs would throw stuff at you or threaten to deep-fry your hand. That's stopped a bit. And it's all a little bit lower key with all the racial stuff. With how things are, you can't upset anybody with what you say, whereas ten, fifteen years ago, it was a bit more . . . tongue in cheek.

I don't know of any chef union or anything like that, know what I mean?

It just doesn't exist. Every other job seems to have a union rep, or somebody like that. A lot of places don't even have HR for the kitchen.

– Would you want that?

Not really, no . . .

I lost one marriage because of it – the cheffing, the lifestyle, tempted by younger waitresses.

It's not great if you're trying to have a family. You'll argue, you'll bite, you'll snap, you'll annoy the other person. You're not yourself, are you?

When I left the wife, I was in a bit of a pickle for money. I just went on my phone, on the banking app, and I was able to borrow fifteen grand. I didn't even have to speak to anybody or nothing. It was just like *there* the next day. That's how easy it was.

I did need a loan, but maybe five grand would have been better, not fifteen. A human would have said, '*Let's try you on five, see how you get on.*'

Not like, straight away, '*Here's fifteen, go on.*' I won't name what bank it was.

But once I left the wife. I was on my own, reanalysing my life. I got with my current partner. I realized that I've got to change my ways and be a more adult human being.

I've grown up. Now I do a lot of freelance work. Becoming a freelance chef has been the best thing I've ever done, because I work when I want to work. If I need a weekend off, I take the weekend off.

I was always like, *I want to be off the stove by the time I'm forty. I don't mind still being in catering and hospitality, but I don't want to be on the stove.* I'm approaching forty, and I'm still on the stove. Maybe if I could be off the stove by the time I'm fifty . . .

I'd like to start my own agency, but an agency run by chefs, not businesspeople. I could get my mates involved and run a good sort of business.

If I do a *chef de partie* job, I get £13 an hour, but the agency is renting me out at £19 an hour. They're making £6 an hour for doing nothing.

I think Covid has helped us. It's made all these businesses open their eyes and realize that chefs are worth their weight in gold. There's a lot of places around my local area that've had to shut and not do any food because they've lost all their chefs.

'*Shit, we've treated them like shit all these years. And now we've got no one and we can't even make any money.*'

They don't make jack shit on booze, like 53 per cent gross profit, whereas food is like 65 per cent at least.

I know we only go to college for one or two years, but so does an electrician or a plumber, and when they're qualified and trained, they're on £15, £16 an hour plus.

If you can be a plumber or a chef, where you're gonna work sixty hours a week, you're never gonna have a weekend off, and you've got to work every single bank holiday, then it's not a great idea becoming a chef, is it?

The chef finds it hard. It's one of the things that ain't gonna change. It is the way it is.

Joiner

(30s)

I didn't want to be an electrician because I hated those small screws. I didn't want to be a plumber because it's the sort of job where you can't see your work. I wanted to be proud of the stuff I've built. And with those jobs you have to keep redoing your tests, but the way you hang a door hasn't changed for two-hundred years.

People ask me, '*How long you been a joiner?*'
I'll say, '*You know Jesus' cross? I made that.*'
It's one of the oldest trades.

I used to help as labour for my dad. He was a brickie. He also used to teach bricklaying at a college. They gave him a lot of the bad kids that the school had given up on. The school said to them, '*Go do bricklaying.*'

My dad, because he's brilliant, he put up with it. But why is it the case that they sent the bad kids to do it? Bricklaying, you can earn really good money doing it. There's a lot of skill that goes into it. But people think you're a neanderthal carrying bricks around.

My dad also used to renovate the houses we lived in. I have these memories of him working, but because I've seen photos and videos of these renovations, I don't know whether I'm just remembering them.

I remember him doing the floorboards and I remember seeing what was underneath.

I remember him repairing the roof on my nana and grandad's bungalow. I must have been five or six. I remember going up a ladder and knocking a saw off the roof and my dad just sort of laughing.

My dad's always been good with his hands, cars and building. And I'm the same.

It's a life hack. If you know enough about building and cars, you never have to pay anyone to do those services. If anything needs doing on the house or the car, I'll do it. It feels normal to me.

After I worked for my dad, I then worked as a labourer for a normal builder, but it didn't work out. When I worked for my dad, he'd be helpful. He'd say, '*Now, you do this one.*'

When I worked for the other builder, you were just cheap labour. I was doing a lot of carrying, sweeping up. They don't care. You don't get much from it other than a pay cheque and being screamed at all day.

You'll also find that a lot of them old-school builders are very rough around the edges. They'll turn up with their checked shirt, nice shoes, jeans, and a pencil in the pocket. They'll say, '*Back in my day . . .*' and then they'll turn out to be a drug dealer on the side and the kind of person who says, '*He hasn't paid. I'm gonna go round and break his legs.*' You think, *don't do that!*

I then did a season working at a funfair. At the end of it, I was like, *well, I've done that now. Time to do something else.* But I knew blokes who'd been there ten years. They'd do the season for six months and then go on the dole for six months and then do the season again. Living in a pokey little bedsit.

Not to poopoo the way they lived, because anyone can live however they want, but I thought, *don't you want to be something?*

I didn't have a plan. I've never had a clue where I'm going. I get that from my dad, he's sixty-nine and still doesn't know what he wants to do.

I just came to the town I'm living in now and I thought, *I'll start doing council work as a joiner.* A lot of it, I just winged. You're better off winging it with council work – as horrible as it sounds – because the standard's really low.

They asked, *'Can you hang a door?'*

I said, *'Yeah.'*

And I went out and bought a plane and a second-hand door. Then I watched a few YouTube videos and practised it at home. My first one came out all right. By the end I was fitting them in about twenty-five minutes.

I already had a van, because I'm very much into my vans anyway.

I borrowed my friend's tools for about a week. He was understanding. I spent the first week's pay on tools. And then I was just able to carry on with the joinery.

If I needed a tool for a job, I'd delay that job until I had enough money to buy that tool and do that job.

For a couple of months it was touch and go, something could have gone so wrong. At the time, we had loans, credit cards. We never got behind on rent or water and gas, but at the time we moved up here, we were about eight grand in debt.

It's horrible, owing something all the time. I didn't have any choice but to put the money I earned doing joinery towards getting out of it. I worked twelve-hour days and I cleared it in a year-and-a-half.

These days, I get up at 6.50 a.m. I'm out the door by 7.55 a.m. I'll get home about 5 p.m. Before Covid, I'd have a quote booked in every night, so I'd go to someone's house after work to do the quote and I'd get back at about 6.30 p.m. Now, I try to schedule a day in the week where I can go round and see everyone in a working day.

I take quite a few breaks, where I'll just walk back to the van and have a few puffs of the vape. I've got a young apprentice with me now. And at lunchtime, we'll sit in the van and talk and look at videos – we're both quite into the gym – and by the time we're done it's been about an hour.

It's hard having an apprentice. I get frustrated because he's slow. I'll say this, *'Do this.'*

He'll start and I'll be like, '*I'll just do it.*'

Things are taking a bit longer for him to pick up, but it's because I can't step back. I'm not a very patient person.

In building, as long as it looks right and is safe, it doesn't matter how you do it. That's what I'm trying to teach him. There are some things where you can be quick. If you're ripping something down with your circular saw and it's going to be hidden, then it doesn't matter if that cut's rough. Don't waste time on things that aren't going to matter.

With the things that do matter, you've got to be logical. You look at something, '*Right, if I did that, what would happen ten steps down the line.*'

My apprentice has the beginnings of this, he just needs to get better.

– What's your relationship like?

It's a relationship where we're mates. Initially, I didn't want it to be like that. But you wouldn't want to be working with someone who you don't get on well with, would you? Sometimes customers don't understand it at all. They walk in and you're throwing sawdust at each other. But most of them laugh about it.

The other day my apprentice was fitting a Belfast sink and he said, '*The legs aren't lining up with the other units.*'

I looked at it and he'd put it in the wrong way round.

He was like, '*How was I meant to know?*'

When I retell that story to customers, I say that it was a fully built unit with the doors on it. I'm always overdramatic with it. But he'll wind me up with things, too.

I'll say, '*Try and fit this bit in here*' and he'll say, '*It won't fit.*'
'*Course it will.*'

When it doesn't fit, he'll say '*I told ya*', with a really smug face.
'*Right, you're sacked now.*'

I've seen him in social settings, and I've seen him at work and he's pretty much the same. I'm an open book with him. When we do jobs, I'm like, '*This is what we got paid. This is what I'm going to pay you.*'

It's mainly fun. Especially in the summer, where you're outside and in a t-shirt. It stops being fun when you get a non-paying customer, or you make an error yourself and you know you're going to be paid £500 less.

And sometimes the paperwork side of things can get a bit much. But the actual physical side of it, when I'm working with my arms and getting dirty, there's never been a time when I've thought of packing it in and getting a normal job.

I can't think of anything worse than putting a suit on and going to work in an office, because the main thing with joinery is that something's broken and then you fix it, and you can see it.

There wasn't a door there, now there's a door.

There wasn't a window there, now there is.

It's a physical thing that you can take pride in. With electrics, say, you chase it in, and you might do the neatest job in the world, but it's covered up by plaster.

I ask the customer if it's all right to take pictures. Sometimes, I'll have to cut round something and I'll do a neat cut first time, bang on. And I'll be like, *oh yeah*. I'll take a picture of it.

I'll zoom in on it that night and be like, *oh yeah*.

I've been a subby for the big housebuilders. A friend of a friend will say, '*We need a joiner.*'

You turn up, put in some roof joists and then you're done.

It's an easier job than doing your own projects. You turn up. Do the job. Go home. You don't have to think about anything. You don't have to think, *were they happy with the job?*

But these guys are trying to put the homes up so quick that the trades can't take pride in their work. You'll say, '*Right, that kitchen's going to take me a week.*'

And the boss will say, '*Can you do it in two days?*'

They'll throw bodies at it, but they all just get in each other's way.

Yes, some of the trades these housebuilders use are shit. But mainly it's the fact that these houses are going up so quick. How can you take pride in something that's taken ten minutes when it should take you half a day?

Two weeks is a nice length job. You can leave your tools on site if you want to. If a job goes on for a month, you think, *back here again.*

I like moving around. My mum and dad say that we've got gypsy blood in us, because even as an adult I only live in a house about three years before I get itchy feet and move.

I just feel like I've stuck around in the same place too long. I feel like there might be something better out there. But now I've got a wife and kids, it's hard getting them on board with moving, especially when they don't understand it.

In my head, there's this dream house. It's modest. A decent-sized townhouse, so the kids can go around on their bikes and walk into town. A four-bed for me, the wife, the cat, the dog, the two kids. A double garage so I could have a workshop in one.

Both my kids had difficulties when they were little. They were both in hospital at times. And my son wouldn't go to sleep, even when he was asleep, he'd scream.

One night, I went to go put him down in a cot and instead of placing him, I dropped him in frustration. Instantly, I felt horrible. I told my wife. I called social services on myself.

I thought, *this ain't right. Why would a father do that to his kids? What sort of human would do that?*

I spoke to my friends, and they said it was normal to get frustrated with your kids. But I'd already called social, so then I had the stress of thinking that they were going to take away my kids. We were absolutely skint at the time. I was working in a factory, taking one box and putting it into another box. It was demeaning. You're left with your thoughts and your thoughts run away with you.

I don't want to go back there.

But I also don't want a fleet of ten vans. I don't want to be on a million pounds a year. I don't want to be any higher than I am. I'm happy. Everything's balanced nicely, work, social life, family, gym, and still time for other things. I know that what balances can easily topple over, but if that happens, I'll deal with it.

Whatever is meant to happen is meant to happen. I try to let life run its course. I try not to mess around with it too much.

CHAPTER FOUR **FIGUREWORK**

Finance director

billing clerk

data analyst

accountant

Finance director

(40s)

This is a nice place to work.

The truth is, if you'd have asked me from day dot when I'd just left school, '*Would I want to go work in a chicken factory?*'

The answer would be, '*No.*'

However, for people who do work in chicken factories, this is actually one of the nicer ones you're going to work in.

Within reason, this is a nice place to work.

The business is a cradle to grave site. We've got about seventy farms across the whole of the region and from 6 a.m. we'll bring in chickens to kill them and process them through the factory.

The kill side is separate to the packing side, two distinct elements on the same site.

You can't just kill chickens and process them straight away, because the bird needs to come down to temperature. We have to chill them for a period of time.

In an ideal world – and I do accept that I can't live in this ideal world – you want full *carcass balance utilization*. When you sell a bird, you sell the whole bird, every component part.

The market and the consumer doesn't work like that. They want fillets. They want thighs. They want portions.

But the minute you cut a bird up, then you've got component parts. Now, the logic is that the price of each component part should equal the price of the whole bird. But it doesn't quite work like that. We lose 50p every time we cut a bird up.

We will normally kill around 120,000 birds a week; 25,000 birds a day. Yesterday, we killed something like 14,000, a massive shortfall that has a big impact in the factory. It means idle staff, no stock holding, *et cetera*.

— Why the shortfall?

We've had issues with catching the birds on the farms, which is a labour issue. We've also had issues with transport, because the haulage industry is having a bit of a meltdown.

We knew this was going to happen because we spoke about it at the 8.30 a.m. production meeting.

Every day, we talk about the same things. We'll go through accidents or incidents from the day before. We'll also go through customer service numbers — the customers we have and haven't delivered to — and production numbers

We want to produce 30,000 packs of chicken a day, 250,000 a week. If we're suddenly behind the curve, then the discussion is about what we're going to do to remedy that.

Poultry is not like making chocolate, where you can just stop supply if you want to. We've got twelve weeks' worth of bird sitting on farms. These are birds coming down a pipe that we can't stop. We can't turn them off. So, against our better judgement, we're still supplying certain retailers at a loss because if we don't then we've got a bigger loss: we've got nowhere to put the birds.

The factory works about twenty-two hours a day. 6 a.m. until 4 a.m. One-hundred people, fifty on days, fifty on nights.

Our workforce is made up of 10 per cent British nationals, 30 per cent Lithuanians, 20 per cent Polish, then probably 40 per cent Romanians and Bulgarians.

These guys have still got families back in their countries. They used to come over here and work and send money back. But now because the pound is so weak, they say, '*Do we even want to come back to the UK?*'

We've lost labour from this country. This is minimum wage labour, cheap labour, but it's the backbone of our industry. For the last thirty years the food manufacturing industry has been built on this labour and it has driven the price of food lower.

We can't forget that.

When there's a shortage of labour, a panic sets in. Competitors in the area offer two, three, four pounds an hour more than we're offering. Your first instinct is, *we need to compete with that.* We can't just rely on robotics or mechanical solutions. That's not what we're about. We need the human touch on our product.

Instead, we box clever.

At the end of the day, all these guys are really worried about – if I'm honest – is the pound notes. So we've left their hourly rate the same and tweaked all the other factors around it.

We've put in attendance bonuses, non-contractual bonuses, forklift bonuses.

That causes more admin for us, a nightmare for our HR and payroll department, but we cannot burden ourselves with an unsustainable labour cost going forward, because then you're burdened with that for life.

I left school with very few qualifications. I'm not putting myself on a pedestal or anything like that, but I say to my kids all the time, *'I'm probably the best example of making the best of what you can.'*

I'm not overly academic. I'm not super intelligent. I'm not out of the ordinary. There are far better accountants than me, but I'm so determined. I'll never give up. If I had said fifteen years ago, that I'd be qualified accountant by now, I'd have laughed at myself.

After school, I dossed around doing retail work. I interviewed for a job in a hairdresser.

One day my mum said, *'Right, you've got a choice, you go and get a job or you go back and study.'*

She phoned up a local sixth form. They were doing business studies.

I thought *oh okay then, education will be a bit of a doss, an easy life*.

When I went to the sixth form, the teachers cared. I probably had the best two years of my life there. I thought to myself, *I find this easy*. I understood the numbers. They meant something to me.

After college, I started off as a purchase ledger clerk for four years. It was the real basics of finance. Matching invoices up and understanding the way a finance department worked.

But I'd have been nearly thirty. I felt I was never going to go anywhere in life. I went to work for a food manufacturer and pretty much everything changed there. The finance director was quite a rough and robust character, straight talking. I thought, *can I work for this guy? I don't know*.

He ended up being a real mentor to me. I was there for eleven years, and I worked for him for eight years. I worked my way up from a management accountant to the head business partnering role.

In that time, he said, '*You've got to get qualified. You have to get qualified. It's not even an option*.'

And he pushed me hard. It was like a father thing. He was harsh at times. He was caring at times.

Studying for the accountancy qualification I'd do a full day's work, nine-to-five with an hour's commute. At home, I would study from 6 p.m. until midnight for two months until my exam. I didn't have a life.

One exam I failed four times. Every time I was two to three marks off a pass. There've been times where you think, *do I need this? Do I want to do this?* But I never gave up. I found a way to get through.

One of my sons is making the same mistakes that I made when I was his age. I'm trying to stop him but it's difficult because he's got that same stubbornness, that same arrogance that I had.

'*I don't need to do all this*', he says.

But you do need to do it. You don't know it all.

Billing clerk

(20s)

I once took a job in a supermarket giving out food samples. I'd stand next to an aisle with a tray.

Sometimes no one would take a sample for five hours. Five hours of doing nothing with no one to talk to.

I had one customer – one of those locals who comes into the supermarket two or three times a day – who used to throw compliments at me. It made me uncomfortable.

I thought, *you're like forty years' old and I'm twenty. This is awkward.*

So I'd just say '*Yeah*' and hope that he didn't come back.

After that I struggled to find a full-time job to be honest. A lot of places were like, '*You don't have experience*.' Part time jobs were fine, but a full-time job – a real job – that was hard to find.

Eventually someone got back to me: a job at a car insurance company. I worked in cancellations.

We took a £50 fee for each cancellation. I'd have to tell people about this fee, and they would never take it well. I don't know if they didn't read the contract or if the insurance sales person just never told them, but it was never a good call.

This place had high employee turnover.

When you have high employee turnover so many people make changes to each customer account on the computer system that each account just gets messy.

A customer would call: '*The police have pulled me over and told* me *I'm not insured, but I was meant to have been insured a month ago.'*

I'd look at the customer account on the computer and it'd be a ridiculous mess. I'd think, *I don't know what to do*, but I'd say, *'You're going to have to stay with me for a while.'*

When you put the customers on hold, we could only put them on hold for two minutes before you'd have to go back to them and say, *'I'm still looking into this for you.'*

You can hear that they're ready to take out their anger on you.

One customer asked me, *'How are you?'* but I didn't realize that he was speaking to someone else and I said, *'I'm good thank you. How are you?'*

He said, *'I wasn't talking to you. Just do your job.'*

There were so many customers who were just horrible. We weren't allowed to hang up the phone, so you just had to deal with it. I thought, *is this what the working world is like?*

Even now, whenever I speak to someone on the phone, I always think back to that job. I think, *ah this person's going to be really rude to me.* But no one's ever spoken to me like that since.

A recruiting agency rang me and said that there was a job going at an estate agent, in billings. I said, *'I don't know what that is but okay I'll go for the interview.'*

I went into the office and spoke to the person who's now my team leader. About ten minutes into our conversation she was like, *'I want to hire you.'*

I said, *'Are you sure?'*

For this job, the training has been so much better. They didn't throw me in at the deep end. They said to me, *'In the first year, you're learning about the billing system, and the second year is when you understand it.'*

I've been there nearly a year, and they still say, *'Oh let's train you on this.'*

I'll log in at home or in the office.

Sometimes the VAT receipts need to be sent out.

Sometimes invoices need to be created.

Sometimes invoices from surveyors need to be printed out.

Sometimes charges need to be raised.

The amounts should always match between the documents and the system. You can't switch off, because if you switch off you end up doing more work.

It's not building a house, but I've still got an objective and I'm still achieving something when I check the invoices, make sure everything's right, and send them off on time. It's a large company and if someone refuses to pay an invoice, that's a big thing. The company's like a wheel and we keep it spinning.

In the Asian community, we're very hard-working people. We know what it's like to be really poor. We have to keep working hard to get places, because we know at the end of the day it's not fair.

My dad's a taxi driver. He used to work nights but now he works from 8 p.m. to 6 p.m. Monday to Saturday. My mum works as a carer at the same time as doing the double shift as a housewife, raising children, cooking, cleaning.

I'll never experience racism as bad as my parents did because the world's changing. The changes are benefiting me, because companies have to make sure they have diversity in the workplace.

Also if I'd been born twenty years earlier, the Asian community would've said, 'Why do you want to work?'

Because of my background, my parents never expected me to work as much as I have. They say, 'Do you not just want to get married?'

I say, 'No not really.'

I don't like the idea of not being financially independent. It's a bit vain but I don't like the idea of going to the shops and asking someone, 'Can you get me this?'

I'll get it myself. It's more satisfying.

I think my parents are proud of me. They won't admit it, but I think they are.

Data analyst

(20s)

In India my family comes from one of the lower classes. My father earns about £100 per month. He's an electrician.

I used to watch him do electrical work. I'd stand behind him to see exactly what he was doing.

I was good at math. In my final year of secondary school, I scored ninety-eight out of a hundred in the state math exam. They put my name on a board in the school.

But I've always been little bit lazy. I have the attention of a butterfly. I'll fly here and fly there, hover around, but I'll never sit on one thing.

I studied mechanical engineering in India. Jobs in mechanical engineering there are pretty vigorous and tough. I once did a project in a forge that made vehicle parts. I thought, *I'm not working here.* It got hot and there wasn't proper ventilation.

I wouldn't have minded doing this sort of fieldwork in the UK, where it's beautiful outside but in India there's a lot of pollution, traffic, road accidents.

I thought, *I'm not risking my life for a job.*

After graduating, I wasn't certain about what to do but I'd done a basic course in SQL, which is a database programming language, and I got to know about working in data.

I then started applying to companies randomly.

I'll tell you the story of my first interview process. The company gave out a notification. *'Today, we will have a walk-in interview for a data associate role.'*

That's it. They don't give you a job description.

I walked into the company's office at 9.30 a.m. There were around fifty candidates sitting there. I spoke to an HR person, and I described to him my experience with databases.

He said, '*Okay, you have a pass to the next round.*'

I waited until 1 p.m. for my next interview. And while I waited, a hundred-and-twenty people walked in for that single role. Some were in their fifties.

I thought, *these guys certainly have more experience than me. Why would they take me?*

In the second-round interview, I met with the manager and told him how I would write certain database queries. As I walked out, he asked '*When can you join?*' and I knew that I'd got the part.

The company's main client was a global computer hardware supplier. When this supplier moved physical assets from location to location, we would move them on the database. A lot of my work was manual. I was cheap labour, £2,500 per year.

When I was working at the hardware supplier, I started doing a little bit of research into foreign universities.

My initial plan was to go to the US to do a master's in data science, but I did a little bit of budgeting and I saw that it was around £70,000 to get into a decent college. And in America, you can only do part-time work on the campus. If you work off-campus and someone finds out, you could get deported back to India.

I'm not risking £70,000 for that. I've never seen that amount of money. If my dad worked seven lifetimes, he would still not be able to earn £70,000.

Here in the UK the cost worked out at around £25,000. It was still a lot, but it was achievable.

The fees for the British student doing my course were £4,500 and I paid around £25,000. Indian students being here is a win win, for the British economy and for us.

The reason I'm here in the UK is because of my uncle. I was looking at getting an education loan from the bank and my uncle said to me,

'*If you really want to do this, we have a small piece of land that you can use as collateral.*'

He gave me the papers and I got a loan for the fees.

After I'd paid the fees, I had savings of around £1,000 when I arrived in the UK.

The rent went out immediately and I was down to about £250.

It was Covid and everything was locked down. It was little bit scary. I was walking around the town centre, and everything was closed.

I had a simple process in my mind. I'll put my studies to one side, and I'll work hard on getting a part-time job.

I used to do seventy applications a day. I had a lot of rejections before I got a job in a supermarket. It was early morning shifts, from 3 a.m. to 11 a.m., which meant I had the whole day to study.

After I graduated, I got a job in the UK as a data specialist at a British product-testing company. I worked on reporting for the marketing department. I'd help write a monthly marketing report, which would be sent out to around three-hundred people.

The report dealt with social media performance, trends for website visitors, email click throughs. A lot of decisions were made on the basis of these reports. I felt like I was working on something valuable.

There was a kind of creativity involved. It was up to me to come up with measurements and insights that we could use in the report. Things like working out the average amount of time a visitor spends on the website, or mapping the journey of an average website visitor.

The data is like a gold mine. Everyone is in the dark, but I am the one holding the torch, showing them the way to the gold.

At this time my parents were not well. I was supporting them financially, whatever they needed, but I wasn't there for them.

I would get paid £2,200 per month after tax. I'd then pay £1,000 as a monthly instalment on my Indian education loan, £500 for rent, £400 for groceries and bills, £150 to my parents, which goes a long way in India. This left me with £150 or so for myself.

The company told me right before Christmas that my contract wasn't being renewed. It was a shocking thing because before that my manager was saying, '*We are going to extend your contract.*'

But at the very end moment they said, '*We can't extend it.*' They gave a very basic explanation related to performance, with a couple of examples: '*You should have scheduled this meeting.*'

It was very generic.

I'd had a feedback session in October where they were going gaga about me. '*You are doing a really good job. The directors trust your work.*'

I was proactive. I was coming up with machine learning algorithms to predict sales and revenue for upcoming years.

It doesn't make any sense, right? They were praising me and then in a couple of months: '*You're done.*'

I do not hold a grudge against them, but I should have been informed beforehand. I had particular offers that I turned down because they said they were going to extend the contract.

A lot of things are on the line for me.

I have to pay back my loan, the interest is mounting up. If I don't pay it'll affect my credit score in India.

My visa is on the line. I have to find a job at a company that will sponsor my visa. The pay doesn't matter to me that much, so long as I get a visa sponsorship and the opportunity to work with data.

I told my uncle – the one who let me use his property – I told him about my contract not being renewed. He said, '*It's just a piece of property. Don't worry about it. You have to take care of yourself.*'

But I know I have to worry about it.

Accountant

30s

I grew up in a deprived city. To use a long word, it was *post-industrial*. My aunties and uncles and cousins, everyone was within a ten-mile radius of the city.

I did well at school and college, top class, good grades, but when I got to seventeen, I was fed up of living there. I wanted to get out, but I didn't know what I wanted to do. I didn't have a burning passion to be this or that. I was just good at passing exams. I didn't particularly enjoy college, but with the EMA, I got £10 a week if I attended every lesson.[3] I'd get halfway through the week and think, *this isn't worth £10.*

I asked one of my teachers what I should do, and they said, *'If you want to study business, you should go to this uni.'* I did what they suggested.

I remember my years at uni as good years. I found it easier than college in terms of passing exams. The course had two or three accounting modules and lots of business modules – marketing, law, strategy.

Half of it was quantitative and the other half, I'd call it *'bullshit'*, but other people would call it *'strategy'*. I had no interest in the managing-marketing-strategy stuff. I'd fall asleep if someone started talking about Maslow's hierarchy of needs or if someone drew a four-box matrix and started putting things in it.

3 Between 2004 and 2011, the Educational Maintenance Allowance (EMA) provided financial support to students aged 16–19 from low-income households.

The lecturer would say, '*That goes in box three.*'

I'd be like, *how? You're plucking numbers out of the air. What are you basing that on?*

The uni forced us to do a sandwich placement in the third year. Again, I didn't think too much about what I was going to do – I really did drift into where I've ended up – but the application processes for these placements, it was like you were applying for the FBI. Verbal reasoning tests. Maths tests. Personality tests.

I applied to two of the Big Four and I ended up getting one of them, an offer to work in audit.

A lot of that placement year was driving to towns on the south coast. Sometimes you'd be staying at a nice hotel on a beach, but often it was just driving and sitting in traffic.

You'd get to the office of the company you were auditing.

The client would say, '*Here's a room for you to work in. Here's a table.*'

And you'd be in a shitty dimly lit office, with leftover chairs, your back killing you by the end of the day. I was just thinking about getting the day done and getting to the weekend.

After the placement I got a graduate job sorted with the same accounting company. I came to London, and I saw the offices of the Big Four and it was like an episode of *The Apprentice*.

You think, *the world is my oyster*.

Then your first job is with a client in Hillingdon and you're getting in early and going home late and you don't see the sun for a week, and you think, *shit, this isn't what I expected*.

The whole audit job is based around the annual financial statements. You've got to walk through the business's processes to identify what could go wrong to cause a mistake in the financial statements. Once you understand what could go wrong, you then get straight into, '*Let's look at the balance sheet. You've got £3 million with Customer A. Can we get confirmation from Customer A that they do in fact owe you £3 million?*'

It's checklists like you wouldn't believe. That's what kills you. You can look at a company and, often, by reviewing the numbers and getting a feel for the business you can smell where the risks of errors in the financial statements are, but the checklists and the forms that you have to fill out put you in a straitjacket. It takes your gut instinct away.

I get it, because you can't sign off an audit saying *'Yeah, I've got a good feeling about this business'*, but going through a checklist with three hundred questions on it . . .

If I'm honest, I didn't really see the value in the service I was providing. The actual service of audit, me coming along and going *'That feels correct'* and poking around someone's office to tell them what they already know, it's not really adding value.

Audit has always been a great foot in the door for the Big Four to unleash their tax and corporate advisery teams. The auditors know when to keep their mouth shut to not upset the client's management.

Later on in my career, I was working at a company that was being audited and I got the impression that the auditors weren't happy with some of the numbers, but they didn't push back. And I think it was a case of the management team wanting the auditors to say something and the auditors wanting the management to say something, but nobody wants to put their neck on the line and say, *'Those figures are garbage'.* Accountants aren't known for being the most aggressive, right?

I wouldn't say I felt fulfilled when I was doing audit, but you feel good getting through it. It's what I imagine military service feels like: maybe you don't understand what it's all in aid of, but you come out of it stronger than when you went in.

After three years at the Big Four, one of my clients offered me a job as an accountant and I thought, *well, I've always wanted to get out of audit.* I took the job. When I took it, I was afraid that one day I'd look back at the people that had stayed in the Big Four and wish I'd done what they did. So much of the conversation at those places is about when you should leave. I've heard it described as an escalator: you've got to decide what level you get off. But that's a negative way of looking at things, because staying isn't the only way of rising.

I didn't have any plan for my career, other than to always keep progressing, to keep getting better at whatever I decided to do, and to keep making more money.

I've made these big shifts in life, and I've never really given them much thought. I've just kind of gone on. It's strange because I'm quite a precise and analytical person in other respects.

I feel an element of detachment, and maybe that's a consequence of working in a corporate environment. There's not much of a community.

I've left jobs that I've put a lot of effort into and when you leave, you don't get a medal, you don't get a plaque saying what a great person you were, it's an anticlimax. *'See you later. Have a good life.'*

Just before Covid, my wife got a transfer to a US branch of her company, and I ended up taking a financial controller role out there. I was trying to keep up. I was stressed and compensating for it by making personal sacrifices. I'd sneak online and do maybe four hours work on a Sunday. Four hours doesn't sound like a lot, but your day is destroyed . . . It was good stress, it pushed me, but I carried it for too long.

America sucks you in. It's like an amusement arcade, full of bright lights that drain you after a while.

I skipped Covid in this country. Covid in the US was nowhere near as bad, especially in the state I was in, and the impression I've got since coming back is that people in the UK seem to be really downbeat, that motivation is at an all-time low.

Perhaps part of it is that Americans talk positively, and British people talk negatively, but it seems more negative than I've ever seen. I suppose if you're working stupid hours in an office, then at least there's a sense of camaraderie. Whereas if you're stuck at home doing that, then you think, *what the fuck is all this for?*

It's very easy to feel lonely working from home. Of course, I don't buy the argument that people don't do any work when they work from home, because if you have a task to do, you'll do it. But I think people have under-estimated how much of their socialization came from work.

They would've complained about it. They would've said, '*I'm sick of Jim bringing in his ham and cheese sandwich every Wednesday*.'

But if you take something away for a long enough period, then you miss it.

I know everyone's on LinkedIn posting a picture of their coffee with their dog at their feet, sun shining in through their kitchen window.

Okay, it looks like you're having a nice morning but what are you like at 6 p.m. when it's gloomy and you haven't spoken to anyone all day?

There was someone at the firm where I trained. He was the golden boy. I spoke to him after I'd come back from the US, and he didn't seem anywhere near as *I'm-going-to-take-over-the-world* as he was.

He'd taken a job as a financial controller at an oil major. A great role, but everyone used to say he'd be partner one day.

It seems like a lot of people have downed tools and said, '*It's not worth it*.'

CHAPTER FIVE **SALES WORK**

Shopkeeper

technical sales engineer

expert network consultant and manager

business development manager

Shopkeeper

(40s)

I took a loan on my house in India and used it to study in the UK. As a student, I worked in nightclubs and doing cleaning jobs. When I completed my studies, I applied for jobs in London, but nothing happened. The recruitment agencies and the companies never gave me feedback. I never had any feedback.

I couldn't find a career, so I ended up working in a petrol station. I worked there for six, seven years. I became a supervisor. The salary wasn't so good, so I changed career and became a taxi driver.

I used to work for a private firm and Uber. It was good money. Working sixty hours, I was making around £400 a week after all the expenses.

Then Covid came and the customers didn't want to risk their lives getting flu, so they didn't come. I got no support from the government. At that time, I got £20 for working ten hours. I thought, *this is not working*. I felt very down. My one worry was income.

I did some work at an airport and at a Covid testing centre. When that ended, my wife said, '*You've got experience working in a petrol station, why not try a shop.*'

We had some savings between us, so we decided to get a lease for this shop.

I wake up at around 7 a.m. First thing, I go to the cash and carry and buy different stock. Every day, I'll buy two or three different products, tissues, alcohol, cigarettes, vapes.

Then I'll go to the bank and deposit any cash that I got the previous day.

I'll then drive to the shop, relieve my staff at 10.30 a.m. and I'll work until 8 p.m. After that, I go home, have some dinner and go to sleep.

I then do the same thing the next day, the same thing every day.

You need to have a good sales space and good customer footfall. Whenever you want to buy any business, you should also make sure there's no competition.

We've got three corner shops at this crossroads. If it was only two shops, this could've gone really well, a career for life, but the customers are spread out between three, and so our sales are low.

I'm putting in eighty, ninety hours and it's not paying me as much as I was earning in a taxi before Covid.

For me, my career has been a bit of struggle. I haven't found the right career so far.

I'm thinking in the future, I could try being an electrician, something where I can get enough income to pay all the bills, something where I can work forty hours a week and still be able to save £400 a month. But it's hard to find a job nowadays.

My mistake has been rushing into things because I've had to pay my bills and rent. My advice to others would be to be patient.

If I look back over the past twenty years, I think I could have been happier in India. But it's hard to go back now because I don't have a solid career. And at least in this country, you can always find driving jobs, delivery jobs, taxi jobs.

The customers are the best bit about the shop. They are very nice. I know the loyal customers by name. I know what they do in their lives.

Somebody runs a window cleaning business. Somebody's retired. Somebody's going to visit their family down in Devon. When you talk to customers every day, they become close and I don't feel tired after working ten, eleven hours.

I found it a bit nerve-wracking speaking to them in the beginning, but it's like an energy that you pass to people, and they pass the same energy back to you.

It's one of the best jobs. And if I was able to make £1,000 or £2,000 more sales a week, then I'd say it was the best career. When I have busy days and I make good sales, I go home happy; it's like when you grow a plant, and you start to see it fruit.

Technical sales engineer

(40s)

At school, I never really bonded with anything. I tried to join the computer club, but the male teacher told me that computers weren't for girls.

We were funnelled towards very passive roles. *You could work in an office as an admin assistant. You could go into HR management.* I remember thinking, *I want to die. Is this my life?*

I made the stunning life decision to get pregnant when I was seventeen. I never went to university.

When my daughter was school-aged – I couldn't afford the childcare before then – I started working as a temporary admin assistant.

I remember feeling nervous when I started the temp job. It was like I was acting in a play.

But there was something valuable about going to work and being valued for who you are as an individual, rather than being valued in relation to other people – as a mother to a child, a wife to a husband. Work retains your sense of self.

A chap I was seeing when I was temping introduced me to this game *Doom*. If the computer didn't work, I couldn't play doom, so I got him to start showing me how to fix the computer. And that was it, I was absolutely in love. DOS, the command line, it all lit up my brain in an incredibly pleasing way. I gathered up computer manuals and read them.

I am drawn to the logic of computers. I don't always understand human beings very well, with their opaque objectives. I'd rather know *yes or no.*

My first IT support job came when I annoyed the guy in the IT department so much that he let me become the helpdesk caller. After six months of that, one of the chaps in IT support broke his leg, and he couldn't go out and do the jobs, so he answered the phone, and I did the jobs.

I worked through a variety of IT support roles. Eventually, I got into networks and firewalls, and I began specializing in that area.

Network support is about getting the traffic to the right place, quickly and cleanly.

Security is about making sure that the traffic is safe as it travels.

Twenty years ago, a hacker was a goblin in a hood, typing in a dark cave, who had to have some skill to be able to hack things. Now, you can just buy malware as a service off the internet. You then buy a database of names, click a button and the malware does it all for you. Mischief used to take skill, now it just takes a malicious impulse.

I then moved to internet service providers and began leading teams. Eventually, I was running security projects for blue chip companies.

The problem with these support roles is that, when you're a junior and there's a problem in the middle of the night, you're woken up at 2 a.m. to observe the fix. When you're promoted, you're woken up at 2 a.m. to help with the fix. When you're in charge of the team, you're still up at 2 a.m. because your team are fixing it. And when you're in charge of a team globally, you're responsible for the problem having happened in the first place.

When I was a manager, I was always a little bit worried that I'd be one of those people that someone would go home and moan about to their other half, moan about how miserable I'd been making them. I myself had moaned about previous managers. I thought, *God is it possible that I'm that kind of manager without knowing it?*

I decided that it probably wasn't possible. I could be an arsehole. I could be demanding at times. But I always got my guys raises. I always sent them on training. And I always got them the best bonuses I could.

One of the worst things I've had to do was actually dismiss someone. That was so, so stressful. At the beginning of the process, HR said to me that what the employee had done was gross misconduct and that I should just dismiss them. That was all the guidance I was given.

I remember after I told the employee that I was dismissing them, I burst into tears around the corner, because it was awful.

The employee appealed straight away, and the company appointed someone to look into all of my actions for the previous six weeks. I thought, *where was this level of scrutiny and effort when I asked for help*. I had sleepless nights. I became very ill. I felt so unsupported by the company.

I remember thinking, *managing people really sucks*. I couldn't do it properly because my heart wasn't in it. And I felt that if I carried on, I would become that person that ruins people's lives. I was worrying too much. I was over-involved.

Management can be a problem for technical people. Sometimes they bring the same approach to people as they do to their keyboards. *If I tap this button, it will do what I want it to do*.

But human beings are distressingly stubborn.

At the beginning of lockdown, I found that I had been so focused on my career that I was plunged into an intense state of isolation. It can be quite dangerous to fill your social life with work-related things.

I was on my own in a little rabbit hutch of an apartment. I went a little insane. I hadn't built anything locally, anything real. I was used to being out and about a couple of nights a week, but it was always with work. All I could think about was work and things related to work.

In white collar jobs, where you have some control over your work, it's up to you to draw the line and enforce it. If you keep working sixty hours a week, it becomes what everyone is used to. You do that for six months and then you try to pull back and people think you're slacking.

I do think modern work can become too entwined in your life. We need to be careful. When companies say, '*Ah we're a family here*', we should treat that as a horrific idea. I don't need work to be a family. I need to be at a good and fair employer that pays me well. An employer that I enjoy working for, but that I don't feel joined to the hip to.

As I hit middle age, I really wish I'd had this attitude of *I have no fucks to give* twenty years earlier. I think it would have done me a lot of good to have been bolshie about things when I was thirty instead of now.

I suppose it's something you learn . . .

Eventually I thought, *I don't want to do this any more. I want a better work–life balance.*

I looked into sales, and I realized that I could halve my hours and double my pay. So I left and moved into technical sales, selling cyber security products. It's commonly considered to be joining the dark side, but I have no regrets. I'm pleased with where I've got to. I'm incredibly well-paid and I do something I love.

Where I work now is also stuffed with women. I love it. I think in the first fifteen, twenty years of my career, I was pretty much the only woman, all of the time.

And when I'd done well and been promoted, some people would say, '*It's because they want a woman.*'

Even this interview, someone said, '*They want a woman.*'

I said, '*Maybe, but I've suffered enough for occasionally something good to come out of it.*'

One of the problems with working in the City is that all the socializing takes place in a bar after work.

I sometimes wonder what it must be like to be a man and not have to calculate how drunk the people are around you. I've been in situations where it's me and twenty half-drunk men. Someone always thinks this is the time to try their arm. Let's say that I don't mind –

shoot your shot, no problem – what I do mind is that, when I say '*No*', they take that as a signal to turn into a raging arsehole for the next six months.

I spend a lot of time with men. Sometimes I'm the only woman they talk to for hours. Some of them get the wrong idea because they don't interact with women at all, and they mistake my friendliness for something else.

At some places I've worked, I've had to isolate myself and not go out for drinks after work. I don't really understand some of these people. They go out with their mates after work and they don't think their mates want to have sex with them, so why do they think I do?

Sometimes men think, *I would never behave like that*, and they don't outright see this behaviour going on, and because of this they find it very hard to believe. But the people that behave abusively or unpleasantly don't do it in front of people that would stop them. They wait until the good guys aren't around. And I think men need to be a bit more cognisant of this. It's not that all men are doing it, it's that one arsehole can upset maybe fifty women a year.

I have left jobs to get away from these situations. I believe it's impacted my career. I've had roles that I've taken only to realize that the reason why my name was put forward was because the guy who put my name forward liked the idea of me working with him, for entirely the wrong reasons.

On one occasion, someone I was working with on a project wanted me to help run a workshop in Europe. I asked if he'd booked the office and he said, '*No, I've decided that you're going to stay at my summer house. It'll be much more tranquil*.' And because I said no, he didn't talk to me for four months and the project became almost impossible to deliver.

Everyone at my current job is pretty cool. I haven't seen any of that behaviour here, which is one of the reasons I'm so happy.

– Tell me about how you sell.

When you sell to a customer, you have to work out who is leading the need, who the tail wagging the dog is.

Is it a network team decision? Is the network guy in charge? If so, we'll talk about speed. I'll draw things out on a board, showing how it all connects together. I'll still make it clear to them that they still have to comply with the data security stuff.

Is it a security team decision? Is the Chief Security Officer in charge? If so, I'd talk to them about regulation, and data security. You talk about more nebulous things like *safety*. You try to work out what he's worried about, and what his Board is worried about.

Or is it a procurement-led decision? In which case, they want to have everything as cheaply as possible. You do try to explain to them how big the GDPR fines are.

I have a stack of notebooks, a different colour for each account I'm working on.

There's something about writing with a pen. Handwriting sticks in my head. I can type fast, but it's divorced from my head, it doesn't mean anything.

In the notebooks, I'll write down: *key relationships, personalities, key concerns, previous activities, the desired future state, level of technological interest, where the conflicts are within the org, who do we like, who do we not like, where haven't we done things well, who seems to be in charge.* I'll draw a few maps in there of how the people I'm working with in the organization interact with each other.

– You mentioned earlier that you liked things to be in black and white. Have you managed to impose that on this job?

Absolutely not, and it is a significant cause of stress for me. People don't say what they mean.

It's something I have to live with.

Expert network consultant and manager

(20s)

Essentially, it's cold-calling, reaching out to CEOs, directors, vice-presidents, and trying to get them to do some ad hoc consulting for my clients, who are primarily private equity firms and hedge funds – it's corporate, but it's not really.

Our clients will give me a call and say, *'Hey, I'm researching X industry. I'm looking to speak to customers who have a specific type of software. Can you and your team source those customers?'*

I then set this up in our CRM (Customer Relationship Management) software. I write screening questions for the experts. My associates will go off and find the most relevant people. After that, I collate the responses and send them to the client, who chooses which expert advisers they want to speak to, and then I'll set up the teleconferences.

The client pays a lot. A lot. Irrespective of how much the adviser charges, the client pays between $920 and $1,300 per call. Some advisers charge £50 per call, so the margins are huge. It's so lucrative. If you can deal with being in the industry, you will make a lot of money, a lot of money. But it's not for everyone.

The industry is heavily target driven. Each associate is given a target every month. I have one as a manager. I need to make sure that everyone's reaching their targets.

I think I'm a good manager because I'm empathetic towards people. But if I'm too nice, then my managers tell me that I need to be pushing more. One of my managers said, '*The associates need to be scared of you.*'

I was like, '*No they don't!*'

It's a double-edged sword with targets. I am very competitive. And when I was an associate, if my manager was like, '*Sorry, you're not doing that well this month*' I would think, *right! What am I going to do to make sure I hit it?*

It's a constant pressure. If you want to make a lot of money in the industry, you hit your targets and then you get commission plus bonus.

A good month would add an extra two grand to your salary.

If a client emailed me at 10 p.m., I couldn't help but reply: *if I don't do it now it's tomorrow's job, our competitors aren't going to be responding at 10 p.m., if I reply now I can get the lion's share of the six or seven calls this guy wants for this project.*

Each bit of commission is a dopamine hit. You're like, *ooh another one*. And the software allows you to see how your peers are doing.

It was like a game, but then like most games, it became less and less interesting.

Before the pandemic, I was struggling badly with my mental health. On a Sunday, things would get dark in my head. It was the only day where there was nothing else going on.

During the week, I'd come home in the evenings and maybe I'd be a bit sad, but I'd still worked that day, I'd still cooked, I'd still kept my commitments, I'd still gone into the office.

I was a bit of a show pony at work. It was this mask that I was wearing, but keeping busy stopped me from falling into that next level of depression. I didn't have time to be sad.

Maybe I could have gone on for another ten years in my career, going into the office every day and distracting myself, but the penny would have dropped eventually, and I'm so grateful that it did. The pandemic gave me the opportunity to feel what I was really feeling.

When the pandemic hit, I thought it was going to be so good. I'd never worked from home before, and I thought it was going to be like a holiday.

But I was suffering from depression, and I started using *'I'm working'* as an excuse not to leave the house. It was like, *my life is this and I can't do anything else*. It sounds really sad, but the only joy I would get would be that *ding-ding-ding* of the commission.

I found that my performance went down. I put in the bare minimum to my work.

My alarm would ring at 8.55 a.m. I'd snooze for five minutes. Then I'd go on my phone and I'd put in some client feedback onto the CRM, so that people would get a notification and know that I was online.

I'd message a few people on Teams and gather the energy to get out of bed and start the day, which would usually happen around 9.30 a.m.

Out of bed, dressing gown on. I did so many calls in my dressing gown. My bed and my desk are thirty centimetres away from each other.

My justification was always *I'm going to work 'til 11 p.m. probably, so if I'm at my desk at 9.30 a.m. that shouldn't matter*.

I was working a lot less if I'm honest – maybe four hours a day. But it wasn't noticed.

A few months later, I asked for a promotion when I hadn't done the work. And that's when the sit-down happened, *'What are you doing with your day? There's not much going on here.'*

I was like, *'Err.'*

This sit-down delayed my progression by a year. I had a few meetings with VPs where we came up with a plan of action. I implemented those changes and eventually I became a manager. My hours then went back up dramatically, 9 a.m. until 11 p.m. some days.

But when I was working from home and living with my friends, I realized that my company was a little bit more toxic than other places. Their days were a lot shorter, their managers a lot nicer.

They could take a two-hour break to go for a walk as long as they got their work done. There was no presenteeism. Whereas I have constantly felt, if there was a lull in my day, *I need to be online, need to be online.*

I didn't understand why my friends didn't have those pressures. If I was offline for two hours, I'm going to get messages. *'Hello? Hello? Hello?'*

My friends would finish work on time, and they'd have lots of meetings about meetings. I want a meeting about a meeting!

We were told – not officially, nothing written down – that if a client emails you before 10pm, you need to respond immediately, because making our clients happy is at the forefront of everything we do.

The reason why we're working so much is because the clients are working so much. If a client wasn't wanting to book calls at 1 a.m., I wouldn't be doing that either.

We're reacting to our client's needs in the same way that lawyers are reacting to their client's needs. It's systemic in the whole corporate world. It's not one company, it's not just consultants, it's not just lawyers, it's the world we work in.

– *What's your priority in life?*

I never want to be out of work, because I'm scared that, if I stop, I won't be able to start again.

I want to have a stable level of happiness, and that desire comes from having been sad for a lot of my life. Also, it sounds so silly, but my biggest priority is to have something that nobody can take away from me, to have my own children, to have my own financial stability. I can find happiness there.

Business development manager

(40s)

I'm a Business Development Manager for an outdoor education company, which I suppose is a posh way of saying that I work in sales. I try to encourage schools to come on residential stays at our centres across the UK.

The majority of the time I'm calling, emailing, and using LinkedIn to approach schools to talk to them about doing a residential course.

I then do quite a lot of account management: for customers that have used us in the past, how can I make sure their experience is the best that it can be? Rather than having them just bring the Year 6's like they did last year, how can I make it the Year 5's *and* 6's?

There can be quite a lot of Zoom presentations to schools and to parents. I'm also always on the lookout for education trade shows and exhibitions where I can set up a stand. And at least once or twice a week, I find myself showing customers around the centres. That's my favourite part of the role.

I have 100 per cent freedom. I check in with my boss fairly regularly, once or twice a week, where I let her know what I'm doing rather than asking permission to do it. But if I didn't speak to her for weeks on end, she'd be fine.

The job has always been field-based. In the past, the expectation would be that you'd be in the company car driving to schools, sitting around and trying to convince them, but because of Google Meet and Teams and Zoom, it's more convenient for schools to go, *'Let's jump on a call for half an hour'.*

There was freedom before, but it's increased since Covid.

My little boy's in a primary school just up the road. I get to take him to school two or three times a week. I pick him up twice a week. A lot of my friends who are dads don't get to do that. They're not getting home 'til six.

When I finish at the end of the day and my wife or little boy ask me, '*Have you had a good day?*', nine times out of ten I say, '*Yeah it was nice*' or '*It was easy*' or '*I saw this excited kid who just ran off the coach because they live in a city and they'd never seen the amount of land that we have.*'

Whatever it may be that's happened that day, nine times out of ten the days are pretty good.

My sister worked for a water company for many years, in a similar role to mine. She said to me, '*Why are you so happy in your job when I hate mine?*'

I said, '*Because I sell fun things. You're selling water.*'

I've always tried to do something that I've at least got a basic level of interest in.

I once worked for a company supplying mobility aids to keep people in their own homes, saving the NHS money. At the time, my dad and my grandma were relying quite heavily on both the NHS and mobility aids, so it was nice to support that in some way. I loved that job.

Then my wife and I had our one and only child, and my dad and grandma both passed away. I was approached by the outdoor education company. By that point, I felt I had doffed my cap a little to the older generations, and I was drawn to something where my son could say, '*My dad does outdoor education and he's involved with all these great things for kids.*'

I walked around one of the centres and it was in a bad place, really bad. I thought, *you know what? I could come here and genuinely make a difference.*

This is a really big-headed thing to say, but I'm a fairly intelligent person, but I'm not intelligent enough to be a multimillionaire. I'm not. I haven't got the next big idea. So I made a decision quite early on in my career to always do something that has a moral purpose to it.

If a company offered me £10,000 more to sell stationery into schools, even though I've got the contacts and I'd probably be fairly successful, I don't think I'd do it. It wouldn't appeal to me. So if I do decide to move, it'll be into something that I hold dear in one way or another.

– Are there targets that you have to meet?

I do have to make sure my centres bring in quite a lot of money. I oversee the south of England, and I have one residential centre of focus, and my revenue target is about £7.3 million. It doesn't really matter how I make that 7.3. As long as I do, everyone's happy.

– Does that target stress you out?

No, but that's probably to do with me as a person. I don't get stressed out about anything to be honest. I've never really thought about why.

I've got that Dr Pepper ethos: what's the worst that could happen? If I lose my job, I can get another one. That's fine. I'm quite financially sensible. I always make sure I've got a year or so's salary set aside.

I'm not a status-y person. I've always said that I'd do what I need to do to earn money. If I had to work as a binman, I'd work as a binman. If I had to work on the trains, I'd work on the trains. If I had to work in Sainsbury's – *cool* – so long as it pays the bills and keeps my family happy.

My wife works two days a week for the local council. They're always saying to her, '*Do you want any more hours? Do you want to climb up to the next grade?*'

She's like, '*No, I'm really happy where I am.*'

It's not that we lack ambition, but it's just that life's too nice . . .

I'm happy, she's happy, and everything just works.

CHAPTER SIX **SCHOOLWORK**

Nursery assistant manager

primary school teacher and former soldier

secondary school teacher

academic

Nursery assistant manager

(40s)

I helped out at a friend's preschool and I loved working with the children. I fell in love with the sector. You watch children grow and develop right there in front of you.

It's so satisfying to talk to a child and to hear them repeat words back to you, or to teach them how to use a pair of scissors – all these life skills that children learn under the age of five. And as much as they're never going to remember who taught them how to use scissors, that skill will be with them for life, which is a very rewarding feeling.

Some are tiny babies when they arrive. You watch them roll over for the first time, learn to walk, learn to speak. Then suddenly you're watching them leave and you know that you're not going to see them again.

It's not like other jobs.

You might have a finish time, but if you can't get out for staff–child ratio reasons then you're stuck at work. You end up spending more time with these children than their own families do. And I spend more time with the children that I look after than with my own children.

You are so wrapped up in what's going on around you, all these different little lives.

Even when you leave, you never switch off. You're always thinking, *what am I going to do tomorrow?*

It is heartbreaking that nursery work isn't recognized as it should be. If you're a qualified nursery nurse – never mind that you've got three years' worth of study behind you and that you're in charge of children and multiple staff – you'd get paid more working in Tesco's than you would a nursery.

You're working 8 a.m. 'til 6 p.m. every day on a one-to-eight ratio, or you're in a baby room on a one-to-three ratio with three babies crying, like a parent with triplets.

You've also got paperwork to do, activity planning to do, updates to parents to do, and conversations with parents at the end of it.

Of course, you're going to make mistakes, and each mistake could put a child's life at risk. There's so many things in the news with poor nursery nurses being scrutinized and criticized. We're under pressure and we're as stretched as far as we can be.

So much support goes out to teachers, but early years' workers don't get that kind of support. We don't get the holidays like teachers do. We don't get half terms and six weeks off in the summer. I remember when there was an issue finding teachers, so the government gave bursaries and bonuses to students to get them to do their teacher training. They need to do the same for early years.

There always used to be enough staff looking to train and enter childcare. But seven or eight years ago, the government changed the requirements for nursery qualifications so that you had to have a C or above in English, Maths and Science. This has killed the sector. Most people who do this job aren't academic, but they enjoy physical work, and it's a very physical job.

We're still not away from the idea that somebody who looks after young children is a glorified babysitter. Now, you might not have a high opinion of a physical job that could have an eighteen-year-old doing it, but these young girls (and I was one of them) come in and do this job with such drive and passion and energy . . .

I think it should be thought of more highly than it is.

When you've done this job as long as I have, you develop another personality. That *high energy, always happy, doesn't get stressed* persona.

Parents will walk into the nursery and talk about how happy everyone is and how high energy everyone is. You think, *yes, because this is our job.*

As an adult, you sometimes forget that a child's world is so new and fresh, you forget how exciting it is. When it's raining, you think *oh my God, it's raining,* whereas a child thinks, *oh puddles to jump in!*

The world is so new to them, and you must have that in the front of your head. Everything is exciting to them, so everything has to be exciting for you as well.

But it means that when I come home, I'm so drained. One of my children might ask me to play a game and I'll be like, *'Can I just have five minutes of not doing anything like that?'*

You walk out of the nursery straight into your own childcare at home. It's work away from work sometimes.

'Let me just have a cup of tea and I'll play with you.'

The kids understand, but you feel mum guilt. *I should be playing with you. I should be loving my time with you because I'm at work so much that I should hold onto these moments.*

It's just part and parcel of being a parent. I think if they told you at school that the one thing you'd feel as a parent, for the rest of your life, is guilt, it'd probably put everybody off having children.

I work for a business that has nurseries all over the world. They give us a curriculum that we follow. The company likes physical documentation to evidence that things are being done, whereas smaller nurseries are quite happy to trust their staff without needing bits of paper to say that this or that has been done.

The company also give us a list of items that we're not allowed to use for health safety reasons. We can't do jelly play. We're not allowed to use tinsel for the under-twos because it's a potential choking risk.

There are so many things we can't do.

It's difficult, because you've got to keep checking your policies and procedures. *Can we do this? If I approve this, am I gonna be put through an investigation and a disciplinary?*

All these extra things that we didn't really worry about before – safeguarding, health and safety – these are important, but it's almost gone to the extreme.

It just feels like there are more and more things being added to the job, pressures that we never used to have.

Primary school teacher and former soldier

(30s)

I floated into joining the army. I can't remember wanting to join. I just did it one day. It was the week after my eighteenth birthday. I would have gone earlier but my mum didn't want me to go and wouldn't sign the release papers, so I had to wait 'til I was eighteen.

I remember going in and reading the oath of allegiance and the next thing I know I'm on a coach. It just sort of happened, like it wasn't me doing it.

The army has messed me up, but in a way it's also made me who I am. I've met some of the best people I've ever met, but I've also lost people that were close to me, and I've seen things I wouldn't want to see.

Life on an army base is pretty boring. You do tasks for the sake of doing tasks. You get up at about 7 a.m. There's a parade at 8 a m, in your best uniform and stood to attention, waiting for the person with the rank to tell you what to do for the day. Often, you'd go up to the hangar where the tanks were and you'd clean and count stores there.

It was jobs for the sake of jobs.

There'd be some sort of physical exercise. A run and an assault course or a gym session. Two or three types of physical exercise a day. Then you'd have a parade at dinnertime and then back to your rooms and we'd go and get drunk, a typical squaddie night out.

– How did the working day differ when you were on tour?

On tour in Afghanistan, every day at about 4.30 a.m. or 5 a.m., we were woken up by the call to prayer – a hauntingly beautiful sound.

You'd have a shave, which was important for some reason, and get into your uniform to go out on patrol. We'd patrol to show our face to the locals, make them feel that we were doing a job to keep them secure.

What else did we do? We built a little school, and we rebuilt houses that had been blown up. We transported things from base to base. And we supported the Afghan National Army, teaching them our ways.

We'd have to teach the Afghan National Army soldiers PT (physical training) and it was like they were made out of jelly. They'd just collapse after five minutes. They were lovely people though. I made friends with some of the Afghans – lovely people.

Before you went out there, you got told '*This is the enemy. They wear a towel on their head.*'

It sounds horrible, but that's what we were told. And when you're there, you're realize that the Afghans are people who just want to get on with life. They'd bring us things like bread and watermelons. One of the Afghan guys we trained even gave me a fighting chicken.

I'd been with him when we'd come under attack. He'd fallen into a river and got his belt caught on the riverbed. I pulled him out and he was really grateful. He said, '*I want to give you this chicken. It's a prize fighting chicken. Make sure you look after it, or I'll kill you.*'

He'd said the last bit in a joking way, but I couldn't tell if he was joking about the prize-winning bit.

The next day I threw some dry rice down for the chicken to eat. After it had eaten the rice, the chicken's stomach expanded, then it collapsed and died.

I thought, *oh my God*, so I put the corpse on the burns pit and covered it up. The next thing I know, one of the stray dogs is pulling one of the chicken's legs out of the pit, right into the view of everyone. I thought, *this can't get any worse* [he laughs].

When you were on tour, it didn't feel like a job.

I did a parachute jump once and my parachute malfunctioned, and I nearly hit the ground before my body automatically remembered that I had to bring the canopy back up. And that's what being out in Afghanistan felt like: it was like we were on autopilot.

I didn't adjust well to coming back. I can't really describe it. I was at home, but I just felt like I should be somewhere else, back where I'd been, with my friends.

At the time, I'd been raring to go to Afghanistan. I thought, *this is a just cause*. But with hindsight, I don't really think it was. I don't really agree with the reasons why we were there. I don't know – I don't agree with going into other countries and imposing our will on them.

I got made redundant when David Cameron cut the army's numbers. It was a week after I'd been put on a promotion course for Lance Corporal.

After it happened, I remember lying on the couch for days on end drinking bottles of red wine, getting really fat and not doing anything. It was proper depression, probably.

If it hadn't been for the redundancy I would have stayed in the army. I didn't particularly enjoy it, but it was a job that I could do. You know what I mean?

– No one enjoys breathing, but they do it. Was it like that?

Yes. I didn't miss it once I was fully out, but if there were a war tomorrow and I could go back with the people I was on tour with – my amigos – I'd go back again tomorrow. It sounds really cliché and cheesy, but it was a band of brothers.

The other day, for instance, it was the first time I'd seen one of them in years, but it was like we'd never left each other.

After I left, I did some resettlement courses through the army, but they were big seminars and not really geared towards you as an individual.

The army promised us a lot of things that never came. In the end, I just cut ties with it.

You do the job. You get messed up by it. And then you're just left. '*That's it. Your time's up now.*'

I don't know if that's true for everybody, but that's how I felt at the time. You're treated like a number, and I don't think that's a secret.

I remember going to the doctor once because I think I was having some sort of PTSD.

He said something like, '*No, you won't be depressed, you just need to change some things in your life. You're probably not happy with your wife.*'

In hindsight, I wasn't happy with my wife, but at the time I didn't think it was the kind of support I needed.

I had counselling after I left. I went off my own back to get it. There were things from the time I'd spent in Afghanistan that were swirling around my head. I couldn't get to grips with them. For instance, I'd helped find a child who'd fallen into a river and died.

For the counselling, I went back through my diary of the tour, and I realized that this memory of pulling a child out of the river was bothering me. It'd really affected me. I think because I had a small child of my own.

I used to dream about a spider in the corner of my room. I'm not scared of spiders. I pick them up. I like them. But there was this spider in the corner of my room. I'd look at it. It'd look at me. It was like this Mexican stand-off. Suddenly the spider would fall onto my face, and I'd wake up screaming with no idea where I was. A real night terror.

When I did this cognitive behavioural therapy, things clicked in my head. I could tell that it had worked, because I went back home, fell asleep, and dreamt about the spider again. It waved to me and walked off. I've never had the dream again.

I first went to work in an animal feed factory, bagging up feed – hard work from 5 a.m. to 5 p.m.

I then got a job at a fast-food chain. I was really embarrassed, because it's one of the threats they use in the army, *'You can leave if you want, but you're going to end up flipping burgers'*, like it was the worst thing in the world.

When I was working there, I used to pull my hat down over my head hoping nobody I knew would come in and see me. It was horrible for about a month but then I realized that I enjoyed it, that I had some transferrable skills, and that I was treated better by the fast food chain than I was by the army.

I got promoted and became quite a good manager. I felt like my colleagues looked up to me, which I don't think I'd ever felt before. My colleagues weren't people I'd normally hang around with, but I grew to respect them and like them. I even met my partner there.

When I was working in the restaurant, I did an access course at a local university. And from there, I did a degree in English.

I've never felt so out of place than at that university, in a place full of eighteen-and nineteen-year-olds who wore berets and talked about philosophy.

I really struggled. I found it stressful to juggle my uni work, my fast-food job, and the forty-five minute commute to the university.

But I knew I wanted to be a teacher. It was the first time in my life when I had a sort of plan.

I wanted to be a teacher because I'd watched *Educating Yorkshire* and there was a teacher on it – I can't remember his name – but he wore a waistcoat. I wanted to be him, that friendly face that the children see and learn things from. He was my inspiration. Him and one of my English teachers from school, the only teacher I can remember.

It's been twenty-two years since I've seen that teacher, but I emailed him recently to say thank you for inspiring me. I mentioned that he once gave me half a house point because I said a word he couldn't define.

He emailed me back to say, *'You can have twenty house points for making me tear up because that was a lovely message to receive.'*

My mum – the recurring job goblin – said that I wouldn't like secondary school teaching because the children will talk back. In my head, I thought, *I probably wouldn't like secondary.*

I did primary and I love it, even though I've not had a smooth ride in teaching at all. My first year was cut short because of lockdowns. The second year was a lot of home learning.

I hated the online learning during Covid. It's not teaching. Trying to teach a primary school class on Zoom, it's just impossible. I was itching to get back into school.

People said don't hug the children because of Covid, but I couldn't think of a world that was worse than everyone standing ten feet away from each other, so as soon as we were back in the classroom I was hugging the children.

The classroom was a safe haven for them, especially the vulnerable children.

Since then, my third and fourth classes, they've been dominated by Ofsted and things like that.

It's a really stressful job.

I get up at 6 a.m., get to school at about 6.50 a.m., and I'll plan one of my lessons that morning – maybe a guided reading lesson, which is a short text followed by five questions and a slideshow about the vocabulary. Then I'll do some admin tasks, some marking and setting up my room.

The children are in at 8.30 a.m. We'll do maths 'til break time, when I'll supervise their fifteen-minute break outside. Then we'll do English and the guided reading.

Then it's dinner. We do something called family dining in our school. The children all sit down with people they don't know, and they serve each other. There's quite a lot of broken homes so a lot of the kids don't have that experience of sitting down at a table to eat a meal. It's lovely seeing them chat to each other.

We come back in the afternoon and from 12.30 p.m. until 3.30 p.m. we've got various lessons, RE, music, PE.

I don't really use the military approach to discipline in the classroom. It's not in my nature to shout or to lose my temper. But when I do PE it's like a boot camp.

Then at 3.15 p.m. the children go, and I'll normally stay and do some planning until 5.45 p.m. When I get home, I'll realize I've forgotten something and do some more work. It is a thankless, never-ending task – well, the kids thank you but nobody else does.

When you're planning, differentiating between different ability children is a big strain on the workload. Some of my low ability children in Year 1 aren't even at a nursery level. You have to think, *what are those kids going to do? Who's going to supervise them? Where are they going to sit?*

I can't imagine doing this when I'm fifty. I think the majority of teachers leave after the seventh year and I can understand why. I mean, I'm getting grey hairs, my hair's thinning.

We had a snow day the other week and I used the time to do some planning. If I had a magic wand, the working week would be four days and one unpaid day would be for planning. I'd have an incentive to get it all done so I'd have a weekend.

I am good at building rapport with the children. They seem to just respond to me. I think it's partly down to my immaturity, because I'm sort of on their level, but at the same time it's partly because I'm a big guy and they're so tiny. It's like a giant walking in a field full of hobbits [he laughs].

I teach Year 1 and Year 2 and I love it. They've got the banter that I thought I'd only get from Year 6. It's back and forth.

Like I'll say things like, '*You do that again and I'll throw you out the window*.'

The kids will say, '*Oh no, you won't do that!*'

Someone might go home and tell their parents, but they all know I'm joking.

When I've got the classroom to myself and I'm not being observed, that's when I feel most alive. It's my little world. But if I'm being observed, I feel like the performance I'm putting on for the children isn't the same. You see teachers who read off a script, a bit robotic, whereas I invest my personality in it. You need to be like a TV presenter.

And if I'm alone, I can act a bit silly and the kids love it and respond to it, like the other day they were regurgitating things that I'd told them a month ago about King John.

I have learned that I'm not as resilient as I thought I was.

I've probably cried in front of my headteacher more than anyone else in my life.

Teaching is harder than soldiering, without a doubt.

There were some tough times in the army, but I've never felt under more pressure and more stress than as a teacher. It was far less stressful in Afghanistan. Get me back to being shot at!

Secondary school teacher

(40s)

I'd always read. I lived in a very busy household as a child. It was a way of escaping reality. I'll read pretty much anything. I'm an omnivore. Toni Morrison, Alice Walker, Shakespeare, Gregg Hurwitz.

I'm a big fan of the Brontë sisters. I once went to Haworth for a day trip. I thought, *how could they write such great literature in such a desolate area?* And that made me think I could achieve anything. It was one of the things that spurred me on to becoming a teacher.

My own experience at school was dreadful.

At high school, the teachers didn't care. One of my English teachers didn't even seem to enjoy reading.

I didn't do well. I didn't pass any of my GCSEs at a decent enough grade. College wasn't what was expected in my family. It was a bit like, *'No, we don't go to college, we get jobs.'* So I left school and worked as a purchase ledger clerk.

I got married young and I had my son when I was twenty-one.

There was never a plan. Never a plan.

After a time, I went to college. I then went on to uni to study English.

In my final year, just before my exams, my marriage dissolved. I ended up not completing my degree. It was only five years later that I did my final year again.

After I graduated, I was just trying to get through life. I was a single mother, and I didn't have any money. I worked in shops and bars, and I did what I could.

But all through this time I was still reading. I used to go to the big libraries in the city centre, big buildings that looked quite scary. I'd always felt at home in them.

I ended up volunteering as a learning mentor at the school my son went to. They encouraged me to do my PGCE and then I became a teacher.

But there was never a plan.

Contrary to popular belief, a good lesson involves quite a lively classroom. One with a lot of collaboration between the students. They're discussing things, asking questions, getting deeper and deeper into an idea.

It's like being a conductor of an orchestra.

One question comes from over here.

An answer comes from over there.

You can go into a text and teach them so much about life. It's about making them see beyond what they already know.

I recently got one of my classes to do some non-fiction writing. They had to come up with an article on their own about how technology negatively impacts their life. Some of them blew me away. Even the kids I didn't think would do that well, did great.

One of them spoke to his grandparents, who said that they felt really sorry for him because, without phones, they'd had a much freer life than he had now. But the kids all stood up and presented their articles to the class, and you could see it was a real winning moment for them. They were scared to present in front of everyone, but they did it anyway.

Inside, I'm cheering. I have to hide my face, because I want to cry with pride. It's good to hold the reins, but the best part of teaching is when you let the reins go.

– Are there classes that you feel you've let down?

Yes, that's just being a teacher. Every single day, I think *oh God, I didn't explain that poem properly and they might need that in the exam and now I won't see them for a week.* The things that you do as a teacher haunt you. If you didn't pay enough attention to a kid, you'll go home and think, *that child might have needed me today and I didn't listen.*

Or I'll have a bad day where I'm grumpy and not feeling it and I won't be as polite as I should be. I'll go home and feel bad. I work in a deprived area, having a grumpy teacher shouldn't be something that the kids should have to put up with.

But it's such a fast-paced environment. One minute you can be teaching English and the next minute it's disclosed to you that a child is self-harming. What's the most important part of your job? To me, it's looking after the child, but sometimes a lesson will suffer because of that.

I don't think we're supported well enough on this front. Look at the amount of school refusers at the moment, kids who are struggling to even leave their bedrooms. When a child has that many issues, educating them is the least of your concerns.

Teachers were teachers when I was at school. Nowadays, teachers are social workers and counsellors and parents in some instances, as well as experts in mental health issues and special educational needs. All with very little guidance.

People say, '*Why are they striking again, they get enough holiday. All they do is sit around and teach lessons and do some marking.*'

I don't think the people who say these things have taken into account the fact that we've got children who are in crisis. A child who's lost a parent. A child who's undergone some form of abuse. A child that's suicidal or self-harming. And whenever something traumatic is disclosed to you, you've just got to back into the classroom and teach for the rest of the day. There's nowhere to decompress.

Honestly, the teaching part of my job is the easy part. We've got too many hats to wear. Every school should have a crisis counsellor. Every school should have a social worker and a police officer attached to it.

And then you've got the data. Every time you mark a bunch of papers, you input data, *data data data*. The school will say, 'Well, *their data when they came into the school was this, and last year it was this.*'

But they're children, not data!

It's another hat that teachers wear I suppose: we're administrators, having to deal with the fifty emails that come in when you're teaching a full timetable.

And that's where our breaktime and lunchtime and after school time goes: responding to emails.

God, I could just go on whinging about the teaching profession [she laughs].

I do know so many really good teachers that have just left.

Left without jobs to go to, because they can't cope with it any more. In my school, there have been ten who have left for different professions this year. One's joined the police, one's a paramedic, one's even a driving instructor.

– *Not easy jobs.*

Yes, it's unbelievable that teaching's so hard that joining the police is considered less stressful. Unbelievable.

Teaching's like nursing, you go into it because you want to help and because you care. But you become stuck in a system that doesn't value you – the government doesn't value you, the general public don't value you. All the while you think, *well here I am looking after your loved ones.*

I'd say to anyone thinking about going into teaching, *have your life first and then go into teaching.* Enjoy your twenties and most of your thirties, then go into teaching.

I've got friends who are thirty-one. They've been teaching for ten years, and they're burnt out. Whereas I have so many memories of my actual fun life to look back on, a time when I wasn't weighed down by the responsibility.

During the pandemic, I changed my relationship with work. Before, I was constantly working, working, working. I'd bring work home and work 'til 10 p.m. I realized that I needed more balance. So I started going to the gym and I started a master's degree. I tried to focus on what I wanted in my life rather than just on work.

I don't have my work email on my phone any more. That's my phone, I pay for it, why should someone be able to contact me 24/7?

I stopped making sure that every single book was marked after every single lesson. There's no benefit to it. Instead, I adapted my teaching style so I was circulating the room more and marking throughout the lesson. This way, the child can see what's wrong straight away.

I also do things like whole class feedback, where if I've looked at five students' work and they've all made the same mistake, I'll stop the lesson and make a point of it.

I began to teach in a way that would mean I didn't have to be sat at home marking books the entire time. But I have to say that doing this has resulted in some issues at work. When you stop giving and giving, people like to remind you that you're paid to give.

I toyed with the idea of leaving teaching this year. But I thought, *no, I'm a teacher. I want to be a teacher. That's who I am.*

Academic

(50s)

My father ended up as a lecturer teaching chemical engineering. In the early 1970s, he took a sabbatical to work on a project in Chile. The whole family went and lived in Chile for a year. I was six or seven and I have very vivid memories of that time.

Once in the summer, we drove to a region called *Los Lagos*, where there are volcanoes and lakes, and I think that's where I became hooked on rocks.

I'm interested in explosive volcanism, in piecing together the processes that lead up to volcanic eruptions, and in the consequences that follow.

Early on in my career I was working on the rock record, the deposits left behind by very large eruptions. These deposits are geologically interesting and quite often well preserved, but such large eruptions are very rare. In fact, in terms of the next volcano that's going to erupt somewhere on Earth, it's much more likely to be a smaller one. And so I'm now working on volcanic systems which have moderate eruptions relatively frequently, but have the capacity to cause significant local impacts.

As an academic, there's a sense that you've had a small influence at certain points in time on the direction that your students take.

It's a privilege teaching in a university, because you interact with capable people at a time in their lives when they're seeing opportunities that they'd never even thought of.

I'd like my students to know how much vicarious pleasure I get from seeing them be successful at whatever they do.

In admissions interviews, sometimes you have this moment when you realize that you're having a conversation with a student who's only ever had that conversation in their own head.

You can see the student think, *'I'm having a conversation with someone else who's interested in the same things as me.'*

It's a tremendous moment when that happens.

Once, I knew from a candidate's personal statement that he was interested in trains. I asked him, *'Can you describe the geological journey you've taken on your train ride this morning?'* Ten minutes later it was clear that this person wasn't going to go away [he laughs].

CHAPTER SEVEN **HOUSEWORK**

Stay-at-home mum

stay-at-home dad and part-time food server

childminder

cleaner

Stay-at-home mum

(30s)

I worked at quite a large law firm for seven, eight years. I tried a few times to get onto their trainee solicitor programme, but I was never successful.

I applied for the programme three times. The first time they said it was between me and somebody else. When I heard who had got it, I thought, *yeah all right, we were never going to get it.* They encouraged me to apply again.

I applied again the next year, and it was the same thing, between me and somebody else.

They told me, '*Definitely apply again*.'

The third time I applied, it was exactly the same situation. It knocked my confidence a bit. I didn't want to put myself through it again. I thought, *maybe becoming a solicitor is just not meant to be.*

I got married, became pregnant with my first child and, to be honest, I was a little bit relieved.

When I went back to the law firm after maternity leave, the hours were fine, but they'd made a few little changes – like parking, for instance. If you didn't get in early enough, you didn't get a parking spot. You'd have to park miles down the road and walk.

I'd have to get my child to nursery in the mornings and then I'd have to battle with parking. It was all those little things, those little added stresses, that made the decision for me.

I ended up leaving. I don't think the firm was that bothered. I was easily and quickly replaced. I was more of number to them.

After I left, I went to do admin in an estate agents for four years. I just wanted a job. I wasn't as bothered about the career element of work. My thinking was, *what hours can I do? What job could accommodate those hours?*

I found out I was pregnant with my second child. Again, I felt a sense of relief that I only had to do that job for another nine months and then I'd be out. And since I've had my second child, I haven't gone back. He's just turned one.

Both times that I went on maternity leave, at the law firm and the estate agents, I did intend to go back to work. I kind of knew I had to go to back, and – don't get me wrong – in some ways I wanted to go back for my independence, for that bit of money, and that sense of identity. But maternity leave just completely changes you as a person and what you want from work.

After my second maternity leave, I didn't really know what I wanted from life. All I knew was that I wanted to be a mum to my kids. Between my husband and me, it was never a case of, *'You're the woman. You shouldn't go back to work.'* We had a chat about it; I've always been a maternal kind of person; I wanted to stop; I wasn't upset that I had to give up my career.

At the moment, I'm finding it difficult to decide whether to go back to work. I don't know how I'll fit work in. Trying to find work that accommodates school hours has been hard. Often I'll look at a job and think, *I like the sound of that*, then I'll look at the hours and *oh I can't do that.* The only jobs that fit the bill are admin jobs, doing the tasks that everybody else in the office hasn't got round to doing . . . I don't really want to be paying for nursery for the privilege of doing people's leftover jobs.

I want to go back to work for me. I know that the kids need time away from me.

But at the same time I don't want to go back to work because I want to be with the kids.

* * *

At about 6 a.m., I get up and hope there's no kids awake. I get showered and ready before the kids even wake up. If they've woken up, I've got no chance. My husband leaves at 7.30 a.m. so I've got a little bit of help until then. After that, it's breakfast and getting everybody out of the door for 8.30 a.m. to take the older one to school.

She's developing this attitude now.

She'll huff and puff, *'No, I don't want to do it! I don't want to do my hair.'*

'Tough. You've got to do your hair.'

After the school run, I'll take the youngest for a walk. We'll get back at about 10 a.m. He'll then go up for a nap. We'll then just play. Bless him, he's got second child syndrome, and he wants to be around me a lot. But sometimes he's happy playing by himself. He'll sit there exploring his toes, looking at a book, or just laughing at himself. Then it's lunchtime. I'll try and get jobs done around the house. Then it's school run time. And then the day is gone.

I enjoy going to get her from school – that moment when she comes out of school, and she's missed me.

Then it's tea at 4 p.m. Bath at about 5.30 p.m. and then it's chill out time before bed – homework, playing. I'm lucky that they play with each other now. They're obsessed with each other. I mean, they wind each other up something rotten, but they will play by themselves and that gives me ten minutes to sort the tea out.

On Wednesdays, my eldest has swimming after school. On Thursdays, gymnastics. The youngest fits in with us.

My husband comes back at about 7 p.m.

I'll be honest, it's tough. I know people do it. And I know it's hard on my husband, being out from 7 a.m. until 7 p.m. at night. But it's bang on bedtime when he comes back and it's hard trying to get everything done ready for him getting home.

My husband is brilliant, bless him. I can't fault him. He does as much as he possibly can in an evening. He'll do tea when I'm feeding the youngest.

He's not the kind of man that expects his tea on the table when he gets home. He'll help me get the kids to bed. But that means we end up eating at about 9 p.m. and then getting jobs done around the house after that.

When the kids are both asleep, there's a little bit of relief and a little bit of anxiety. *Who's going to wake up first?* My son is still up every night, not sleeping through. At the moment he's teething. It's been awful. We'll go through these odd weeks where he's a nightmare. He'll go to bed at 6.30 p.m. At 9.30 p.m. I'll go up to feed him. I'll do the same at midnight. He'll be up again during the night. And then I'm up at 6 a.m.

I'm trying to survive on roughly four hours of broken sleep.

Apart from two hours where I had a couple of drinks with the girls, I haven't had any time to myself since he was born. Two hours, that's literally all I've had in about a year. At the minute, the only time I have to myself is going to shops.

Mum guilt is horrendous. It's a horrible, horrible thing.

I question everything. There'll be one little thing that I do that means me and one of the kids fall out and that little thing will sit with me the whole day, outweighing all the good stuff.

I used to drop my daughter off at the nursery and she'd be crying. To then have to do the journey to work, and to sit in an office thinking about the child that you've left screaming . . . It used to make me cry.

The guilt of sitting in an office when you could have been sat at home with her, it's horrible.

Today, for instance, I've taken my son to nursery so that I can have a day of getting on with things without distraction. I've left him crying – horrible.

But at the same time, I come home and I think, *thank God for that, I've got a day to myself.* And then you feel guilty for feeling that.

It's this constant questioning, this constant analysing of everything, you know?

I feel a sense of *you should want to go and have a career.* And I feel guilty for not wanting that for myself. But at the same time, I'm quite happy being a mum and fitting what work in I can.

I'm happy for my husband to have his career. He's doing well, progressing. He's funding me now, which then makes me feel guilty that I haven't got my own source of income and that I have to rely on him. It's a difficult thing to go from having a full-time job that paid well to having to ask for money for the daftest things, like swimming lessons and gymnastics. He doesn't hold it against me, but there's always that guilt. Life, I suppose, is about finding a way for the two of you to appreciate that both jobs are just as hard. It's hard all round.

But parenting is lovely. I know it sounds like all I've done is complain. But I do enjoy it. Picking her up at the end of the day. The times when they need you. It makes it all worthwhile.

I know that there'll come a day when my son doesn't want me in the night, and I'll be very upset about it.

Stay-at-home dad and part-time food server

(40s)

I'm currently a stay-at-home dad.

Before that, I was a complaints manager for an insurance company. My inbox in that role was never-ending. I'd probably get a couple of hundred emails each day. Managing eighteen people, a portfolio of four-hundred clients, with complaints and disputes to process and allocate to the team. The stress that went with that was immense.

Some days, it probably knocked me over the edge, and I'd think, *really, how can I do this?* I was quite thankful to leave.

I left employment so that my wife could start her new career as a primary school teacher, and so that I could homeschool my children (we were in lockdown rules back then). I decided to take the hit so that my wife could fly in a new direction.

I was on about £35,000 a year. It was quite a well-paid role, the highest salary I'd ever earned. We cut the money coming in quite significantly.

There were struggles, don't get me wrong. That's why I picked up a little bit of work. We looked at our outgoings – insurances, take-aways, shifting from Tesco and Sainsbury's to Aldi and Lidl – and we went back to spending the bare minimum.

I also work a few hours each week at a pizza chain. We needed a bit more cashflow. It brings in just under £1,000 a month to help with everyday spending.

I'll be honest, at first, delivering pizzas to people's tables wasn't my idea of keeping my brain busy. But in a weird way, I kind of enjoy it. I can shut off from the house. I can have adult conversations and interactions with other people, people that I wouldn't ordinarily meet.

When I was working in insurance, I wasn't really getting family time. I was in the office at 8 a.m. every morning and I was leaving at 6 p.m. every night, shattered. I couldn't switch off from work. The girls were in bed as soon as I got home. I didn't have a family life.

But that's completely turned on its head.

The girls are up before me. My eldest goes downstairs at about 6 a.m. My alarm won't go off until 7 a.m., and by that time both of the kids are downstairs playing, screaming, annoying each other.

My wife is out the door by 7.30 a.m.

I'm then getting both the girls dressed, teeth, breakfast. Out the door at 8.10 a.m. to drop the eldest one off at school at 8.35 a.m.

Then, depending on the day, I'll take the youngest one and we'll go swimming, to a parents' club, or shopping.

I'll shove her in the trolley and take her round Aldi and Lidl. She'll drops toys on the floor and take things off shelves.

Then we're home for lunch: unpack the shopping, have a bite to eat, put the washing machine on, empty the dishwasher, change a nappy, sit down with her for half an hour and make sure she's entertained.

Then we're out the door by 2.50 p.m. to pick up the eldest from school. It takes me about thirty minutes to get the youngest ready, so I'd have a reminder on my phone at 2.15 p.m. to get the youngest one ready to go.

Shoes on.

Then she'll kick them off.

Shoes on again.

Go to the toilet. Out the front door. Make sure the youngest doesn't sleep in the car or she won't sleep later on. Walk to school. Let the youngest play in the playground. Have a bit of a chat with the some of the parents.

Leave the playground at 3.20 p.m. Back to the car. Back home.

The first thing my eldest will say is *'I'm hungry.'* Give her a bit of fruit. She'll challenge you for chocolate and crisps.

Then it's homework. I start the evening meal, making sure it's on the table for when the wife comes home.

We all eat together. It's the one thing we do as a family. We'll go round finding out what the best part of everyone's day was, sharing stories.

The kids will ask my wife, *'Did that child do this today? Did they chuck a chair at you today? Did they write naughty words on the board?'*

Afterwards, we have about half an hour of downtime.

Then it's bath, brush teeth, pyjamas on, put them to bed at 7 p.m.

Then, depending on the day, we'll have a bit of telly or I'll be at the restaurant working. But every day is different. Tomorrow, for instance, is swimming night. Friday is football club after school.

You should see my phone: I've got alarms for everything.

– Do you consider it to be work?

Absolutely, because it's got to be done.

But it's the best job ever really, making sure that the girls and my wife have got everything they need. I love it.

– Have you felt lonely, being at home the last couple of years?

No, I keep myself busy. I volunteer for a local charity as a budget coach and debt adviser, helping people that are in debt. All for free, all for love, and for helping other people and keeping me busy.

Throughout the week, I'll meet some clients and help them with their budgeting. I'm also a church organist, so I'll take a choir practice once a week and at the weekends I'll go to church. That has been a real deep joy and passion that I've had since I was a teenager.

*   *   *

Although my wife loves her new job and she loves the fact that I can be there to pick up the girls and take them to school, she feels that she's missed out on two years of their upbringing, two years where she hasn't been the one taking them to school and picking them up.

She feels she's been robbed of that responsibility and pleasure, of that element of motherhood.

It was only a few weeks ago that we were talking about this. It was a difficult conversation. But we came back to the fact that she decided that she wanted to become a teacher. At that time, it was the only way we could do it.

I've spoken to other guys, colleagues at my church for example, and they've said that they would've appreciated having the experience of being at home, having that exposure to the upbringing of your kids, rather than being the working man all the time. My wife and I have experienced both sides of the coin and it's made each of us stronger.

When I was working full-time, if the girls wanted anything, they'd always go and see my wife. But the girls tend to gravitate towards me now, because my wife's quite busy with her job.

It's *'Daddy, Daddy, can I have this please?'*

They always come to me first. Even if it's getting up in the middle of the night, if they feel cold or not quite right, they always come to my side of the bed.

– How does that make you feel?

We've both experienced that feeling of not being wanted as a parent. It's a horrible feeling. It's like I said a moment ago: I think in the back of my wife's mind, she feels that she's missed out on certain elements of being a mum in the past couple of years.

But I haven't answered your question about how the girls gravitating towards me makes me feel. I'm not quite sure how to answer that actually.

I just do the doing, I don't stop and think.

Childminder

(40s)

My dream job would have been to be a nurse in the RAF. It was always, always my dream, from when I was knee-high. But I had to put those plans to one side when I was twenty. I had a bad accident at work. I was working in a residential care home and one of the residents hit me on the back with a walking stick and knocked me down. To this day, I'm still troubled with my back and shoulders and one thing and another.

But anyway, I had to get on.

I went back to work in residential nursing homes. I then fell pregnant with my first child, so that was grand.

I found a job working part-time in a primary school. I was still living at home, so my mum was looking after my eldest. I was bringing in a few pounds working at the school, but I was missing so much of my child's life and I'm quite sure he missed me. Oh, I felt guilty. Big time.

Then I fell pregnant with my daughter. I thought, *right, I have to do something about this, because I'm not going to miss out on her milestones.* So I decided to get into registered childminding.

I open Monday to Friday. I have a couple of part-time families, here two or three days in the week. I open my doors at 6.30 a.m. and it could be 6 p.m. before they're collected.

I sort them all out with breakfast. I have three wee ones who are potty training at the moment, which is *exciting*, but we roll with it. The week before last, one of the younger ones says to me '*Me pee-pee*' and we went over to potty without a problem. The penny had dropped. *Oh gosh*, I feel excited just talking about it. I'd go to the extent of saying that I feel more excited now than I did years ago, because you come to know that every child is so different.

This morning, I asked another wee one, '*How many blocks tall can you make that tower. One? Two? Three?*'

He made a tower that was taller than he was.

'*Stand up next to it. Look it's taller than you are!*'

The next thing, the tower toppled over.

He said, '*Oh no!*'

'*Try making it two blocks thick.*'

Ninety-nine per cent of the time I'm on the floor. I try to get down to their level and we do things together. We have a laugh, and we make the most out of every day. Whether it's building towers or dens, counting and watering the flowers, watching them grow, or watching caterpillars turn into butterflies. And when you see the butterflies, '*Oh my goodness. Look at the colours!*'; the excitement of it all; it warms your heart. I love my job, so I do.

I remember one of the first children that I looked after when I first became registered. I had him for about three years, from when he was a young baby. He didn't get into the playgroup in my village, he got into the one in a neighbouring village, so he went to another childminder, and it broke my heart.

You've been through everything with them, especially when you have them so young. It's devastating.

But whenever I bump into the family at the chippy, he says '*Hi, how are you?*' and the arms come flying round you for a big hug. It's truly uplifting. You think, *wow, I am still something to that child*. It's very rewarding.

Each year, on an annual basis, we get inspected by a social worker that has been assigned to us.

There's twenty-nine policies that we have. *Equal Opportunities.*

*Walking Home from School. Alcohol and Drugs. Toilet Training.
Providing Food and Drink. Safeguarding. Child Protection.
Confidentiality. Managing Children's Behaviour. Partnership with
Parents. Children with Additional Needs. Personal Care. Children's
Participation. Taking and Using Photographs. Data Protection.
Managing Emergencies. Whistleblowing. Management of Records. Baby
& Sleep Policy.* I could go on. They're to cover my own bum, for want
of a better word.

– Do the families read these policies?

I don't mean this flippantly, but that's not my problem. They have
their copies and it's their responsibility to read them before they sign
them.

The paperwork has got so much stickier over the years. I've had a
few people in recent months ask me questions about being a registered
childminder. One was a slightly older lady that asked me about how
to get registered. I says to her, *'I don't mean this awful, but if I was
starting out I wouldn't enter the industry, simply because of the paperwork.'*

We have to keep registers as to what kids are here and who picks
them up. I had to get three filing cabinets installed for my paperwork, big monster units in my kitchen, and that's before you go to
my attic . . .

A policy folder for each child and each family, their accident bump
forms, medication forms, observations . . . every bit of paperwork.
And we have to keep everything for a minimum of twenty-one years.
Can you imagine the amount of stuff in my attic? God forbid there's
a fire. That'd be me scuppered, because I can't afford to have fireproof
storage.

I've never done any paperwork when I'm working. I tend not to
do anything when the kids are here, but it means that I do it afterwards and I lose family time with my own kids.

I'm a member of the Northern Ireland Childminding Association.

I think the membership is £135 for the year. But it covers all your insurance. Say I was taking the kids down the park, and they had an accident, at least the children would be covered. And if, God forbid, anyone wants to sue me, so to speak, at least I would have some form of cover in place.

God forbid. Touch wood that never happens. In almost seventeen years, I haven't had any accidents. Thanks be to God.

I'm on a registered childminder forum. Our membership has dropped from about 1500 to around 850.

On a daily basis, you see posts saying, *'Thank you for your help over the years. It's time for me to hang up my boots.'*

Childminders aren't appreciated for what we do. We're a home away from home childcare. We're the cheapest form of reliable and safe childcare.

Looking back, I've regretted not being able to go into nursing. But by another token, I'm thankful for what I have. I have a lovely family. I have my house, and bills like everybody else. I have a good network of friends and family around me. I have the joy and satisfaction of my work on a daily basis through the relationships that I have with each family.

So I do think I'm extremely lucky. As the years go on, I'm content with what I'm doing.

Cleaner

(50s)

I wanted to be in the building trade, to be a bricklayer, but in the 1980s that wasn't the done thing for girls, so I trained as a hairdresser.

I then had two children. I didn't work for a period after I had my kids because I was looking after my elderly grandparents at the same time.

Caring for them was how I got into care work, and I was a domiciliary carer for a while. Part of the care work was cleaning for the elderly people, and I loved cleaning, so I used to get sent to all the cleaning calls.

When I was a carer, I ended up having a breakdown and having six months off work. I lost a lot of the elderly people that I cared for, and it had a real emotional impact on me. And care work is twenty-four hours a day. It was taking me away from the kids. I couldn't always go to parents' evening or sports day or things like that.

My doctor told me that when I went back to work, I should go back and do something that I love. I thought, *well if I did cleaning and worked for myself then I can pick and choose when I want to work.*

It was a bit of a leap of faith because I had two children, and I was on my own. My husband had died when I was thirty-one.

I thought, *if this doesn't work, I'm gonna be in trouble.* I think the breakdown made me a bit more reckless, more willing to take chances.

I had £200 in the bank. I got some cards printed and put them round the village near where I lived. I took the hoover out of my cupboard, put it in my car with a bucket and some cleaning stuff, and I went out to work.

If I met someone thinking of doing the same today, I'd tell them to do it and not think about what people might say, because it's none of their business.

I got some ironing work from a builder and businessman who did insurance jobs and he said to me, '*Would you like to clean the houses after I'm finished with them?*'

I am a big believer in fate and things happening for a reason. I think I was meant to meet him.

I started cleaning his offices. Then people who rented his offices wanted me to clean their houses and it sort of snowballed really. It all grew a lot quicker than I anticipated. Within a couple of months, I was working sixty hours a week. Then there were floods in the nearby town. The builder was busy. I was busy. It went mad for a long time.

I ended up employing a couple of people part-time. That got very stressful when they didn't turn up or called in sick and there was no one to do their job. I didn't want to say no to anything, because I thought that if I said no, then work would dry up.

It all came to a head when I had to go into hospital to have a procedure on my heart. I couldn't work for a couple of weeks and the girl that was going to take over from me let me down. I thought, *no, I'm not going to employ anybody any more. I'm just going to do it on my own.*

That was fifteen years ago. I promised myself that I'd just do the cleaning until my kids left school, then I'd go and get what my mum calls a *proper job*. But it never really happened. I just love working as a cleaner so much. I get a real sense of fulfilment when I look back at a room I've cleaned. I think, *oh yeah, lovely*.

I always do the kitchens and bathrooms first. I like to get the wet work done first, so my hands have time to dry before I go back outside into the cold.

Then I start at the top of the house and work my way down, dusting, polishing, doing the windows. I always leave the floors 'til last.

It's nice to think that my client will come back to see their house absolutely spotless. I do feel really proud. I have one customer that always texts me on a Friday night to say, '*The house is wonderful. Thank you so much.*'

I take real pride in my work.

I've got arthritis in my back and spondylosis across the top of my shoulders and spine. I don't think it was brought on by cleaning, but it's obviously making it worse. But I think if I was in an office all day, I'd probably be in more pain because I wouldn't be moving.

I don't think I could work all day and not listen to something. I listen to audiobooks when I work. Mostly crime thrillers, detective stuff, horror stuff. Sometimes it's factual books about dog training and dog psychology. We've got three dogs and three cats.

People think that cleaners are uneducated and maybe that cleaning is the best they can do for themselves, which isn't true. I can't speak for every cleaner, but I give a high-end service and although I haven't been trained as such, I still think cleaning is a profession.

You certainly wouldn't treat any other professional the way people treat cleaners. I mean, what would the world look like if there weren't any cleaners?

Historically, it's always been women that have been cleaners, and I suppose that's because it's what we do in the home. We've always placed little value on the things that women do. If you work for a cleaning company, they'll only pay you £9.50 an hour. That's not a proper living wage. You can't live on that.

I'm a middle child with two very successful siblings, and they've got quite highly paid jobs, whereas I haven't. My mum definitely thinks that I've not fulfilled my potential. But when I look at my sister and see how stressed she is, I think, *oh I don't want any of that.*

– *Do you think that you've not fulfilled your potential?*

Sometimes, yeah. But then when my customers say, '*We couldn't do without you*', you feel like you're making a difference in someone's life. I've got one customer that I went to yesterday – I've been cleaning for her since 2008, I've watched her kids grow up – and she really appreciates what I do.

Some of the customers want to talk, especially the elderly ones. I'll sit and have a coffee with them. I used to love being a carer – I'd love to go back into it, but I can't afford to – so I enjoy providing company as well.

On Thursdays, I drive an hour and twenty minutes to the city I used to live in. I don't earn a lot of money out of it, and everyone says, '*Why do you do it?*'

But for me, it's fulfilling because I clean for one friend with schizophrenia, and he doesn't see anyone except me and his family. It's nice to see him and put the world to rights. Then I clean for an elderly lady that I used to care for, which is a highlight, because I really feel that she's given me something that no one else could and I've given her something that no one else could.

Sometimes I'll have done everything that needs doing for her, and we'll sit and watch an old Emmerdale. It feels good, that element of being there for people.

I won an election once. I was a Liberal up against a Labour councillor that was already there, and I thought *we've got to get them out, because they're just lazy.* I had to dress like a grown up. I had residents coming to me saying this and that.

I could relate to them, because I'm working class and a single parent, and I've been on benefits, so I knew how hard life could be for people. People would say to me, '*You're a bit gobby.*' And I am very gobby, but if I believe in something, I'll shout it from the rooftops.

When I go back to the city on Thursdays, I clean in the same area where I was a councillor, and it's nice to see the things that I implemented still going on. It's a little bit of a legacy.

I say to my kids, '*Do something you enjoy and if you lose your job, don't worry, you'll get another one.*' I think if you've got a good work ethic, you enjoy work, and you're nice person, then you'll always have work.

CHAPTER EIGHT **WARDWORK**

Matron

midwife

doctor

prison healthcare assistant

Matron

(60s)

I'm very parochial. I've only ever lived in the area where I live now. And since I was a small child, I wanted to be a nurse. It's all I ever wanted to do.

I was born with a septal defect, and I spent a bit of time in and out of hospital when I was younger. I liked being in hospital and I needed to do nursing. I don't know . . . It was just what I was always going to do. Always.

I don't think I've ever thought about why I wanted to do this job. I know this sounds odd, but I think people who work in the NHS do so because they've got an innate need to do it. We certainly don't do it for the money. Whether that need is empathy, compassion, or whatever, I don't know. But I think you're born with it. I don't think you can feel that need if you weren't born with it.

I attended a grammar school. I was a voracious reader. This sounds so pretentious, but one year I remember being thrilled because I got a set of junior encyclopaedias for my birthday. I used to sit up in bed reading them at night. My dad was a fisherman. He was interested in wildlife and geology.

After I'd finished my O levels, I had to go see my head of year who wanted to know why I was wasting my career on a nurse's job. My decision to become a nurse went down like a lead balloon at school.

I started at sixteen as a cadet nurse in a hospital that I could see from my home. My dad said I would last 'til coffee time and my mum said I'd last 'til lunchtime. I lasted almost fifty years before I retired last year.

It's all I've ever done except get married and have children. The proudest my mum and dad ever were of me was when I said to them, 'Oh by the way, you're talking to the new theatre matron.'

Nursing has been a fantastic career. You thrive on the fact that you know you're doing something that makes a difference.

Up until retirement, I worked in an operating theatre. The first time I ever scrubbed up for a case on my own was in 1970. The surgeon was lovely. He said at the end of it, 'I'll give you nine out of ten for that.' I had to squeeze my head through the door.

We did a lot of breast cancer patients and reconstructions. To see women being made whole again, having that horrible alien disease taken from them, it's very life affirming.

I specialized in IVF for a few years. And again, that is the most wonderful thing you could ever be part of. Scanning someone and saying, 'Oh look there it is!', that child that they've waited so long and gone through so much to have.

You get more from it than you give.

But you also have to have a wall. You learn how to build that wall. You learn how – not to build a wall exactly – but how to leave things behind, or else you'd be drowned.

There's times when I've sat in the changing room at work and cried. For instance, when you scrub for a c-section and the baby's dead, you don't just feel it for the parents, you feel it for you.

I had three miscarriages, but I still worked in an operating theatre where they did terminations. I would never judge those patients. I used to think it was unfair on me, but I still didn't judge them. You can't judge people. You have no right to unless you can live their lives. And you can't live their lives.

There's a small core of colleagues who've been there for a long time. You have that depth of understanding with them. We've lived through a lot of change, a lot of upheaval, a lot of White Papers from the government, a lot of changes of government, changes of management.

If we ever get half-an-hour for lunch as a group, you'll sit down around a big table and it'd be, '*Do you remember when?*'

The younger ones sit there and say, '*You did what!*' Like one Christmas when we'd been called out and everybody was starving, so we decided to try cooking a Christmas pudding in an autoclave. Only the pudding blew up. We had to clean the whole bloody autoclave.

It's a nice thing that shared history.

– What would you change about the job?

I think I would make nursing less about getting exams right and more about connecting with patients. I think taking nursing to a degree level has taken us a bit away from nursing somehow, a little bit away from the humanity of it.

Once I said to a student, '*Pass me that mop, pet.*'

She said, '*I'm here to watch not to work.*'

I said, '*You're here to work the same as the rest of us, and you can mop the bloody floor yourself.*'

She wanted to be a manager, but she didn't want to put the hours in.

Of course, you do need a degree of intelligence to do this job. If you're doing a drug calculation you don't want to get it wrong, especially when you're feeding a two-and-a-half-pound neonate.

Yes, you need a degree of intelligence, but you also need everything else that goes with it. You need to have the humanity, shall we say. I don't want to come across as *holier than thou* but that's my opinion. I'm old-fashioned. Millions of others will disagree.

I think we've lost a lot of people who made good hands-on nurses because of these changes. The paperwork as well. There's a lot of paperwork. Things you did routinely but never wrote down now take five pages on a computer. Things that were done because it made common sense you now have to write a ten-page report on.

But at the same time medicine is now much more nurse-led.

It's been recognized that nurses have a lot of valuable skills and knowledge. We've gone from being perceived as doctors' handmaidens to being autonomous. We used to do things as theatre nurses, stitching skin and assisting surgeons, that we weren't recognized for.

And without nurses taking on the junior doctors' jobs – taking bloods and being able to prescribe medications – the NHS would have collapsed.

That's what the nurses striking want recognition for. They want better pay, and because they're doing a lot more work, they deserve it.

The NHS has also become all about getting numbers through doors. This started with the introduction of targets. When they came in, we used to have a meeting on a Friday morning where patients who were coming up to their 'twelve-week wait' target were labelled as *urgent* and shoehorned in: *'You've been given this date. Please present your-self to the hospital.'*

Before, patients would be pre-assessed and if they were fit for surgery, you would say to them, *'We've got these dates . . .'*

The patient might say, *'I've got a holiday then.'*

'Well, do you want to come before? or what about two weeks after?'

And by involving them, you'd get very few patients who didn't turn up.

– At the bedside, the patient has more autonomy than ever before, but on the administrative side, less than ever before.

We're all a bit unhappy about the way things have gone.

For example, we used to have a purpose-built day unit for surgery. It had a high patient turnover and a high success rate. We had an MP from Scotland come down to visit it, because it was classed as a model of excellence.

It was a streamlined service, where one nurse took care of you virtually the entire day. She admitted you. She went to the anaesthetic room with you 'til you went to sleep. She was there when you woke up in the recovery room. She discharged you. And she rang you up the next morning to make sure you were okay. She was a face and a person you could relate to.

But two of our managers on the board of trustees went to America and saw a hub-and-spoke hospital system, where patients go through just the one door. They decided to try that at our hospital trust, which meant closing down the day unit.

I was part of the team that set up the new hub system. At the time, I said to the trust board that I didn't agree with what they were doing, but I had no choice but to do the best I could to make the new system happen.

Patient numbers started dropping. They weren't getting the degree of care they were getting before.

And lo and behold, a hospital in a nearby city to ours has just opened a state-of-the-art day surgery unit on exactly the same model as we used to have.

It makes me very angry, because it wasn't fair to patients to close that unit.

An answer to the NHS's current problems is staring people in the face. It's so bloody obvious that I could smack them when they come on the TV and say, '*Oh we can't do this, and we can't do that.*'

All they need is discharge wards for patients who are well enough to go home but who haven't got any social care in place. You put them in a ward with very few staff, two trained staff and a couple of auxiliaries, and somebody to put the social care in place or to chase the social care. And then you won't have all these ambulances sat waiting for beds.

That's just my idea.

I think it makes common sense.

– *Tell me about a typical shift.*

Most recently, I worked at an elective surgery site, so we used to work 8 a.m. until 6.30 p.m. Every day was different. You might have gynae-cology, general surgical list, breast cancer, hip replacements.

You'd get up on a morning, 6.30 a.m., quick shower, cup of coffee then straight to work. In by 8 a.m. We used to have what was called *brief*. All the surgeons, consultants, everybody would meet in the anaesthetic room.

Once you'd found out which theatre you were allocated to, you'd go to that theatre and introduce yourself to anybody new. *'My name's Mr Smith and I am a surgeon.'*

If things seemed a bit heavy, I'd say my name and *'I'm the scrub nurse, but you can call me gorgeous.'*

It's important to have that degree of irreverence, but it's never to the detriment of the patient. Your job is to support the surgeon and the rest of the team. But if things are getting a bit tight, you can do things to lower that tension. You can say to the surgeon, *'Just hang on. Give yourself a breath. Why don't we try . . .'*

After we've introduced ourselves, we then go through the lists for each patient, pointing out anything out of the ordinary.

By 8.30 a.m., the patient would be in the anaesthetic room, and you would be scrubbed, getting your trollies ready, and making sure that everything's sterile. Then the patient would be wheeled onto the operating table and that was it – get cracking.

The anaesthetist is at the head of the table. Your surgeon would be at the left or right of the patient with his assistant next to him or opposite him. You are on the opposite side to the surgeon with all the instruments.

We'd have every kind of music on in theatre. We used to put Greatest Hits radio on and if a song came on, *'Stuck in the middle . . .'* You'd say, *'Stealers Wheel'* before the surgeon could. That was just the thing you did with them.

I used to work with surgeons who used to throw instruments and all sorts. I once stood in front of an orthopaedic surgeon who was swearing his head off at me. I wouldn't let him bring in another patient because we didn't have enough equipment.

I just took it.

I then said to him, *'Excuse me, but I'm not used to hearing language like that. I normally work with gentlemen.'*

It shut him down straight away. He came and apologized. All he wanted to do was to look after a patient. It's very high pressure. But there's much less of that now. The consultants are friends now, not just colleagues.

After the surgery is over you do counts. You count every single thing that you've got out during the surgery, the instruments, the swabs, the sutures, the needles, everything. And you do that at least twice.

Once the patient's awake, you have cleaning up to do, floors mopped, and then the theatre's ready for the next patient.

Like anything, you develop different skills as your career goes on. Because we're wearing masks – and particularly for hip replacements, where the air you're breathing is scrubbed and you're wearing these great big helmets that make you look like spacemen – you become very good at nonverbal communication.

Put it this way: you can say a lot with a look.

Being in surgery is something that I loved doing. I loved my job. I really did. It wasn't just a job, it was something that I loved.

I couldn't go back to doing the job now. Physically, it's too much, it was too much.

It's not just a mental job. You lift the patients. You lift the trays of instruments. I don't think you'd meet a nurse who's been in job for over twenty years that hasn't got a bad back. It's the same with bricklayers.

I was about to retire when the pandemic happened. I stayed on. I wasn't going to leave my colleagues.

Covid was the most horrendous thing I've ever seen. It's not something I'd like to live through again.

It wasn't a shambles where we were. It was handled as well as it could have been. But there was just so much conflicting information. One day, you heard one thing, '*You can't go in that room.*'

The next day, '*Yes, you can go in that room.*'

The day after, '*No, you can't.*'

It was an unsettling time, when people became much more aware of their own mortality. Some of our doctors died. Some of our staff became quite ill.

I carried on working in theatre. Because of my age and the fact that I'm asthmatic, they wouldn't let me into the ITU (Intensive Therapy Unit).

We were working twelve-hour shifts, a sixty-six-year-old working a twelve-hour shift, driving three-quarters-of-an-hour there and back, then doing it all again the next day. It was physically hard. I was scared. I knew if I got Covid it would kill me. But people did what they had to do. It was like during the war. You couldn't well walk away and leave it.

After Covid, I felt a bit resentful when I retired. I knew it was the right time, but I had a depth of knowledge and a breadth of knowledge that very few other people had. I was teaching junior doctors their theatre etiquette, how to scrub up, how to handle instruments, how not to have your hands shake the first time you scrub up, how to hold the scissors steady. Silly things like that. And that knowledge isn't getting used now.

I was very good at what I did.

I did it for long enough that I should have been. I don't want to come across as another Florence Nightingale – though I was around when she lit her lamp.

I don't regret one minute of my career. I'm very proud of what I did. And I think the NHS is one of the greatest institutions that's ever been designed.

Midwife

(20s)

My whole life I thought I'd be a nurse or a doctor. A lot of my aunties and cousins are nurses and doctors. I was that child dressed up in the nurse's uniform.

When I got my GCSE results, my school pushed me towards medicine. But when I was doing my A levels, my dad was unwell. There was only one medical school in Northern Ireland and if I didn't get in, then I'd have to spend seven years away from my family. I thought, *I can't do that. They need my support.*

When I was sixteen, I worked in a nursing home. In private nursing homes, it's all about the money. There'd be fancy furnishings but not enough pads and creams and skilled staff on the floor. It put me off care work.

I then did some work experience with my local community midwife. I saw an ultrasound scan for the first time, and I remember feeling – and it's so cringy – but I felt a calling in a weird way. I felt so privileged. I left that day feeling ecstatic. *I want to look after women as they become mothers. This is what I want to do.*

Five-hundred people applied for thirty spaces on my midwifery course. I didn't think I'd get in. School leavers didn't generally get in. One of my teachers saw my mum in town and said, '*There's no way she's going to get in.*'

In one of the assessments for the course, it was an actor playing an elderly woman in a supermarket. She was crying. What do you do? I went over to her and asked if she was okay. She told me it was her first time in the shop since her husband died. I said to her, *'I'm so sorry.'*

It really broke my heart – the actor was amazing, you'd have thought it was real life.

I empathized with her. I told her about my granny dying and how my grandda was so lost at first, but he ended up going to a grief support group.

At the end of it, I asked her if she wanted a hug. She said, *'No, sorry, I'm not a huggy person.'*

I thought, *oh my goodness, that was so inappropriate to ask for a hug. They're going to think that you have no professional boundaries. You haven't got in!*

I did get in and I could stay in Northern Ireland for the course.

The first time you see things on placement – obstetric emergencies, a baby coming out flat, a postpartum haemorrhage – you don't understand why they've happened. You panic. You think, *did I do something wrong?* You're afraid to ask questions in case you should know what's happened. Of course, you're being assessed as well.

I spent a lot of my course thinking I should have studied something else. I would have been better off financially. I would have had a means-tested grant because my parents were on benefits. And I would've only had class a few days a week, so I could have worked. Instead, I got a bursary, which meant that I was ineligible for a grant. But at the same time, I knew I was lucky to have gotten into this university and for them to have put in all this money to train me.

One of my grandparents died in my second year. The university told me that I was allowed to go to the funeral, but I couldn't go to the wake, because it'd take up too much time. I remember being so angry. I thought, *this is so unfair. How can such a caring profession be so cold.* My grandparent died and I went on placement in hospital the next day. When I look back, I was taking too much on. But I kept thinking, *if I leave this course, I'll be a failure and the people who said I couldn't do it are going to be right.*

At the end of that year, I took a year out, because I couldn't cope financially any more and because I realized that I'd spent my whole life worrying about other people.

I got a job as a care assistant to save some money. I did some courses I was interested in, reflexology, aromatherapy, massage, yoga instructing. I had felt like my whole identity was wrapped up in midwifery and that if I didn't do that then I wasn't worth anything. But when I took time away from it, I realized it didn't matter if I finished the course or not. There were loads of other jobs I could do.

In my third year, I had a fantastic mentor. If it wasn't for her, I wouldn't have qualified. She gave me constant feedback about how I was doing. I knew where I stood.

'You're doing really well. This is what you could improve on. Next week, I want you to be able to do this.'

I'd had mentors before who didn't tell me what they expected of me. Once when I'd been a first-year student, there were no patients on the ward, and I'd been in the tea room with my manager and another midwife. They didn't speak to me the whole time. I organized the store room. I was trying to be useful. I asked, *'Is there anything I can do?'*

But they didn't speak to me. I remember going home after that shift and just crying, because I felt like there was something wrong with me. Looking back on it now as a midwife, I would never treat a student like that. Never.

Every time I see a new student I say, *'Hi, it's so good to meet you. I'm one of the midwives in the delivery suite. What's your name? How many births do you have? If I have a woman in labour, I'll let you know so you can get a delivery.'*

Now, I'm a registered midwife. I get up at 6.30 a.m. and I leave the house at 7.30 a.m. I can cycle to work in twenty minutes. I'll drive if it's raining. I can park in the nearby housing estate, and because I used to live there, they won't slash my tyres.

If I park in the staff car park, it costs £5 a day. You can apply for a staff permit, but it takes something like five years to arrive.

I'll have a cup of tea and I'll always get something into my belly, a banana or some chocolates on the staff table. You never know how long you're going to be away from food. You could go into a room and have a patient that's pushing for over two hours and the heat's on full blast and you're wearing all your PPE. It takes a lot out of you.

After that I'll go to the nurse's station and see where my name is on the board. We've got fourteen rooms, and twelve midwives on shift, but not all of those rooms will be in use. You go to your room. Knock on the door, introduce yourself to the woman and birthing partner, and get handover from the midwife. If the room's nice and calm, you'd get a full handover, you'd let the other midwife go home, and then you'd do a full assessment of the woman.

Whenever I walk into a room for the first time, I'll say *'Hello, I'm going to be looking after you today and hopefully meeting your wee baby. How are you feeling? How's your night been?'*

I'll ask how her pregnancy's been. I'll try to get an idea of her emotions and how she's feeling. If she's been up all night and she's sore and exhausted, I'll empathize.

I'll say, *'I'm sure you're exhausted and can't wait until this baby's out. As soon as this baby's here, we're going to make you the best cup of tea you've ever had.'*

You're trying to motivate them and keep them focused.

I'll then say to her, *'What do you want?'*

If someone's in the zone, you don't need to give them lots of encouragement. Whereas if someone's panicking, you have to bring them back.

Since Covid we've only had one birthing partner in the room. It works better than having two, where sometimes the granny can take over and the dad feels a wee bit lost or sent in the corner.

Since I've started my training, the paperwork has definitely increased. There's so much litigation in midwifery and maternity care, because the child has twenty-five years from the day they were born to sue the hospital trust.

We need complete contemporaneous documentation. As things happen, we need to write them down. It's really time-consuming. There's a saying, *'If you don't write it down, you might as well not have done it.'*

Even things like massaging someone's back. You write down, *'Massage given with consent. Patient reports good relief from pain.'*

Every time you change their pad, you have to write that down along with the colours of the waters. These are things that you wouldn't have written down years ago, because they would have been a given. But now you write everything down.

The patients always say, *'God, you have so much paperwork to do.'*

It's non-stop. I try not to make it a barrier between me and the woman. You do get used to it and you get to know what you can do in advance of the baby being born. But it never stops.

Once, I was off night duty and one of my friends asked, *'How was your night?'* I said, *'It was busy. I had two deliveries.'*

She was like, *'Oh, that's not so bad. Do you not just hold their hands and rub their back. I'm sure the doctors do the work.'* And that's a lot of people's perception.

They don't realize that the midwife provides all the care during labour as long as everything's within the realms of normality.

The job can also be emotionally turbulent.

You could have a day where you look after a woman who's given birth to a stillborn baby in the morning. It's completely heart-breaking.

And then in the evening you're delivering a healthy baby, and you still have to be just as happy for that couple as you'd normally be, even though in the morning you were looking after a family who are going through the hardest thing imaginable.

– How do you cope when things like that happen?

At the time, it's so important to show empathy but at the same time to not get too involved because it's not about you. It's not you that's lost a baby or has had a really traumatic birth. It's someone else's trauma.

I had a day where I can remember doing an antenatal check and there was no fetal heartbeat. Through my whole shift, my priority was caring for that woman and her family. I texted my partner that I was having a really hard day. And when I got home, I couldn't talk. He had dinner made. I just started crying. I just needed to be held.

After the cry I was fine.

Anyone that's a partner of a nurse or a midwife is definitely a hero themselves. We can be so emotionally fatigued that, when our partners tell us about their problems, we're not as engaged as we should be. That can be frustrating for them. It's not to say that their day isn't important, but it can be hard to empathize because you're so drained. You just eat and go to bed and do it again.

And, as midwives, we are each other's counsellors. If we were going to therapy, it would cost the NHS an absolute fortune. It's the understanding you get from your colleagues that you don't get elsewhere. Your friends and family won't understand what it's like, but with a colleague, we'll go for a walk and talk about the things that have happened.

The other day, I've come onto day shift, and I've seen one of my colleagues still sitting there writing their notes.

I asked, *'How was your night?'*

She said, *'I'm exhausted I haven't had a break'*

I go out and make her a cup of tea and bring her breakfast.

'You're exhausted. What do you need me to do so you can get away? I'll clear your delivery trolley.'

You've got to be supportive of each other, because the next day it could be you staying for an hour after your shift. Sometimes you could be leaving an hour-and-a-half after your shift ends because you wanted to stay, because that woman needed you to stay, or because you could see the baby coming. Even though you're leaving late, you think, *I'm so proud of her.*

The NHS survives off the good graces of the staff a lot of the time, but I never think, *I'm getting paid to do a job.*

I don't see my work as a company paying me to do a job. I see my work as *the women need me to care for them*. My duty is to them rather than the NHS as an employer.

I still get the flutters after every birth. I always think, *oh my goodness, I've just seen a new life come into this world*. I don't want to ever get to the stage where I'm like, *this is a normal day in the office*. If I don't feel some kind of elation, that's when I know I shouldn't be doing the job.

Doctor

(30s)

You make the decision to be a doctor when you're fifteen or sixteen. That is a huge decision. People told me, *'You'll sacrifice a lot.'*

And it's true, you are going to spend a good fifteen years of your life sacrificing a lot to do this. But you don't have any perspective on time when you're fifteen. You think, *oh, it's gonna be great.* And yes, it will be, but there will also be weekends and nights that aren't your own any more.

Who you meet, the events you go to – birthdays, weddings, funerals – all of that is dictated by the job.

My best friend asked me to be the godfather to his daughter and I couldn't go to the christening because of my rota.

You can't imagine these things when you're younger, not until you live it.

There are no nights for me this week. There's no on-call emergency work. My work this week is all work that can be planned. In that sense, it's a good week.

I'm on 8 a.m. starts, but I get into the office a bit earlier. The day starts with handover. If you're lucky there's nothing to be handed over. If you're unlucky, there may be a serious emergency handed to you immediately.

The job itself isn't always that difficult. You are trained to look after patients and to understand how the body works. But managing interpersonal relationships, systems, organizations, politics, that is all definitely very stressful.

Sometimes it can be quite tribalistic because of limitations on services, things like beds. There's a lot of politics. This can surprise people who thought that this wouldn't be the case in an altruistic career.

The management responsibilities escalate every couple of years or so. By the time you're more senior, your time is 50 per cent clinical, 50 per cent management.

I can see that the management side of things is important, but at the same time I sometimes feel frustrated that I'm not using my skills and training.

I don't really know what the solution is. There aren't enough staff for us to have dedicated managers and dedicated clinicians. We all have to take management responsibility, something which becomes more and more important as the NHS becomes more complicated.

But I don't think there can be any replacement for the job satisfaction that clinicians get from seeing patients getting better. When you see someone that's suffering get their life back, when you see a sick child get well enough to go back to their parents, you can't put the feeling it gives you into words and you can't put a value on it.

I was always taught by one of my mentors that you have to go and see your patients after you've done anything, and when you make time to do that at the end of the day and you see a change, a complete 180, then it's so rewarding for you and your team – the nurses, physios, anaesthetists.

One of the biggest weaknesses of our training, and of the medical system, is that it focuses on the times when things don't go well. Ninety-nine per cent of the time, things go well. And that should be brought up and highlighted and celebrated, but a lot of the time things are only brought up in meetings when there's a problem.

Doctors are expected to overachieve and to do everything fantastically well, but nobody can function perfectly for ten years with a lack of sleep, with all the pressures and stresses. Eventually there'll be a drop in performance. It happens to everybody at some point in their career. It's not nice to see. And doctors don't necessarily talk about these things, which doesn't help.

As you become more senior you get closer to seeing medical negligence litigation. You see the effect that it has on people who've gone through it, the effect on their personal and professional life.

It does perhaps alter your perspective. You do your best, but there's also 1 per cent of your mind thinking, *let's risk manage. What's the safest thing for the patient but also for the practitioner?*

In the press there was a story about a paediatric junior doctor who was managing multiple wards by themselves. The consultant wasn't on site. Something went wrong and the junior doctor was suspended from practising.

At times, when staff are on sick leave, staff shortages like the one that junior doctor experienced are not an untold occurrence. But the NHS still has to operate. You have to find a way, and so you stretch things to fit.

What should you do? Do you say you're not going to work that day because you don't feel that you have enough support? There'd be repercussions for making such statements. You have to think about your career.

These things are quite scary.

In medical school, they create simulated environments where patients die. They tell you, didactically and academically, how to process these things.

It's not until later, in real life, that you understand how it can affect you. I remember the first horrific and tragic death of a patient that I saw. Before that point, my career as a junior doctor had been looking after elderly patients with multiple comorbidities. I'd never seen anything like this death. Someone bleeding out of every orifice. The body was shutting down. There was blood everywhere. We were doing resuscitation. There was one other junior doctor there. One of us was charged with making notes and I was charged with putting the cannulas in.

This was in the days when doctors wore smart clothes with white coats. You finish a scene like that, everyone's covered in blood, and then they say, *'Well, I'm going back to work.'*

But senior doctor looked at both of us and said, *'Go have a coffee for half an hour.'*

We went to the doctors' mess and we just sat there looking at each other. *What's just happened? Do we just go back to work?*

You're expected just to get on with it. You find whatever solace you can. You have your colleagues, and you talk about these things afterwards and the next day you go again.

I remember one woman just crying when we told her that she had a tumour and that she would never have a child again. Afterwards, the consultant I was with just nodded and said, *'Shall we get the next patient in?'*

What else could he do when there are another ten patients waiting to be seen? It can be difficult. These experiences leave small scars on the doctors. You get trained to bury these things deep down, because otherwise medics wouldn't function.

– How do you go about breaking bad news?

There are things that I've practised and picked up along the way.

You should have as much information as possible.

You should be in an appropriate environment. A room to yourself and a nurse with you. Tissues. Chairs for them to sit down. Don't have multiple bleepers and phones on you, give those to someone else to carry.

And go slowly. You have to make time for it. People know bad news is coming before you've opened your mouth. Give them an opportunity to ask questions. Let them know that you're sorry for their loss and that you empathize.

It's one of the worst parts of the job, to be honest.

You may have ways of suppressing that empathy for your own self-preservation, but you can't not feel sympathetic and empathetic and sorry for people who have gone through something tragic through no fault of their own.

– Soldiers often talk about there being a veil between them and civilians. Do you feel that?

Yes, and I'd say I use that veil to cope. I tend to surround myself with non-medical people because it's a chance not to talk about medicine. It can become all consuming. My wife is medical. She finds it hilarious that I go to a party, and I enjoy talking to the man who works in accounts. *'He's the most boring man in the world. Why are you so fascinated by him?'* But it helps me block out what I need to block out.

Once upon a time it was accepted that though doctors might not be paid a lot by the state, they were given great accommodation in the junior years, and later on they were given time to work in the private sector to compensate for their relatively low salary.

Whereas now, there's so much pressure on the NHS that it's very difficult to give doctors that time, even though the NHS salaries for those doctors have barely changed in the last fifteen years.

And there are other little things. Should NHS staff have to pay for their own parking? Or the fact that there's only expensive food available for them to buy at the hospital.

When you get lots of these small factors and you put them together, you can get a system where people don't feel that they are appreciated.

This matters when you go to conferences and there are recruiters from New Zealand, Australia, Canada, where they want doctors with our skill sets and they are making every effort to attract them.

When I started, we would happily stay late. It was like a band of brothers and sisters. It was just what we did, and we did it because our senior colleagues did it. We felt that camaraderie.

People loved what they did and so they had this tunnel vision about work.

This goodwill was keeping the NHS going. It was papering over the cracks in salaries, in funding, in staffing.

Now, there has been an erosion of that goodwill, because things have become so stretched, and because of the pandemic, where people felt that doctors and nurses weren't supported – the lack of PPE, for instance.

People think, *should I spend all this time at work? Shouldn't I have some sort of overtime pay so that I can pay nursery fees?* People look at the job a lot more objectively. They look at it not just as a vocation, but as a career, as a job.

These are the people that were on the frontline during the pandemic . . . and I don't think the gimmicks – *clap for the NHS* and that sort of thing – sat well with doctors. They didn't want claps. They wanted equipment, funding, and resources.

And now there is a constant element of crisis in our hospitals. Senior management communicate this regularly.

They'll say, '*The hospital is in a Red Crisis*' or '*Black Crisis.*'

But it happens so frequently that crisis can become the norm. It isn't something that shocks you any longer. You expect it. You expect that, once you get to winter, you'll be in crisis for the next four months.

We were managing these crises, and then a pandemic came along and the things that we thought that would never happen have now happened . . . Mass deaths. Not having oxygen. Treating patients in corridors.

I've been fortunate to see healthcare in different countries and on different continents. Nothing is perfect, but when you're sick in the UK, the NHS really is there for you in a way that is unlike any other country. We're fortunate to have it. I hope we don't only come to realize this when it's too late. We should do everything we can to keep it.

Prison healthcare assistant

(50s)

I just love my job. I once worked eleven days on the trot, thirteen-hour days. I love walking through the prison gates. When I'm not working and I'm at home, I don't know what to do with myself.

I get up in the morning at 6 a.m. I leave my house at 7 a.m.

By 7.10 a.m., I'm walking through the gates of the prison. I go to the nursing hub, have a coffee, and we'll talk about what's been happening in the night-time.

After handover, I'll look at my ledger to see what there is for me to do for that day.

Usually the day consists of giving out medication, mainly methadone. This isn't a five-minute job. You'd be surprised by how many prisoners are on it. I'd say 40 per cent are on methadone and 70 per cent are on medication. It takes us quite a few hours to administer it all.

Once that's done, I'll go and do my social care. We have a ward in the prison for the sick prisoners. I look after the dementia patients. I'll make sure that they've had their breakfast, that they've washed and dressed for the day, that they've got plenty of fluids and that there's no health concerns.

If needs be, I'll do basic observations, blood pressure, temperature, make sure there's no infections or pressure sores, taking bloods, that kind of thing. I'll also make sure their rooms are tidy and safe. One patient, I have to put cream on his feet, so I'll have to wash them before I can do that.

I never thought I could do this sort of caring. I only realized I could do it when my dad was dying. He was in hospital, and I had to see to his personal needs because there weren't the staff to do it. I didn't realize I had it in me. I never realized I had a caring side. I always thought I was a bit uncaring, unfeeling, *cold as ice* . . . *'willing to sacrifice our love'.*

There are some prisoners that want to be helped. We give them all respect and we expect respect in return. People tend to assume that they've made these choices, but some of these prisoners don't know right from wrong. They haven't been taught that. They see their parents behaving in a certain way and they think that's the norm.

I've learned not to judge people. I say to them, *'I'm not an angel. I just haven't been caught yet.'*

And when I speak at the prisoner inductions, my last words to them are always, *'You'll see me walking up and down the wing. Please don't feel afraid to approach me. Just talk to me. I'm always here for you.'*

There's one, Michael, who's always nice to me. He always high-fives me and he always makes me a cup of coffee when I'm on the wing. Bless him. He'd gone months without any front teeth and one day I came onto the ward, and he was there smiling. I thought, *there's something different about you.*

And he said, *'Do you like my new teeth, miss?'*

We talk about what he's going to do when he leaves prison. He's got a trade and he's going to go into business. I'll say, *'You've got so much to look forward to, but the hardest part will be keeping on that right track.'*

He'll say, *'I'm going to do that, Miss.'*

In a previous job, the healthcare IT system had all the information about why a prisoner was in. We don't have access to that information now, but you do get to find out about the bad ones.

The dementia patients I have are paedophiles. When you're with them it crosses your mind, but first and foremost they're my patients.

It's the same when a prison officer starts talking to you about things that are happening with a prisoner. I say, *'Look, he's your prisoner, he's my patient.'*

One of my dementia patients has been unwell lately. We thought he was a goner. The other day he was sat on his chair crying, '*I don't want to be in this world any more.*'

I got him a cup of tea and a chocolate biscuit and said, '*Don't talk like that. Tomorrow is a different day. You'll feel different tomorrow.*'

I'll be sad when he goes.

In between administering medications and doing the social care, we might get a code blue, which is a radio message saying that there's been an incident on a wing. A hanging. Self-harm. We'll need to go with the medicine bags, oxygen.

We have a mental health team in the prison, but they have to listen, and they can't give advice like we can as healthcare assistants.

We've got the freedom to say, '*What have you done that for, you silly bugger? You've only got yourself to blame.*'

It's not my job, but I do also ask the prisoners, '*On a scale of zero to ten how do you feel?*'

And, '*Do you have any intention of committing suicide?*'

There was one prisoner that said to me, '*Miss, no one's listening to me. I'm gonna kill myself.*'

Between me leaving him to go and get the help, he tried to commit suicide. Thank God I had reported it. I saw him later on that day and I told him off and he started laughing with me.

But there are some that don't tell a soul and they go and do it and it's too late. Sometimes I go home worrying about it. Sometimes I have sleepless nights over it. *Have I done enough? Are they going to be there tomorrow?* And the first thing I'll ask when I go into work is, '*How is so-and-so?*'

I do think about them. I know I'm a little bit too soft. I need to harden up a bit. To say to myself, *it's just my job. That's life.*

I don't understand the prison system. In my mind, these prisoners get rewarded for bad behaviour. They have phones in their cells, Xboxes, laptops.

A lot of them go to prison on purpose, because the lifestyle is better than the one they have on the outside. What's that all about? I think they need to go back to the old-school type of prison. Locked-up all day, with simple food. Take away the TV and all the luxuries, and make them work for what they have.

You've got to remember that the prisoners can manipulate. They say nice things to you to get your attention. You've got to be careful.

One prisoner, every time he comes to the serving hatch for his medication, he says, '*Miss, I've got chest pain. I've got pain going down my arm.*'

He's on medication for all this, he's had three heart bypasses, and he's a paedophile who just wants to go to the hospital to see children. Every week, he's blue-lighted to the hospital, where they're sick of it.

I also think prison healthcare should be done in-house. The prison should have a say in how it's run, because at the moment they have no say. It's a private healthcare company that has the prison contract and it's absolute chaos. There's a lot of bullying and I don't think the higher-ups really know what's goes on on the ground.

For instance, there's a logbook that tells you where you're on duty, and people are always going in there and changing it because they want to go work in a certain department. It's totally wrong.

I'm employed by an agency. They charge the prison healthcare provider about £45 an hour. I get £24 an hour. It's not too bad.

With this job, you either love it or hate it. There are no half measures. It can be very, very difficult for some people, walking through those gates and knowing full well what there is on the other side.

But I can't ever see myself working anywhere different than in a prison. I just love prison work. It's so different. Every day is different.

CHAPTER NINE **ROADWORK**

Delivery rider

courier

lorry driver

taxi driver

Delivery rider

(40s)

I'm on a full-time contract, which is good because my company is the only big delivery company to pay hourly.[4] We receive £10 an hour with some bonuses.

My background is in Greece. I have only been in the UK for four years.

I started as a live-in carer, but my family – my partner and my son – came over and I couldn't stay as a live-in any more. I decided to resign and bring my family to London. Before that, I was travelling back home to Greece a lot. I couldn't keep up. It wasn't good for me.

When we arrived in London, I was looking for a job as a carer, but it was impossible to find one due to the lockdown.

I found this delivery rider job. I applied and they accepted me after two days. I didn't expect after two years to still be here, but since it's a proper job with wages I've just kept it up.

You need to give your availability to the delivery company a week in advance. It's quite flexible. If you're on a full-time contract like me, you just have to cover thirty-five hours of availability every week. Then you wait for the company to give you the exact times.

To be honest, the way you sign your contract is quite controlling. You sign a zero-hours contract for three months. And then they won't

4 A few months after we spoke, his company revealed that it would be getting rid of its salaried delivery riders and treating everyone as a self-employed contractor.

ask you whether you want to renew it, they'll just send you an email saying, '*Because you're working hard for us, we have decided to renew your contract.*'

– *Do they have to give you thirty-five hours' work?*

Yes, they have to do that. But sometimes when there is no demand, in like July or August, they say, '*Unfortunately, because we do not have enough demand, we cannot give you many hours.*'

– *Do you feel well treated?*

Overall, yes. It's good that a delivery company gives you a standard wage. Depending on how many hours you work, you can get £1,500 monthly, which is not bad at all.

And they give you the bike and the equipment.

But because you're being paid an hourly wage, they can't leave you for a minute without orders, so they send you all over – from Shoreditch to St Pancras to Camden – and there's nothing you can do about that.

You can do many miles during your shift. It is quite exhausting. In two years, I must have done 15,000 miles.

I'm a remote courier, which means that I don't have to visit one of the company's centres to pick up a bike. It stays in the house.

To start my shift, I ride down to an order hotspot. I wait to get my first order on the app. When the order comes, the app has the restaurant at the top with a map and the delivery point at the bottom.

You turn the navigation on, and you go to the restaurant.

The app estimates the time it will take to go to the restaurant and drop off the order. But – and this is a problem with all the delivery apps – if you have to wait five minutes at a restaurant, there's no way of recording that on our app, so you are behind on the time estimate and you have a feeling that you're always late with your orders. It is quite stressful.

I think it's intentional. They want you to ride quickly because customers are quite demanding. If it takes you two or three minutes more than they expected, the customer will say, '*Oh, why did you stop?*'

I think that customers should know that we have traffic, we have waiting times in restaurants, and sometimes it's very difficult to cycle if the wind is blowing.

We also have traffic lights. There is a traffic light at Blackfriars Bridge which lasts seven minutes. When you have to go through those lights, the application will tell you that you have five minutes to drop off an order one mile away, but it's more likely to be fifteen to twenty minutes because of the lights.

Sometimes we have two orders to drop off. If the app tells us to '*Go to McDonald's first and then to Costa*', the McDonald's customer will always be grumpy because he's waiting two or three minutes more.

'*Why did you go there first? Now my food will be cold.*'

But we need to follow the instructions. It's not our choice to go to one restaurant first and the other second. The app says, '*Go there first.*'

Also, I used to think English people were more patient when driving than Greek people, but it's not the case. I've had three falls in two years. The first one was a bit stupid. I was sitting in the corner at a traffic light. I wanted to go straight, but the car behind me wanted to turn. The driver was new and quite stressed. She didn't wait for me to go, and she turned into me.

I kept my mind, let my bag go, and prepared myself for ending up on the floor. I didn't have any injuries.

And there is a group of burglars around here. Five guys, nor more than fifteen years old, covered with balaclavas. And they are always riding their bikes on the wrong side of the road, snatching phones.

I was nervous last time I saw them. I was on a narrow bike path at a red light. They were coming down the opposite way. I just clutched my bike. They are moving so fast that you cannot catch them. It's like a movie.

– What do you and the other riders talk about when you're waiting at a restaurant?

We talk about our companies, about our lives.

Other delivery drivers are always saying, '*Why is it taking so long? It's always like that in this restaurant.*'

I can understand how stressful it is for them, because they're being paid per item, but I find the complaining quite boring. When I need to wait three or five minutes, it's a good time to relax, because pedalling all the time is not easy.

Most of the restaurant staff are also quite friendly. Many times they have offered me drinks. But they get pressure from the delivery companies as well, so they sometimes mark their orders as done before they are really done. Then the delivery company starts texting you, '*Your order is ready to collect – why are you still inside the restaurant?*'

I see people at other delivery companies working for five or six hours to get £10 or £15 in total.

It might work for them, because on their busy days they can get £100, but I could never do it.

Those riders feel the pressure to deliver because they want to get paid. I've seen them riding on the pavement at a very high speed to avoid lights. I can understand why. But it would be very bad if I did that – an £80 fine and I would lose a whole day's pay.

Some of the riders at these other companies say to me, '*I would like to earn £10 an hour like you.*'

But others don't want to be restricted by shifts. The good thing with the other companies is that you can go out whenever you want and stop whenever you want.

They can go for a week or for a month without riding and it would be fine. But if I decided to cancel my shift today, I must give a very good reason.

There is a union for riders that talks about these things, but I think riders in my company are not really getting involved.

We are working very hard, and we don't really have time. Some riders are also just students. And some riders may not feel confident in the language.

When I'm working on the bike, I usually end at 1 a.m. Sometimes you end up ten miles away and you have to ride back home unpaid.

And if you've ridden fifty or sixty miles in five hours, you don't have any energy.

I'm still doing some care work in the mornings, so whatever time I get back at night I have to wake up the next morning by 7.30 a.m. It's quite difficult.

I see my family every day. We'll have a quick breakfast together, just for half an hour. Then when I come back from my caring job at 1.30 p.m., I will see my wife. She's working from home, so I'll see her, but I won't talk to her much. Then my son comes back from school at 3.30 p.m., so I then have an hour with him before I need to start my job with the bike again.

It's not many hours with my son, one or two. But sometimes at the weekend I don't have delivery shifts, those are good days.

Other weekends, I work both days. This weekend I'll do Saturday and Sunday from 4.30 p.m. until 1 a.m. It really depends on the delivery company's order volume, which gets busy after November until early May.

It's difficult.

Feeling tired is the worst thing about the job.

But, on the other hand, if you ask for working hours you have them. In Greece, this is not the case. Sometimes you are begging for hours and not getting anything. That's the big difference between there and here.

When I'm feeling tired on the bike, I just try to think about good moments, like being in Greece in the summertime. Family moments, you know?

Heavy rain is the worst experience on the bike. When it rains, it's a nightmare.

You just want to get off and throw your bike away.

But when the weather is nice, and you see people inside the restaurants and – I can say – you can feel the vibe of the place. It's quite interesting.

Just to ride through Central London on my bike has been a good experience for me. It's a chance to see the sights. I've crossed Tower Bridge a hundred times. Three years before, I could never have imagined that.

When I was in the care business as a live-in, sometimes you had too much pressure from the people around your client, their siblings, daughters.

They would say, 'You should do this. You should wake him up like this.'

Of course, I know that I have to do my work and be good at it, but I want to feel free in my job.

And if you're on the bike and you're doing your orders quickly, you don't have too much pressure from the company.

You feel a freedom on the bike.

You are not strapped to a desk.

That's the best thing.

Courier

(40s)

I've driven for a big parcel courier company and for a big e-commerce company. Both types of company give you a van to rent and a mobile device.

You turn up at 10 a.m. and load all the parcels. We did two hundred and fifty to three hundred parcels a day. Once you had them, you'd be sent to a town to deliver all of the parcels within a ten-mile radius.

I enjoyed seeing the different places, the different towns and cities, and I liked that I didn't have to pay for anything. They gave you the van, the device, the uniform. You just had to deliver.

For the e-commerce company, it was £90 per day, regardless of how long it took to deliver the parcels.

Let's say you start your first delivery at 11 a.m., some days you'd finish at 5 p.m., other days you'd finish at 8 p.m., but you'd still get £90 however many hours you worked.

I have to say, working for the e-commerce company, it felt like an independent job.

There was no pressure.

I'd always have nice music playing.

I'd do my deliveries and go home.

The courier company was a bit different. They paid me £1 per stop.

The parcel deliveries were also time-limited. The device would say, '*You have to deliver to these twenty houses between 11am and 12pm.*'

But they didn't know or care about roadworks or traffic. You can let them know that there's traffic, but if they let you off once, they'll then start pushing you to finish your deliveries.

You end up driving like crazy, rushing and running.

The company will find out if you throw parcels from the van or leave them outside without ringing the doorbell, because the customers complain. The company can then track down the driver who made the delivery.

Drivers only do these things for two reasons. One, if they want to lose their job. Two, because they feel under pressure to make the deliveries.

Working at an average speed barely gives you a minimum wage, so you rush. If the courier companies were fair with the drivers, then they wouldn't throw the parcels.

Delivery driving is physical work. Coming up and down out of the van. The steps you do each day . . .

It's demanding. I'm getting old now and I can't do three hundred parcels in a day.

When you load your van up with parcels, the first thing you think is, *what the hell?* [he laughs]

Will I be able to finish on time, or am I getting home at nine or ten o'clock at night?

One driver saw his van filled with thirteen massive bags of parcels and asked, '*Do I have the whole month to deliver these?*'

But you tend to calm down as soon as you start emptying your van, and you can save time when you're familiar with the houses in the area. After all, when you finish quicker, you get paid more per hour.

. . . when you're self-employed, it never feels permanent. You don't know when the company will turn around and say, '*We don't need you.*'

So if you like driving, you're better off driving a taxi or a bus, jobs that are better paid and not so physical.

Lorry driver

(40s)

Sometimes I leave for work at 3 a.m. on a Monday morning and I won't get home until 7 p.m. on a Friday.

But you're only paid for the hours that you're on-tacho, when you can work a maximum of fifteen hours three times a week, and thirteen hours twice a week.[5] Those are the hours that you're on the clock. But you're also physically at work for every other hour during those five days: you're camping in the lorry all week long.

All the time you're driving, you've got to consider the road users around you. They're in their own little world because *they've got to get from A to B in five minutes*. They might make a rash decision. And the result of their rash decision might be you crashing into them, causing a massive accident and all sorts of devastation behind you.

It's quite a demanding job.

Here's a bizarre thing: nearly all drivers you speak to – especially what we call *trampers* (long-distance drivers) – nobody sleeps on a Sunday. Even though you're tired from being on the road all of the previous week. You get an anxiety. You sleep with one eye open. I can't tell you why.

---

5 'On-tachograph.' Tachographs are used in commercial vehicles to record data on the time spent driving, speed, distances travelled etc. This recorded data is then used to make sure that the driver is complying with working time regulations.

– How are you paid?

We're paid a weekly rate, but it's made up of all sorts of cleverness. There's certain dispensations you can get that you don't have to pay tax on. And companies will try to pay you as much as possible tax free. It pays good money.

For example, your living allowances, meal allowances, overnight allowances – all tax free.

We get £25 a night stop out allowance.

£10 a day meal allowance.

£35 to stay away from home for a day.

You're also not using your own electricity and fuel and water and all the rest of it because you live in the truck. But some of the toilets and showers at services are some of the most horrendous places you can imagine.

– What are the customers like?

Some customers are so grateful and appreciative. There are others who barely acknowledge you. There's one particular customer who treats us like sheep, like sheep going to slaughter.

You're pushed down a path by these signs.

Go through the gate.

Turn left.

Right through that door.

And if you miss a sign, all of a sudden you're in the wrong place and someone will say, '*You're not supposed to be here. Did you not see the sign? You've got eyes haven't you?*'

Eventually, you park your truck in the bay, walk across the yard, give the guy your reference number, push your papers through a hole in the wall.

He never even looks up. '*Write your trailer number and registration on there. Then go wait in your truck.*'

You think, *go wait for what? For how long?*

You're just a number to these customers. And that's why you get the drivers who say, '*If you can't be arsed, I can't be arsed.*'

Then the working atmosphere becomes unpleasant. I call it yard politics. On the group chats it'll be, '*It's all right for him, he's got a nice run up to Carlisle.*'

Everybody's bothered about every job except their own.

In my dad's day, that chatter used to be on CBs.[6] There's a new version of CB out there. It's on an app. But you get so many horrid people on there, treating each other with disrespect. Some driver will post something on Facebook about the kind of food they're eating or about the load they're pulling, and all of a sudden on the CB somebody will say, '*Did you see so what so and so posted?*'

That poor bloke then gets wind of the fact everyone's talking about him, and he has a horrid day. It's horrendous. Let's hope he has a thick enough skin, because if he hears this and takes his eyes off the road, we've got a major catastrophe on our hands.

I just keep away from it all.

When you first start driving, every Monday is like, *wow I'm off*.

But then you realize that your home is still your home. And someone still has to run that home. And by driving all week you've put more responsibility on your wife.

This is particularly the case since we've just taken in some Ukrainian refugees and our dog has gotten ill. It all falls on her.

So when you get home at the weekend, you should be resting, but you've got to do all the jobs that she's not had time to get to. It does start to put a strain on your marriage.

All my life I've wanted a feeling of independence, of no holds barred. That's what I've been looking for.

And in many ways, this job gives me that freedom.

---

6 'Citizens band radio.' A short-distance radio system popular among lorry drivers.

On a night, I'll park up and find a new pub if I can. I'll walk over, have a couple of pints, meet the locals, and come back, get my head down and do it all again.

Taxi driver

(50s)

There aren't many taxi drivers who actually have music on in the car. I find it strange.

On Saturday nights my job is not like a job, because I'm actually out experiencing that Saturday nightlife as well. I'm listening to the radio with the tunes on.

Life and work are intertwined.

I'll have Capital FM on and it's got the tunes and people are like, '*Ah I could stay in here all night!*'

I listen to everything. Music to me is music. It's just got labels so that you can identify it. It's crazy, but if I hear it and I like it, I play it.

It's a spirit-lifting thing.

And it's that vibe. Keeping them on that vibe.

'*This is the best taxi I've ever been in!*'

I know they're just saying that, but when I myself go in another taxi and they've got no music on. They're not talking to the customer. They've got their headphones in, talking to somebody. There's no music. It's just dead.

To me, that's a weird experience.

I left school when I was fifteen. I worked as a pot washer. Someone didn't turn up to work. The manager said, '*You're gonna be live tonight.*'

I became a full-time chef. It's a hot, hard job. But I'm glad I did it because it made my brain able to think fast.

And driving at night you have to see things before they happen. There's people that drive when they're high on drugs, drunk drivers. There's a lot of strange things that happen at night.

These young people race like they're on *Fast and Furious* and sometimes I see crashes. During the night, you'll see cars crashed into walls.

I've seen a lot of that.

Recently, I took some people from a pub who were all dressed up in their Halloween costumes telling me that they won some competition. We're driving up the road and then I looked in my wing mirror and I see a motorbike doing over a hundred miles an hour.

I saw it and then it was past us, chased by armed police.

These women are like '*Oh my God! what is this?*'

But this is normal. We see things like this all the time.

Then we turn right, and we see the same motorbike hurtling right towards us. So he's lost the police. We see the police like five-hundred yards down the road.

This bike's on a scramble. It's like something on a film.

You never see things like that as a person who just drives from A to B.

I remember picking up two guys who got kicked out of a nightclub. There was one guy sitting in the front, a really big guy, and then a guy sitting in the back. They were upset.

One guy said, '*They don't know who I am! I'm going back to get my gun and come back and shoot 'em.*'

I said, '*Mate, you don't need to do that. You know what I mean? It's not worth it.*'

And he goes, '*You're not even bothered are ya!*'

Where I'm from would be classed as the ghetto, so I know characters like that.

Somebody else could have been very scared of the situation because they're not used to those characters.

I'm lucky in the respect that I grew up in a ghetto environment, but I've worked in the corporate world, so I can adapt to both worlds.[7] Whereas if you didn't grow up in that lifestyle, then these rowdy guys can feel that energy. If you're scared of them, they might turn on you.

I never have any problems in the taxi, but there are taxi drivers who get attacked. A lot of taxi drivers are not from that ghetto culture. They don't understand that the rowdy person is just a rowdy person, they don't mean harm.

But a taxi driver might see it as, '*Oh, they're trying to attack me!*' Then he escalates it and then it becomes a problem.

It's down to your attitude as a taxi driver. As long as you're cool with them, they're cool with you.

The taxi trade is like working in a bar. You meet every kind of person from every kind of background with every kind of story. Some of them are funny. Some of them are bad. Imagine being a fly on the wall? You hear conversations that you shouldn't hear. You see things that you shouldn't have seen.

It's a rewarding job, for the customer I'm providing a service, but for me I'm learning a lot about people.

You are part of the community as a taxi driver. There are stories of taxi drivers what would kick you out if you ain't got 10p. I'm not one of those.

I just make sure I see them go in their house. I remember dropping a guy off. It was like minus four outside. He went up some stairs to his house and I didn't see the door open. I'm waiting for the door to open, so I can see he's gone in. I don't see it open, so I got out my car. And when I'd got up there he had fallen on the step. He was drunk. It was a good job that I'd got out to check, because he would've frozen to death out there.

*   *   *

7 He had previously worked in a sales role in a delivery company's head office.

People say, 'Do you taxi drivers go out for a drink?'

No, we're all solo artists. We're all doing our own thing. You don't meet up, you know?

– Does that bother you?

No, not at all. Not at all. There's no time, because your work goes really quick. If you work in an office and you do eight hours, it feels like twenty hours. When you work in a taxi you do twelve hours and it goes really fast.

And that's because you're always moving. I'm driving to a job ten, fifteen minutes. I'm driving with the customer ten, fifteen minutes.

Time is ticking all the time.

But it's not stressful. There's no pressure. You can only go as fast as you can go.

You can't go, '*Oh, I've got to do this job quickly, because I've got to get to the next job!*'

There's nothing like that.

Being a taxi driver, it's a job where it's live, everything's live.

You don't have to worry about tomorrow.

CHAPTER TEN **SITEWORK**

Site reliability engineer

plumber

electrician on a production line

construction site manager

Site reliability engineer

(20s)

When I was eleven or twelve, my friends and I wanted to play games together. The game we wanted to play was Minecraft. I was the little nerdy one in the group. I said, '*I'll figure it out.*'

I set a server up and we all played on it. I then realized that if I could code then I could make the game do what I wanted, so I started learning Java. And that's where my interest in tech came from.

I taught myself a lot between thirteen and sixteen. Linux networking, Linux systems, how to script, how to use Bash, how to use Python, how to make a website, how databases worked.

I was mostly playing around and experimenting, but I also ran a Minecraft server, which is like running a games community.

On that Minecraft server, you'd have mini games and different modes. I'd sell stuff to players that they could use on the server. In the run up to Christmas, the server would make six to eight thousand pounds a month. And after Christmas, all the kids' Christmas money would start coming in.

A lot of the money I made went straight back into the server. I'd have to pay developers for plugins, pay people to build maps for me, pay server hosting companies. I had a rack in a data centre that I had to pay for. This stuff wasn't cheap to run.

And then there was a listing site called Minecraftservers.org. I could be bidding thousands to get my server to the top of that site. That's two grand on advertising in a month.

I wasn't in it to make a tonne of money. I just liked logging in in the afternoon and seeing six-hundred people on my server. If you'd have asked my parents, they would have had no clue what I was up to, because I wasn't buying things.

Eventually, I panicked and shut it down when I realized that I might have to pay all of this income back in tax . . .

I speak to friends of mine who say, '*I wish I'd learned to code.*'

And they try. They'll write a script, but they never see the script do anything substantial. But in Minecraft, when I made a mod, I could see it in the game. I could see that what I was doing was making a difference to the game my friends and I were playing.

When I left school, I worked at a college in the IT department for six months. A month or so in, I was in the college on a Saturday, doing some work in a classroom while the students weren't there. My boss was in there. He was talking to one of our IT contractors, who was running all the Linux infrastructure for us, and who was leaving.

I ran into my boss's office ten minutes later and said, '*I know Linux!*'

I did the interview and got the promotion. Three months into that role, a colleague, the network engineer, got blue-lighted up to London for a heart transplant. I then became the network engineer for the college at nineteen. I was responsible for the network and the Linux systems for thousands of students across three different campuses. And I'd not been to university. I'd taught myself all this. It was nuts!

I now work as a SRE (a site reliability engineer) for a managed service provider in London. We host websites and apps for lots of household names.

SREs are the firefighters of the tech world, responsible for keeping things online. Something will break at 3 a.m. and I'm the one getting the call to fix it.

If I don't know what to do, I'll go to my boss. If he doesn't know what to do, we're screwed. Hopefully, I'll look at something that's completely broken and then an hour later it's back working, and I can see traffic flowing again.

I wake up between 8 a.m. and 8.30 a.m. I'll log-on for fifteen minutes, read the news, and see what's going on that day. Then I'll walk to the office. I'll say hello to everyone. I'll have a look at the traffic we received overnight and see if there's anything suspicious.

I'll see what's in the support queue to see if anyone's screaming at us. By then it'll be 11 a.m. and I'll start on a ticket from the support queue. Some of these tickets can go on for six months. For instance, one might be: *build a system that can handle thirty million requests a year.*

My work for the rest of the day depends on what comes up. It could be an incident that we have to deal with, or it could be working on building that new system.

It's not physically straining this type of role, but it is mentally straining.

If you're dealing with an incident, with everything going on, time just flies. I forget to eat. All of a sudden it's 4 p.m. and I haven't had lunch yet. If you're dealing with an incident, with everything going on, time just flies.

If I spend two months building something, it's a great feeling when you see the first visitor hit the website and you know that it actually works and it's not going to fall apart. I have a dashboard where I can see the graphs and numbers ticking up. Seeing things go live, it's such a great feeling.

I can be in a room with my friends, and 70 or 80 per cent of people in the room have used something that I've built in one way or another. It's surreal.

– *What drew you to the job?*

It's the scale of it. If I cock something up and something goes wrong, and the website and app for the company I'm working for goes down, then it could be hundreds of thousands of people who are affected.

It's horrible to be woken up at 3 a.m., but I love it at the same time. It's a thrill.

*　*　*

My parents were care workers. They didn't have loads of money. But I now have the ability to look five years into the future and think, *I want to try living in New York*. None of my family ever had the chance to try something like that that. They've barely flown. It's amazing. I never expected to be able to do half this stuff when I was playing Minecraft.

I look back at some of the people I was in college with and they're still in my home town. Some of them have become druggies or alcoholics or whatever. There are jobs there but there's no careers.

– *What are you afraid of?*

I'm afraid of going into management. Luckily as an SRE I can stay on the individual contributor route.

– *Why do you fear it?*

Dealing with people. I like working on the tech, doing stuff and breaking things. If I go into management, I'm missing out on the nitty gritty. I don't want to be in meetings all day, doing one-to-ones with my team. I want to be doing tech.

As soon as you become a senior developer, your chair is just spinning because you're in meetings the entire time. I don't want to be dealing with HR problems: '*Oh, I'm not getting on with Bob.*'

I don't want to be dealing with that.

I want to be thinking, *I can't work this problem out, I've got this bug, I've just blown up the website*. That's what I want to be dealing with.

Plumber

(20s)

I learned to read behind everyone else. When I was five, I was told I was autistic. I then got to secondary school, and they told me I was going to fail my exams.

When I was in Year 9, I started the first year of a construction course. It was a BTEC in *Construction and the Built Environment*. I was taking it seriously, but the school didn't realize how rigorous a course it was.

They put it down as a course for all the 'challenged' students. It went downhill. You had students who were destroying my work, nearly burning down the school, and clogging drains by pouring concrete down them.

I was just going home and reading the textbook.

I got a merit, someone else got a pass, and there were ten fails. School was the worst time in my life. It was a Catholic school. I was gay. I had a lot of self-hatred.

I became interested in the construction industry by watching videos online. I'd watch an American show called *This Old House* and the plumbing fascinated me. Construction became the focus of my life. It got me through school, because it was a way of ignoring the rest of what I was experiencing.

With my autism, order is important to me. I find it interesting to consider fine points of information in the various regulations. You've got the Building Regulations, which contain so many contradictions and things that don't make sense, and those are overridden by the

Water Regulations, which completely contradict the Building Regulations. And then both of those are contradicted by the manufacturer's instructions for a product. It's really funny. The people who write these regulations have not a clue in this world.

Construction is seen as a joke in this country. People think plumbers are overpaid morons, but they don't realize that we have all these laws and regulations to follow.

Tony Blair told us all that working in an office was the key industry in this country and so people started to believe that the construction industry was for morons and for jokers who have failed at school.

But people don't realize that getting into the construction industry is hard. Anyone can get a job in a warehouse tomorrow, but to get a job on a site as a basic labourer, you need health and safety qualifications, you need to be certified as *competent*, and none of that is cheap to do.

– *Tell me about the construction site.*

On a construction site, everybody is a straight man. If you're a woman, if you're gay, it's a big issue. Most of them are civilized blokes, professionals, but some of them do a lot of, *'Have you seen this bird? She's got nice whatevers.'*

I don't like it. It's disrespectful and frankly it doesn't interest me.

The way I speak when I'm at home is different to the way I speak at work. The way I speak at work is not the true me. At home, I speak a bit more posh or a bit more gay, if you get what I mean.

At work, it's *'Oi, mate' 'Yes, mate' 'No worries, mate.'*

If I call somebody *'Pal'* at work, it's *'Oh, that's gay'* and *'Are you flirting with me?'*

I'll be honest, it's not easy being autistic and gay. I receive a hell of a lot of abuse on a daily basis. I've tried to hide being gay. I've tried it. It's not something you can hide. People eventually figure it out, so if you're honest it makes life easier. People see it as something very foreign.

This week I was sat at work, and I received these messages from one of the plumbers I work with:

'*What are you doing at Unit A? Looking at gay porn on your laptop? . . . Are you going to start work or just sit there all day with your finger up your rear?*'

'*Fuck off with your homophobic tone.*'

'*But you told us you were gay . . .*'

'*What the fuck does that matter? Your text was homophobic and offensive.*'

'*Get a life queenie.*'

'*Bigot.*'

It's not just this, it's every little comment when I walk past. There were always comments about watching gay porn. They're all older than me, but they're all children, really.

All of this blew up because I mentioned what they were saying to the client's site manager. He told my manager and then I got shouted at.

'*You should have told me. You shouldn't have told him.*'

In his defence, he's done a lot for me, and he was hurt. My manager then told the managing director, who called me. I almost threw up when I saw that I had a missed call from him. I took the next call, and he summoned me to a meeting at the company headquarters the day after. I carried on working, trying not to pass out.

– *What were you thinking about?*

I was thinking, *oh my God, if I jump off a building I won't have to go tomorrow.*

Earlier that day, I'd been told by a colleague that four people would lose their jobs because of me, even though I hadn't reported them.

These four guys then made allegations against me for sexual assault. They were completely false. Instead of admitting what they had said to me, they were trying to go for the nuclear option: to cost me my job before they lost theirs, so I almost got sacked because I'd been abused for the last six months.

I saw the company director. It was standard director behaviour: trying not to accept responsibility and trying not to say anything that'd get him sued.

He said, '*I can't say that you should pretend that you're straight. It's not acceptable for them to say that at work. And, as far as I'm concerned, their allegations are just allegations*.'

It was nice to find someone who accepted that the abuse had happened. He was upset that it'd been going on so long. I offered to resign, to get my tools and walk out. He said that he didn't want that but that he couldn't '*Wave a magic wand and fix this*.'

I don't enjoy confrontation. It's hard for me.

Electrician on a production line

(30s)

I did a couple bits of work experience through school, one as a plumber and one in office admin. I preferred the plumbing because it was hands-on. So in my last year at school, I applied to do a plumbing course. It was full, but the college mentioned that there was space on the electrical course.

I said, '*Yeah, I'll do that*.'

That's how I became an electrician, by chance.

I hated school. Hated the academic stuff. I couldn't wait to be an adult and go out into the big, wide, nasty world.

When we went into recession in 2008, I was an apprentice. Where I had been working, we did a range of everything. No two days were the same. We could be working in a school one day, a steelworks the next. And the person who was teaching me on site was brilliant. He was patient. I still got a bollocking when I messed up, but he was really good. I still keep in touch with him now.

During the recession he said, '*We're going to cut your hours and you'll be on three or four days a week*.'

I said, '*I can't afford that. I need to be working*.' There was another company offering forty hours a week, so I jumped ship without really thinking about it. It's probably one of the biggest regrets of my career.

I left for a company that did a lot of domestic wiring in council houses.

I hated being in someone's house all day. I hated having to tidy everything up at the end of each day. I hated the pressure you were put under by supervisors to get the job done quickly. There were a lot of unskilled people running jobs they shouldn't have been.

It's quite easy to get another job in our industry. You're disposable labour. You could finish a job on a Friday and start somewhere different on Monday. I've been regularly in and out of jobs. And when it comes to work and money, I'm not the best with my finances. If I get it, I spend it. I haven't even got a pension. So it's always in the back of your mind, *how long is it gonna be 'til the next job?* My dad was in the steelworks all his life, so he never had to worry about that.

Financial worries are always on my mind, but I just bottle them up.

People say, '*Ah you tradesmen you don't talk about your feelings. Everything's just "yeah I'm all right"*'.

That's true, but people's feelings are coming out a lot more now. You have toolbox talks on mental health. But I think there's still a stigma where people bottle the feelings up and it eats away at them.

– Where are you now?

It's a brand new factory, twenty minutes' drive from me. I work 7 a.m. 'til 4 p.m., self-employed. It's clean, it's warm, it's dry. If I was working outside, I'd be screwed. I'm tall and my knees and back are knackered.

It's a production line where you start out with a few bits and by the end of it, there's a fully built kitchen unit, shrink wrapped and all taped up.

It's like Lego, and that's what I like, hands-on, nuts, bolts, spanners, screwdrivers. I have a big pile of metal on the floor and by the end of the day I've built a big frame and put sockets on it. Before I build something, I see it come together in pictures in my head. I'm not one for writing much down.

Sometimes I'll be on my own, and I'll have earplugs in and music on, other days I'll be working with someone, and you have a bit of craic with them.

The days they just fly by.

The atmosphere I like at work is when it's like being in the pub with your mates, but you're on site and getting paid for it. You give each other shit all the time. It's just banter, but it's rude and vulgar and probably even racist at some points.

You don't really care what you say because you're all in the same mindset.

It's character building, innit? I wouldn't want to work a nine-to-five job where I've just sat on my arse all day, bored. I like to be mentally stimulated and that's having a laugh with your mates.

It makes the day go so quick that you don't even feel like you've done it.

Eight, ten, twelve hours' graft just flies by.

Whether you're a dentist or a high-end lawyer, you've got to go to work with a good set of people, have a laugh, do the job and go home.

But I think things are changing. We've had apprentices on site in the last two or three years and you can't say anything to 'em, because when their assessor comes out, they make sure that he's not bullied on site and that he's not been made to do stupid things. I don't think I'd enjoy doing my apprenticeship now because of all this box ticking.

When I'd been at this kitchen supplier two or three weeks, I left to go to a job at a refinery. I was sat at the induction on the Monday, and I was there for two hours, and I thought, *this isn't for me*. I texted the gaffer at the kitchen supplier, '*Any chance I could come back.*'

He said, '*Yeah course you can. You're a good lad. I were gutted you left.*'

I was back the next week.

The gaffer at the kitchen factory is so laid back. You have got your targets and deadlines, but he's not on my back all the time. He doesn't even come round and see us much, because he knows we're capable of doing the job fast and to his high standards.

. . . I need to settle down, but I don't want to because it's not me. It's not as though I chase the money.

It's hard to explain unless you've been there and done it, but I just like being here there and everywhere. Like a loose firework or something.

Construction site manager

(30s)

A lot of people I work with, there's an ancestral line of relatives that have worked in construction. Their dads are in it, their grandads are in it. But I'm the only one in my family in construction. I fell into it. It chose me, so to speak.

I got into construction because of school. I didn't enjoy sitting in classrooms and being told what to do. That wasn't how I learned. My handwriting was atrocious – I still get laughed at for it today – and computers, I didn't get on with at all.

All I wanted to do was kick a ball about and ride a bike with my friends. And that's what I did seven days a week whenever I wasn't at school.

From that friend group, we're all in construction now, so part of me getting into it was led by them.

When I left school, I thought plumbing would be the best paid and I wouldn't have to think too much. *That's what I'm gonna do.*

I did a part-time college course in plumbing for two-and-a-half years from sixteen. That was three days a week and the other two days I worked for a friend's dad who was a small builder. I got to see a bit of everything, groundworks, bricklaying, roofing, carpentry, plumbing, electrics, decoration, carpet-fitting.

At the time my friend's dad seemed – not a scary figure – but a don't-get-on-the-wrong-side-of-him kind of guy. Looking back, he had so much patience with me, so much patience. He was the first real role model I had. He made me think, *okay, work hard and get your head down and you can become something without sitting behind a computer every day.*

Compared to a lot of other industries, you have to grow up quickly in construction. You're working with things that could quite easily injure you or someone else. And doing something wrong costs money straight away.

You have to be savvy and practical, on your feet and learning. Early on, I learned that if you don't understand something, you've got to just say so, because you're going to get a lot more of a bollocking for trying to muddle through.

Every Friday, he'd take us to lunch. You didn't talk about work. You talked about what you were doing at the weekend. You had that brotherhood, with everything that comes through that, the banter and the laughs and the jokes.

When the plumbing course ended, my friend's dad said, *'Look, I've got enough work. You can work full-time for me.'*

Then, about two months later, it was 2008 and the credit crunch hit. His work dried up. I had to stop working for him.

At that time, the Olympic Park was one of the biggest employers in the construction sector. One day, I got the train down there and waited outside the gates until someone needed a worker. It happened to be groundworks, and it was a massive change from doing tiny extensions. I was there for three-and-a-half years. I was eighteen and they were paying a good wage. I thought, *this is great. I don't need any master plan.*

But it was prison-like. You start at 7.30 a.m., break at 10 a.m., back at work at 10.30 a.m., and on and on. If you were five minutes late, you got moaned at. There was no freedom. You felt like a number. I don't think people should feel like that.

I'll always remember one day, the day before my twenty-first birthday, when I was stood there in the pouring rain – it was a day like today – freezing cold – in a trench up to my knees. I looked around and thought, *what am I doing? This is not what I want to do. This is not where I want to be when I'm fifty years old. It's no good.*

I didn't want to be a body, *'Go and dig that hole.'*

I wanted to feel, every day, like I could go back home and look my family in the eye and say, '*I've made a difference today. I've got over this hurdle, that problem.*'

At this time, I met my wife. Her dad had a good job in construction and her godfather owned a small construction firm.

Her godfather needed a handyman and within two weeks I was working for him. So I went from the Olympics, a massive site where you couldn't breathe without having to sign a bit of paperwork, to a small main contractor, doing jobs from £500,000 to £5 million, and that was where my career took off.

Had I not met my wife I don't even know whether I would have stayed in construction.

Now, I work as a site manager for one of the biggest main contractors around. It's difficult to define what a site manager does, because every day is so different. I tell the younger site managers to only have a plan for two to three hours of your day, because the rest will be taken up with problems that come in, and you'll get nothing that you've planned done, and it will stress you out.

I'm the first one here, 7 a.m. I open the gates up. I try to use the first bit of the morning to rattle through some emails. I set aside two to three hours a day to tackle them. I've got sixteen-hundred unread emails in my inbox.

They're a massive, massive problem. You can't have a conversation with a guy on site without recording it in an email. If you take someone's word that *we'll be done on Friday*, and you don't write it in an email, then you'll bring in the next trade on Monday and they won't be able to start, and your company's paying ten guys to stand around and do nothing.

'*You said you'd be finished on Friday.*'

'*Prove it.*'

At 8 a.m., I do subcontractor inductions for half an hour. By that time, I've probably got five or six missed calls about problems on site.

Yesterday, one of the brackets didn't fit, so I had to trawl through drawings to see whose problem it was. Then I sat down with a quantity surveyor, the one who deals with the money, to talk about this problem. All of this took a couple of hours.

Then I spent some time going through our site records putting a case together as to why a subcontractor doesn't need extra time or more money.

We had a new member of the team that's started, so I was taking him on site, at the same time as solving a few logistical issues and doing a few quality checks. We then had a look at where we could accelerate the programme. All of that took a couple of hours.

Then we had to handover some beams that have been painted to the dryliners, so that they could start on the walls. I was there to make sure that the beams handed over were correct. All of this is recorded.

That takes me up to 1 p.m. The mechanical and engineering contractors had issued a new programme, and I also had a quality check sheet from the window contractors, so I had a look at that while eating my lunch. I made some comments and sent them off.

I then had an email from some suppliers saying that their people were delayed due to the weather. I looked at that and thought, *what can we do about the weather?* I ordered a couple of pumps to help with water ingress.

Then from 3.30 p.m. until 5.30 p.m. we had a meeting about the timings on this job. The clients have added so much extra stuff to this job as we've gone on, so we talked about where our justification for a time extension could come from.

At 5.30 p.m., I shut my laptop and went home. I try to avoid looking at my phone. Now I've got kids I'm a lot better at switching off from work, but there's always that time when they're in bed and before I go to bed. I always do it. I do it on Saturdays. I do it on Sundays, but I can't help it.

It's like an addiction. Sometimes I'll be there at 10 p.m. replying to emails, because they come in at such a rate. The wife goes mad.

As a site manager, you are relying solely on other human beings doing their job and doing what they've told you they'll do.

If you were relying on computers, you could know that a deadline would be hit. Whereas construction doesn't work like that in the slightest. You've got to think, *what are these people capable of?*

How many people can we have working in that area?

Are people going to be working above them?

Do those subbies need to go in first because of the drying times?

What if the weather isn't hot enough for it to dry?

If it isn't hot enough, do we need to re-programme?

If I need to re-programme, do I need to speed up these guys, or do I need to tell them not to come in?

It's a mess.

People think it's just putting one brick on top of the other, but it's this massive, complex machine. You can spend a week of your time trying to reorganize something because of one problem, one lorry breaking down with a delivery of bricks in it.

There's no chance that construction can be solved mathematically. No chance. Not a chance. I call the planners '*calendar technicians*', changing the programme every day only for something else to crop up that requires more tweaking, and wasting so much time doing that. A programme is only as good as the person writing it and the person carrying it out.

For example, if we just take this recent weather – the cold weather, the rain – it's probably stopped 40 per cent of the work happening on site this week. We can't do the roofing because it's raining, and because the roofing hasn't been done all that water is going down into the building, so we can't do anything inside.

Every single building has its own constraints. Even those housing developers building the same house twenty times over, those houses have been built on slightly different bits of land, the falls are different, the drainage is different, and that's all got to be calculated.

Everyone saw what happened at Grenfell. That was a long line of human error. I don't want to say, '*People taking short-cuts*', but I can't think of a better phrasing.

And Grenfell has accelerated changes that were already coming in the industry.

Now, you have a lot more people involved in a single item of construction. For instance, fire breaks and insulation. For these, you now have fire technicians and fire engineers who have to make sure that every system you install is certified.

Even a piece of plasterboard connected to a steel frame counts as a *'system'* that needs to be certified. And if it's not built in the same way as it was when it was certified, then it all needs to be taken down. Before, all of this would have been overseen just by the architect.

Say you're building a wall. It takes the same amount of time as it ever did for that wall to be built. But to get to a point where you're in a position to build that wall takes a lot longer now than it once did, and that's because of all the health and safety legislation, quality legislation and updated building regulations.

You can only close that wall up after a competent person has come and checked that the inside of the wall has been built correctly. If that competent person is busy for a week, you've got a week where that wall's staying open, waiting to be checked.

There also aren't the skilled people coming into construction any more. There's a massive gap of skilled labour. We go to school events, out of a thousand pupils, ten are interested in construction. Of the ten, you probably get two that want to be involved on the *operational side*, the actual building sites, the frontline. The others want to be sustainability managers, or involved in the design.

Why would people come into the industry? Construction is long hours and hard work. That's the bottom line. My contract states that I should 38.5 hours a week. I do that by Wednesday and I'm on a fixed salary. Fifty or sixty-hour weeks are completely normal. It's what's expected to get jobs done.

And for a lot of the big construction sites, it's hard to get onto them, with all of the certification you need. You can spend anywhere between £30ish for your basic construction skills certification card to £3,000 for your qualifications.

For instance, you have to be Firecrest accredited to install anything to do with firewalls. That qualification alone isn't cheap, and when you're self-employed that's coming out of your pocket. For someone coming into the industry, you can't just get on with it any more.

A lot of the workforce is between the age of forty-five and sixty. If you talk to them, they'll tell you two things. One, the quality of materials is worse now than it was. Two, there's no real money in construction any more because of all the legislative hoops you have to jump through.

And what used to be done on a handshake now has quantity surveyors involved, who will take every penny they can to make their client more money.

Or you'll have a client that knows everything. If you've lost four days because of rain, they'll say, '*In this contract part blah blah blah blah, you should have notified us on the first day that you were going to be delayed. And you should have put prevention measures in. What have you done to prevent it? We're not accepting this delay.*'

All of this means that there's this massive clog going on in the background.

To this day, there's no denying that it's a very alpha-male-dominated industry. If people see a weakness, often it's '*He's no good*' or '*Unbelievable – how can he not know that?*'

You've got to be very thick-skinned to come into construction. You walk in and you probably hear more swear words than non-swear words.

When I first came into management, I worked with a site manager. You introduce yourself. He said, '*Pop the kettle on.*'

I said, '*How do you take your tea?*'

He said, '*It's very specific. Tea bag stays in the water for four minutes. You squeeze out the tea bag. Take it out. Then you add the milk. Then you add one sugar.*'

I thought, *fair enough he wants milk and one sugar in his tea.*

I splashed the tea bag in there, bit of milk, bit of sugar.

He took one sip and poured it out on the floor in front of me.

'That's the biggest load of shit I've ever drunk. What did I ask you to do?'

'Make you a cup of tea.'

'No no, I want the specifics. That was not made how it should have been. All you're going to do today is stand there and when I ask you to make a cup of tea, you're going to make me a cup of tea.'

For a whole day I stood there and made him cups of tea. I thought, *Jesus Christ what have I come into?*

He said, *'Look, if you can't follow a simple instruction how can I trust you to do anything out there?'*

I thought, *you know, he's got a point.* It's always stuck with me.

You couldn't do that now. You'd get pulled up by HR, but at the time this was how youngsters were treated coming into the industry.

But once you've got someone's trust in construction. That's it. You're at the frontline, you're in it together. When your directors are coming down, you know that you two are on the same page, and as long as you're on the same page, you're good.

This matters because a lot of site management is making quick-fire decisions. You don't want someone behind you going, *'Oh, I don't know why he's doing that.'*

You want someone to stand behind you and say, *'Yeah, I agree with him. I would have made that decision',* even if they wouldn't.

That's the bond you have with each other, ten hours a day, and that's where the jokes and the brotherhood comes from. I spend more time with the guys here than I do my family.

It's high pressure.

There's a lot of self-harming, suicides, especially in construction management. This is openly spoken about now. In the last few years, it's become very different to ten years ago, when the directors would come down to site and say, *'It's your fucking problem. You fucking sort it out or you're getting sacked on Monday.'*

Now, it's sitting around a table. It's still unpleasant conversations, but you don't feel that axe hanging over your head.

There was one job I did. I was two months into working for a company. It was the biggest job the company had on at the time. It was understaffed, the design wasn't there, I had a poor team around me. We had a meeting one day, and the main owner of the company came down. He tore us all to pieces. He went round the table asking, '*Who wants to be on this job?*'

Everyone said no, apart from me. I had just bought a house and I needed a job.

Then everyone started arguing with everyone else around the table. It was horrible.

The next day, my personal phone rings and it was the big boss. He said I was going to be the only one staying and that he'd get a new team around me.

But I wasn't experienced enough for the job. It ate me alive.

One day, I'd done everything I could, and I remember the area director coming to site, walking round, saying '*We're still missing things here.*'

I just broke down. All the emotions like you wouldn't believe, pouring out. Tears running down my face. It's quite a macho industry and I was distraught. I thought, '*I can't do this job any longer.*'

I remember another site manager saying, '*Are you okay?*'

'*No.*'

'*Mate, just get yourself and go home. This job is not worth it not in the slightest.*'

I remember sitting in my car, head on the steering wheel, thinking, *what am I going to do? I've got a wife, a young child and a house.*

I looked at all sorts of ways that I could get out of the job and still earn enough money to keep the house and the lifestyle we were accustomed to. It had got to a point where I was taking sleeping tablets just to sleep at night. All I could think about was the job and how it wouldn't get done.

They brought a new site manager to the job. He was fifty-five. My phone was ringing I reckon a hundred times a day, because I was the only who knew the history of the job. When my phone rang when I was with him, he said, '*Fucking hell, why are you still answering phone calls after 5 p.m. All the trades are going home. It's gonna make no difference. What difference is it going to make answering that call now rather than eight o'clock tomorrow morning. Why are you so stressed? You're nuts.*'

I remember driving home angry about it almost, *he's a bit of a lazy wanker*.

As the weeks went on, I was sitting across the office from him, and at 5 p.m. every day, he would put his laptop down. I worked with him for just under a year and it was one of the best things that could have happened to me. That mentorship, that arm on the shoulder. He'd seen it all before. When he was there I felt relaxed. *Yeah, this job will get done.*

He'd say, '*Them guys on site are gonna do what they're gonna do. You can try and point people in the right direction but that's all you can do it.*'

When he was there I felt relaxed. *Yeah, this job will get done.*

To this day, we still talk. We talk like mates.

Without that circle of people, the work would swallow you up. I've seen so many people that get swallowed up by it. You see it in people's faces, they're gone.

It's given me a career and it's given me a good life.

You can plan and plan and plan, but ultimately it only takes one person to ruin all that planning, so don't get stressed about it.

Close the laptop.

Go home.

Enjoy your life.

CHAPTER ELEVEN **NIGHTWORK**

Nightclub worker

police officer

postal worker

Nightclub worker

(20s)

I was a regular at this nightclub as a student. The youngest people working in the club are eighteen, nineteen. The oldest behind the bar is thirty-two. The management are in their fifties and sixties.

On a workday, I nap from around 2 p.m. until 7 p.m. I get in the shower, get ready, leave the house just before 10 p.m. I walk up to the club, and I start setting up my station, which changes night by night.

You can be on bar, on shop (which is the cloakroom), on the door, or you can be a shot girl. I get there at about 10 p.m. The shift starts at 10.30 p.m., so I do half-an-hour without being paid.

You do a lot of work at clubs that you don't get paid for. Management justify it by saying that you have to be set to start work when the club opens at 10.30 p.m. and it takes at least half an hour beforehand to set up. I tried once to get there for 10.30 p.m. and it was very stressful. Once the club's open you can't leave your station, so I had to radio people to bring me things. It impacts everyone else.

If you've got an illness, you can request to be on shop or on door, where you're sitting down all night. They're the easiest jobs.

But I like being on the bottom-floor bar. It's busy. You're always talking to people, interacting with them, and when it calms down you get to muck around a bit with the people who are also on the bar.

A lot of us are – like – autistic or have ADHD, so we'll be dancing to the music but not in a normal way. It's just fun being together.

You really have to know how everyone else works, because on a

Saturday there'll be a crowd four-deep in front of the bar – and it's not a big space behind the bar.

People will be shouting at you, *'I've been waiting here for half an hour'.*

So you have to move quickly, in-sync with each other.

When we're cleaning down the club at close (1.30 a.m.), we're supposed to finish within an hour-and-a-half. On busy nights, it's not possible to clean the entire club to a good standard in that time, but we stop getting paid after that hour-and-a-half is up. So that's our incentive to do it faster.

It's a zero-hours contract at £9.20 an hour. You tell management your availability and they do a rota about a month in advance.

I don't know anyone who doesn't have a second job because they don't give you enough hours and we don't get paid enough. The older people who rely on it as their main job take it a lot more seriously. There's one guy, Tom, who takes it very seriously. He does a lot for the club that he's not paid for. He does it because he feels like he owes something to the club for hiring him and keeping him on.

Like any kind of hospitality, it's a high school environment. Everyone seems to sleep with everyone and there's always some drama going on. The staff are split into people who prefer drinking and people who prefer doing things that are illegal. There's only two people on the staff at the moment who absolutely refuse to do drugs, which is fine.

In the nightclub environment, it's an unsaid thing that all of us struggle to some degree with alcohol and substance abuse. When you work difficult hours most of your social life becomes each other. And although we know everything about each other's lives, we never talk about our relationship with drugs and alcohol . . . it's kind of ignored.

– Do management know about the drug-taking and the drinking?

Yeah, they do. They don't encourage it on shift, but at the afters (after-party) the managers are doing it themselves. The club owner is notorious for always having way too much stuff on him. He'll be like, *'Here you go, have this. Let's do it together.'*

The afters are supposed to end at 11 a.m., when the day shift come in, but if it's a bank holiday or Christmas or New Year we'll have a special staff party.

Last Christmas, we started our meal at 2 p.m. and we were still in the club at 3 p.m. the next day.

It's a surreal environment to work in. Everything's so casual. You're not cutting up lines on the side of a bathroom in a regular workplace, are you? So it's a certain kind of person that works here.

They hire you based on whether you have this . . . this craziness. Everyone's a bit psychotic and I'm sure most of us struggle with our mental health or with trauma in the background of our lives. You can overshare and it doesn't matter. We laugh about it, *'This has happened. Oh well. Oopsy daisy.'*

It's light-hearted coping, I guess.

The staff turnover is very high. Most of the new staff tend to last a couple of months. We're constantly hiring. It is a difficult place to work.

With the hours, your sleep is all over the place. I've only stuck around because I need the money.

All the nightlife has been shutting down in the town. So we're flooded with people that used to go to the other clubs. It's a complete clash of people. And 70 per cent of them are on something.

Drugs are cheaper than alcohol and – at the minute – cheaper than food even.

The customers are good and bad. The women are a lot easier to interact with.

They're the cliché of drunk white girls, *'Oh my God, you're so pretty. I love your hair.'*

They make you enjoy what you're doing.

The men tend to be quite creepy. Most of the time, they're trying to hit on you, asking what time you finish. You just have to laugh it off, *'Oh, ha ha.'*

We can't even have female members of staff on the floor of the club cleaning and picking up glasses, because there've been too many incidents of female staff being assaulted by the men. A week or two ago, a customer kissed a new member of staff while she was on the floor.

She was all in a tizzy, *'I've got no idea what to do. I'm so freaked out.'*

We radioed management, they checked the cameras, the doorman kicked the guy out, and he was barred.

You have to be a completely different person when you're on shift. After work, I'm not able to sleep until midday because I have to decompress, to calm down from the persona that I put on to get through the job.

I have to be upbeat, bubbly, Betty-Boop-like, all smiles and happiness. *'Ha ha! So funny! Yay!'* Because if I'm myself, if I don't put on a performance, then I'm not going to get tipped by customers.

I've been off substances for six months now. Weed's fine, but I don't support anything that's sniffable. I've seen first-hand the effects of addiction and how difficult it is to overcome.

But now I'm not taking drugs at work, time goes a lot more slowly. It's harder to keep up the mask around customers.

When I was on drugs, it was like I wasn't there, I was just acting on instinct and I seemed to know exactly what I was doing.

When I'm sober, everything feels very real. The music's really loud. I can hear and feel everything. And the creeps looking at me and hitting on me, they make me way more uncomfortable now than they used to.

It's a lot harder than it used to be.

But I now know that I don't want to work here for ever.

Police officer

(50s)

There is one thing that has always been in my head, even today.

It came through on the radio and they said to me, '*You need to go to this address. We believe it to be an auto-erotic death.*'

I went up the stairs. He had put the noose around his neck, from the loft hatch. Mirror in front and mirror behind, and he was in the middle.

I went back downstairs. As I was going down the stairs, I saw pictures on the wall of him in a suit proper. You wouldn't even think twice that this is what he did.

I went into the front room. I said, '*I'm so sorry, ever so sorry. Is there anything I can do?*'

His wife said, '*No.*'

She was distraught.

She said, '*You know what the worst thing is? I knew he did it.*'

I left. I went to another job, and I finished my shift at three o'clock in the morning. It's dark. As I'm going towards the car, I stopped.

Who's sat in my seat?

And all I could see was that man who'd hung himself. I could see him. I could see him sat there. Of course he wasn't there. It was just me. But I could see him.

I unlock the car and I lock the car. I unlock the car. I lock the car. I could still see him.

I've got to get in. I've got to go home. What am I going to do?

I thought *just be brave and get in the car*. I open the car. I didn't look. I go in, shut the door, start the engine, put my music on, chat to myself.

I'm chatting to myself on the A-road. I look next to me and there he was.

For about six months, I was doing that. I was re-living. It was constant. Every night I'd see him. I started talking to him. I used to say to him, '*How was you day?*'

And then after about three or four months I thought, *I can't do this I've got to let go.*

Sometimes even now I see something on the telly, and it comes straight back. It's like I can see him there.

There are certain things that have always remained. Other things too. This was the most recent thing.

But there are so many things that you see, and they just never leave your brain. It's somewhere locked up. But it's there. Constantly there.

I left school when I was sixteen. I then went to work in a biscuit factory for two years.

I decided to apply for the police. That's what I'd always wanted to do. It was just something that took my fancy.

To join we had to do the fitness test. I managed to get through all the sit-ups, press-ups because my upper body strength was perfect at the time. But the shuttle test . . .

The pass was level 8.4 back then. I had been a smoker from quite a young age, and I only managed to get to about level 8.0.

Three months down the line I went back, and I got to 8.2, so I failed again.

They gave me another three months: '*This is going to be your last time; if you don't pass this time, we will have to give you a year before you can apply again.*'

I was so determined. I was in the gym day and night.

I went back in, and I managed to do it. 8.4. And that was it. I just dropped dead. It felt amazing. I thought, *I've got it, that's it!*

I've always remained in frontline policing. People were saying to me, 'It's time for you to progress. Either move on to the detectives or become a sergeant.'

I did do my sergeant's exam but once you start going from sergeant into inspector, you're always taking a backseat. It's more office work. Whereas I always liked being out doing frontline policing.

Policing is not just about going to arrest someone and taking them into custody, it's about getting to know people in the community, and then people getting to know you.

I worked in the same area for many years. There was a young lad who was into drugs, he was into crime, into everything. I used to arrest him almost every week. Whenever some officers were looking for him – he was such a lovely lad – I used to see him and say,

'You're wanted, you know that? People are looking for you.'

'Yeah, I know. If you're going to take me to KFC, then I'll come with you.'

'Jump in.'

I used to take him to KFC, then take him to custody. And I would say to him all the way to KFC and back to custody, 'What are you doing with your life? You're fourteen, fifteen, sixteen, seventeen . . .' And then he got to the age of nineteen – you grow up with them – and he committed a burglary. I arrested him. I brought him in. He was good as gold, bless him.

I said, 'You haven't got any more chances. You're going to be spending time in prison. Do you really want that?'

And then one Christmas day a few years later, I was working, and I went down to his mum and dad's. He was there,

'I've turned my life around!'

'Never!'

'Yeah, I've got a girlfriend and she's pregnant and I'm gonna be a good dad.'

I thought, good for you, lad. Only to find out a few years ago that he was found dead. He ended up in a fight in the town centre. Someone stabbed him.

You try and you try and you try, and then this happens.

Policing is not what it used to be. Policing changed about seven, eight years ago. It changed for the worse. We used to parade thirty-five to forty police officers on a night shift, but over the last ten or eleven years we ended up having no more than ten officers on shift.

I remember one day we went into a training day. We had the Assistant Chief Constable come down because the numbers had dropped – the arrest rate and the numbers of vehicles visible in the community – he came down and said, 'We've got to start having you all single-crewed.[8] We want more cars out and about. We want more police officers on the street.'

The Home Office wants to make sure that there is more visibility. But more visibility doesn't mean having more officers, it means PCSOs (Police Community Support Officers), and it means single crewing. So, you'll see ten cars arriving outside your house, but it's only ten officers, because five of them have to go and do an area search, two are doing house to house, and the others are just coming to speak to you and whoever else is in the house. You might have ten cars, but it's not actually a huge incident; it's just what you see.

And there is part of me that thinks we're not really looking after the public.

The statistics show that we're doing really well as a police force, but as for the actual offences . . . I went to a burglary. We didn't know what had been taken because the owners weren't there. I called to put it down as a crime, a burglary. The officers at the station said to me on the phone,

'But we haven't got anything stolen?'

---

8 One police officer per patrol car. 'It is awful – you're on your own. You've got no back up.'

I said, '*Not that I'm aware of because I can't speak to the owners.*'

'*It's not burglary then, is it?*'

'*What is it?*'

'*Criminal damage*'

I said, '*How am I going to put criminal damage when they've ransacked the house? I've got to put it down as a burglary.*'

'*No no no, until we find out what has gone, if anything, we put it down as criminal damage.*'

We crimed it as criminal damage. That happened on a number of cases. How does that look? We're going down on burglaries, not because they're not happening, but because we're criming them as criminal damage.

How can we manipulate something to make us look good and make the Home Office look good? That's wrong! People should know, the public should know. You are there to protect, to prevent, and to tell the truth, not to do the opposite.

These are some of the things that make you think, *that's not what I joined.*

The Home Office wants the numbers, the statistics. Every month in briefing you'd have ten or twelve officers sitting around the table. They'd bring up the projector and it'd have all the PCs on shift.

It'd be: '*You've done eight arrests, you've done four arrests, you've done three, you've done eleven, you've done one.*'

A lot of us became arrest hungry. *I'm going out tonight, and I'm going to nick the first person I see*. It'd be a £1 KitKat that someone had stolen, but you nick 'em, bring 'em into custody.

Is that really proportionate? But you bring them in and what you say to them is:

'*If you say you did it, I'll give you a caution, and you'll be out within an hour. Is that okay?*'

'*Oh okay, what do you want me to say?*'

'*Just say "yeah it was me, I did it, sorry".*'

You go in, do the interview, and they say exactly what you've

told them to say, because they're thinking, *I'll be out in an hour.*
But that caution remains in the system, it remains with them. It's
not fair.

And when I go back to see my sergeant, I've got a tick in the box,
and that tick says, 'Well done, you've made an arrest. Another one
tomorrow, yeah?'

And then you do the same thing tomorrow.

A few years ago, I had to go and arrest a member of staff. As a frontline officer, you don't normally get involved with internal incidents.
I was asked to go because I was a female officer.

We were asked to go and speak to the personal assistant to one of
the senior officers. We went in and she was panicking.

'*I've come into work. I've gone downstairs and this man* [a senior
police officer] *has followed me. He's been following me for the last five
years . . . Last week, he was following me at the supermarket. He knows
the registration number of my car. He's done checks online to find out
where I live.*

*Today he really freaked me out . . . I was going to get my coffee in
the canteen, and he stood behind me and he started to push himself
against me, and then he just put his hands on my shoulders, and he
started to massage me . . . I turned around and said, "Please stop!
leave me alone".*'

I did some investigation on the same day. I said to the lady who
was the alleged victim,

'*I have spoken to a number of people. I have got the information.
Now, are you willing to give me a statement? The way I'm going to
deal with it is by arresting him for harassment, which has escalated
because he's now not only bothering you at work, but he's also bothering
you outside of work. And it's been happening for a long time. And
today you got to a stage where you had a panic attack.*'

She said, '*Absolutely*'.

I phoned professional standards, and I explained the situation.

They said, '*You deal with it the way you would deal with if it was anybody else.*'

Perfect. I booked the custody suite. Everything is done. At 5 p.m., the senior officer came out and I said:

'*There's been an allegation of harassment against you. This is what's happened . . .*'

'*Okay. Yes, I know the lady.*'

'*What we'll do is: you'll come with us. We'll go into the police station of a different town, we'll go into interview, and you can explain to me what this is all about.*'

He said, '*No problem.*'

I got to the custody suite. Booked him.

I got a male colleague to search him. On him, we found a diary. It said that he was going to follow the victim at 5.30 p.m. the same evening. It had the registration number of the victim. He also had her address.

There was also a photo in the diary. It was taken somehow through binoculars. It was my victim standing, getting changed in front of her bedroom window.

I put it on the table of the custody sergeant's desk.

I said, '*Sarge, I think we need to do a Section 18 search just to have a look and see what this is all about.*'[9]

He said, '*Yeah, no problem.*'

But – no word of a lie – as soon as we went through to go and do the processing, I got a call from the custody sergeant:

'*Come back.*'

I went back.

The custody sergeant said, '*Custody is no longer authorized for this man . . . The superintendent has asked me to close the custody record as if I've opened it in error.*'

I said, '*What's going on here? Something's not right.*'

---

9 S. 18, *Police and Criminal Evidence Act 1984* – the power to search '*any premises occupied or controlled by a person who is under arrest*'.

He said, '*Don't argue. Bring him back. You need to go upstairs to the canteen and wait for the superintendent. The superintendent's coming down to speak to you.*'

'*But how can I release him? How am I going to put a crime when I haven't got any evidence?*'

He said, '*You're not putting a crime. I have opened this custody record in error.*'

This senior officer was released with immediate effect. Don't ask me why because I still, to this day, haven't found out why.

The superintendent came down and said to me,

'*We don't arrest our own people, do we?*'

I said, '*With all due respect, if we suspect that someone has committed criminal offence, we do.*'

He looked at me again and he got close. He was quite a big man.

'*We don't shit on our own doorstep, do we?*'

. . . I couldn't sleep that night. I took this senior officer home. I dropped him off.

I had to inform the victim that he'd been released, and when I informed her she burst into tears over the phone.

Two days later I had my locker searched. The custody sergeant who had released him went off sick.

I was taken out of the area that I been in for five years, and I was single-crewed in a completely different area. All because I challenged the superintendent's decision.

The superintendent said that my arrest was unlawful. Now, in order for an arrest to be unlawful, you must have no evidence. I requested an investigation. Everyone on my team started to go, '*Don't touch it. Leave it alone. Stop what you're doing.*'

I can't! I've got to find out what is going on.

I didn't challenge the decision because I felt like it. I challenged it because it was wrong. The release was wrong.

I couldn't get the Independent Police Complaints Commission to investigate it, because as a serving police officer you can't request that.

The only investigation that could be done was me challenging via the Chief Constable. So, yes, I challenged it. I took it to the Chief Constable.

It got to a stage where for about two years I was fighting to find out what had happened.

As it happened, the investigation concluded with my arrest being unlawful. '*Reasons unknown.*' They never gave me an explanation as to why.

The Force had to pay this man money for an unlawful arrest. That was the end of my career. I thought, *no, two years fighting for something . . .*

For them to say that my arrest was unlawful, that was the end. I never had any complaints against me. I never had any issues with my job. Nothing. I had an impeccable career.

In law, I had done everything by the book.

After that, a year later, I went off sick and then I got my retirement. I thought, *that's it. I've had enough, I can't do this any more. Because this is wrong. So wrong.*

Since I was eighteen, I joined the police so that I could do the right thing. I would have loved to have stayed there another ten years; to retire and then come back as consultant, a probation tutor.

There is a lot of corruption in the service. People will say there is no corruption now. But I listen to the news, I see the papers, and I think, *seriously?*

What do we, the police, learn? Nothing. We make mistakes, but we don't learn because we don't tell people what mistakes we've made. What did they learn from this? *Nothing.* They always say that there is '*a lesson to be learned*'. There shouldn't be any lessons learned any more.

Postal worker

(40s)

It was a crazy time, the night shifts: 12 a.m. at night 'til 8.10 a.m. in the morning. You can do as many nights in a row as you like. I was doing five – if you're lucky, six – nights, and overtime on top of that. If my boss said '*We need a walk prepping*' or '*We still need the parcels sorting, can you do a couple of hours*', I'd say '*Yeah I'll do it*', and you'd do it until 10 a.m. or 11 a.m. in the morning.

With nights, when you first start doing them, you think you can take on the world. But I was caning it a bit hard.

I was smoking.

I was drinking a lot.

I didn't think I was drinking a lot – but, a bottle of whisky a day, on the whole it *is* a lot.

I also wasn't sleeping that well. I'd get home at ten o'clock in the morning and that would be my night-time. The missus'd take the kids to school. She'd come back and I'd have the windows open and music blaring.

I'd get to sleep about four o'clock in the afternoon, and get up again at 8 p.m. And that got smaller and smaller. I was going to bed at 6 p.m. and then getting up at 8 p.m.

As far as I was concerned, this was something that I could stop doing at any time. It suited the moment. I kept the missus happy, kept work happy, and I kept myself happy.

But it wasn't the way to be.

I had a stroke. I didn't know a thing about it. I came downstairs and I've tripped over one of the stairs. *That's a bit weird.*

Then I made a cup of coffee. As I was stirring the coffee, in my head I'd stopped stirring it, but my body was still going. Everything seemed a second or two delayed. And everything seemed to take forever, even to put your trousers on.

I went outside to go shopping. I shut the door and I'd left my cigarettes, my phone, my keys – all inside.

I sat down on a wall, and I thought *I'll have to go to her mum's.* I started to walk but the floor was on a slope. I know it's not, but I can't help but walk like it is.

I got to her mum's. My missus turned up and she phoned the ambulance. They arrived and I thought it was funny. I just didn't understand why they were there.

They took me in to hospital and I said, *'I've got to get back to work so can we hurry up and diagnose me.'*

The doctor turned around and said, *'You've had a stroke.'*

I just wouldn't have it and I said, *'I don't know what you're talking about . . .'*

I was waffling on, talking absolute rubbish, and it took the doctor two or three times to say it to me until I realized.

He then said, *'six months off.'*

'No way. I can't do it. I've got to work.'

I was off six months.

You hear about having a stroke in the news and it's a life-changing thing for most people. I really did come off lightly.

I got away with something, but I don't know what.

– *Tell me about your current shift.*

I get up at around 3.15 a.m. I brush my teeth, have a wash and that, and always have a coffee. I check the weather to see if I need to take any different clothing, and then I get on my bike and cycle for about a minute to the depot.

When I get there, I'll sit down and have a cigarette outside with anyone that's there, mostly the night staff. Sometimes you get the non-smokers come out and stop and talk. The people are quite a good bunch. But you've got a few moaners and what have you.

– What do you talk about?

Mostly work. We're all a different genre. Most of the people came up like me in the eighties and nineties. And you get a few of the old boys there who can tell us this and tell us that. The conversation is pretty good.

Before the stroke I used to be so full of chat. Like, I knew every song, every sample – you name it, I could tell you when that song came out.

Since the stroke, I don't care about that stuff any more.

I don't know what's happened. I've taken a back step and I love to listen to people talk about what they've got to say and what it was like for them.

After the cigarette, I go inside to prep two walks, my walk and my partner's walk.

I throw letters into a big frame full of slots, each slot a numbered house. Then I'll check to see if there's any parcels for us.

My partner comes in at 7.30 a.m., because he's part-time.

We go and get the PDA units. They've got their locations on all day and if these guns sit still for more than fifteen minutes, they start vibrating.

The management can look at the PDA data. I don't know whether they do to the extent that Amazon do, but we're going along that wavelength. It will come in soon.

Then we set off in the van, head to the destination, and I start my walk. My partner is in the van dropping the parcels off. We meet back at the halfway point. Then we go onto his walk, and we split it. Then we empty the letter boxes. And once we've finished – at about 12 p.m. – we go back in the van to the yard.

That's it.

I cycle home. I get in at about 1 or 2 p.m.

My son's normally awake – he's one – and he jumps all over me. I get my phone out and sit with him. I make some tea and try not to fall asleep. I take him out for a walk, something to keep me and him busy.

I get us back, do the dinner, sort the other kids out, and by the time they're done going to bed it's half seven.

I'm in bed at 8.30 p.m. with a cup of coffee and a cigarette. Crazy.

Nothing's like it used to be because of the pandemic. When the pandemic first came about, I was happy working. Then I got an email to say, '*You've got to go home. High Risk. Blah blah blah.*'

Naturally, you just panic – *blimey*!

I showed it to my boss, and he said, '*Right, get your stuff and just go home until we know any different.*'

So I went home and told the missus, '*I've got to stay home.*'

'*Why?*'

'*Because of my stroke.*'

My boss phoned me two or three days later and he said, '*If you feel that you're in danger or anything like that, you can stay at home. That's fine. But we'll have you back whenever you're ready.*'

And so with that I said, '*Yeah fine I'll come back.*'

I went back as soon as possible. A few of the others did too, but quite a few didn't, which I can't say I'm surprised about. Some were scared, some saw an opportunity. They still get paid. I don't know what's happened but some of them are still off.

So I don't know what people are talking about when they say, '*Lockdown this, lockdown that.*'

I was working.

It blew every Christmas out of the water, because the amount of parcels that came. There was truck after truck after truck. The stuff that we were delivering was just phenomenal. Watering cans. A single bottle of bleach. We were cramming it in.

But, in the same breath, as big as that job was, it was different because the roads were empty.

Every postman will tell you, it was heaven.

We were the only ones on the street, piling down there. And everyone was in, so you never had a problem with receiving parcels. Just put it on the door, ring it, they'd open the curtains – *lovely* – and go. And so it made everything that much easier. No traffic, no nothing.

Walking down the street and people would bang on the windows. '*Hello!*'

'*Wave to the postman!*'

'*Thank you so much for the work you do!*'

We were getting biscuits, drinks left outside, cans of coke. It was really nice. And to an extent you felt like, *at last, getting some praise.*

But like everything, it doesn't last. And I think as soon as we came out of lockdown that was it.

'*Oh, it's the postman.*'

'*Don't worry about him, just leave him to it.*'

Amazon, DPD, Hermes, they're all on top of their drivers. At Royal Mail, they'll tell you, '*It's got to be done by this time, but if you don't, cool.*' No one's gonna screw their face up.

But if Amazon is doing it, then you know full well we're going to be doing it. We suddenly seem to be trying to play catch up.

The letters are dying out. They're concentrating on parcels. They've opened a massive, massive parcel hub in the Midlands.

You only have to look around you to see the amount of packets that we deliver now. And they're making the walks bigger. We never had to empty the postboxes before. We now do collections.

But personally, I don't think they're asking that much.

The perks and the benefits of that Royal Mail have got are so rare. All sick pay, the works. Working four days for two weeks, five days in the other two weeks. And most of the time you're home by three o'clock.

By far this job massively outweighs my old job.[10] You are paid ridiculously well for it, so I don't understand what these people are moaning about.

When you're at this level, as a postman, unless you can change it or you've got something strong to say, you're better off not saying anything and keeping your wits about you.

Because, ultimately, these other postmen all moan about it but carry on anyway . . .

– Will you be at Royal Mail until you retire?

Yeah I will, sadly. And I think I'll spend most of that time wishing I could have been something more. But I think realism puts you in your place. My bed is made here, and I like it.

But that said, it's not the be all and end all of living is it? It's my job, and I know it's important, but my life and what goes on outside of the job is also important . . . and being a postman gives me time I never had.

---

10 He was the manager of a fast-food restaurant *'working fourteen-hour days.'*

CHAPTER TWELVE
UNDER-THE-SKY WORK

Dairy farmer

gardener

roofer

Dairy farmer

(60s)

I'm a farmer's daughter. Quite unusually for people nowadays, I've only ever moved fifty yards.

Even when I was a little girl, I knew I wanted to be a farmer.

My grandfather cherished his grandchildren. He was always bringing gifts. One day he came back from market with a donkey.

I loved the donkey, but he was a bit naughty. He could open doors and he'd let the cows out. You'd get a knock at the door,

'*Your cows are all around the village!*'

My dad said, '*that donkey's got to go.*'

And of course I was very upset.

Then my grandpa brought me a lamb. I used to take the lamb for walks around the village. He died and I was devastated. I was invited to a birthday party on the day he died. I almost couldn't go because I was so upset.

My grandpa then brought me down two young female pigs, followed by a boar a few months later.

As you might expect, the two pigs were going to have piglets and my dad said, '*We haven't got room for all these pigs. They're going to have to go to market.*'

They went to market, and again I was upset.

And then my dad said, '*Why don't you go and choose a female calf? Then it won't have to go.*'

I went out to the shed and named them all after characters in the Magic Roundabout. My favourite calf was Dougal. I used to get her out of the pen and walk her round the village. This was fifty years ago, so we've had quite a few Dougals since then, but *the* Dougal, I kept her 'til she died, and she's buried at the top of the field.

And the house that I live in, the house that we built, it's called *Dougal's*.

I went to a grammar school, did my A levels, and there was an expectation to go on to university, so I did agriculture and economics at a time when agriculture was a very male-orientated industry.

My dad assumed I'd get a job somewhere once I'd got my degree, but I said, '*Well, I'd like to come back and work on the farm.*'

He said, '*I don't think it's a thing for girls.*'

So I went off to interview for various jobs. I went for a job with a feed company in their HR department. At the very end of the interview, they asked, '*What would your ideal job be?*'

And I said, '*Working with animals.*'

I didn't get the job.

My dad let me come home and work on the farm. He thought I'd do a year and say, '*I can't do it.*'

Fortunately, I did last. I'm here and I'm a farmer in my own right. I've thoroughly enjoyed it, and with each year that goes by, I realize it's the only thing I could have done.

To start with, working on the farm stopped me getting married, because if I got married and had children, well, goodness, then I'm admitting that I'm a woman.

I felt I had to prove to my dad that I was as good as a man, that I could do the work of a man, that I could run a farm.

But I found a modern man and I carried on farming. He brought the children up.

My dad found it quite difficult that a man was staying in the house, but he was quite happy to come and eat my husband's food.

In the end, my dad was very accommodating. He treated me as, almost, an equal.

But a family business is quite difficult. We were all – my dad, my two brothers and I – working on the farm, nearly a thousand acres.

You're working with people that you love, so you can't speak to them in quite the same way as a colleague.

You become the child that you were. For me, I always felt slightly inferior because I'm a woman. I'm quite happy to stand up in front of a load of men and give a talk, but my brothers made me feel slightly like I wasn't an equal.

When we were all working together, I saw my parents and brothers nearly every day. And then when you see them at Christmas, you don't give them a hug or a kiss.

But when my husband's parents or sister visit, they haven't seen each other for months, so they hug and kiss and they're genuinely pleased to see each other, whereas farmers . . . it's a different relationship.

I think it's a healthier one when you're not working together.

– Do you want your children to take over the farm?

One of them is very interested and is managing the farm with us. Fortunately, the other two aren't interested.

My husband and I are thinking about retiring, but she's dragging us along.

I think women have got a different approach to looking after animals than men. I was helping my daughter make a pen the other day. She had eight calves in one pen. As we were going to move them, I said, 'That Hereford calf's not well, is it?'

A healthy cow's ears are there [she puts her hand next to her head] and her ears were at quarter to three. You notice things about cows, about how they walk, how they hold their head, how they hold their ears, how they breathe, how they moan, how they lie. You've just got this in-built sense. My daughter's the same, and if somebody was to say, '*Well, how'd you know there's something wrong with that cow?*', I couldn't describe it, but I know there's something wrong with her.

I'm sure that there are men out there that have got the same sense, but they always seem to be a bit harder. When I was farming with my brothers, I think they thought, *Oh, she's being silly about that.* But now, with animal welfare so much at the forefront, this really is how you should treat animals – with respect.

Poor old cows. We expect a lot from them. When I had my first daughter and I was breastfeeding, producing milk was absolutely exhausting.

I thought, *my God, the cows should be out in the field on their back with their legs in the air, producing all this milk.*

So I know it's a bit sexist, but I do think women are good at looking after animals. We treat them as we would want to be treated.

Technology has also made it easier for women to be involved. There's machinery that can make hay and silage. You used to have to manually put the wheat stooks and small bales onto the trailer and manually throw them off when you get back to the farm.

That was jolly hard work.

– What do you think about when you're going about your tasks?

I'm thinking of all the things I've got to do, and the order in which you've got to do them. *We need to do this, we need to do that.*

My daughter is up at the farm at 5 a.m. Two other people will be there as well. One does the milking. One scrapes the yard, mixes the feed, and puts the feed out.

There's twenty calves to be fed. We calf all year round, so there might also be a cow to see that's just had a calf.

The three of them will be finished at 9.30 a.m. They'll come back and have breakfast for an hour, then they go back out.

Oh gosh, there's so many jobs to do!

In the summer, when the cows are out, there's moving the wire to put them onto fresh grazing. There's always cows coming bulling, so they need to be artificially inseminated.

Cleaning the sheds, as well. I probably clean them out every eight weeks.

The cows will be milked again at about 3.15 p.m.

Then the calves have to be fed again, and the yards have to be scraped again. They'll finish up by 7 p.m. It's a long day.

And my daughter could also be out at 10 p.m. calving a cow, or giving a cow colostrum. I spend a lot of time calving cows late at night. I'm an owl rather than a skylark.

Today, I haven't done much on the farm. My husband and I can't do a day like we did ten or twenty years ago. We're sort of more management, go-for, filling-in, and paperwork.

It wasn't a very farmy day. I did a bit of feeding for an hour. Then I went to the milking herd where my daughter was freeze-branding some of the heifers, and I helped her make a pen.

I filed some passports (each cow has to have a registered passport within twenty-eight days of it being born).

Someone's coming to buy a calf tomorrow, so I got the documents ready for that.

Then I brought more feed back, before my daughter's horses escaped and I got those in.

– Do you think of it as work?

I suppose it is work, because sometimes it's so relentless that it doesn't always give you time to enjoy it.

If you had a normal job, you'd have a review every six months. I've never had a review. Nobody's ever told me what they think of what I do.

It's very unstructured.

It's also a tough road ahead. We're dairy farmers but we're not on an aligned contract. The supermarkets have got dedicated farmers that supply them with milk and they give them a guaranteed milk price, and there's an element that they allow for profit. For everybody else that's not on an aligned contract, you're on a lower price, but you're doing the same work.

We didn't make a profit last year, and we only just made a profit the year before. Hopefully things are on the up, because our milk price has gone up 4p in three months – absolutely unheard of.

Every penny to us is £15,000.

Somebody once worked out that if milk had kept up with inflation, we'd be on 70p a litre, but a year ago we were on 27p.

And because of Brexit, the government are trying to change so many things.

All farmers get a basic farm payment, which depends on your acreage. If they didn't get that payment, many farmers wouldn't make a profit. It's helping keep food prices down.

When they remove it, food prices will have to go up. I think it will knock a lot of farmers out. It will possibly result in farms being a lot bigger, which is what people don't want.

The way that we can survive is by selling our milk at the farm gate and making cheese.

We started making cheese in 2001, when there was another recession-depression in agriculture. A lot of farmers got out, but we thought, *maybe if we try and add value to our milk.*

We make a quarter of a tonne of cheese every week and I think we've only ever thrown two batches away. We're quite innovative. If something goes wrong, we write it down and we create a new cheese, which is why we've got twelve different cheeses.

Farmers never throw anything away, because there's always a day when you might be able to use it. Never throw it away! Call it something else! As long as it's edible . . .

We also took out the bounce-back loan and we've now got two vending machines at our gate. One sells fresh milk, the other we've filled with our cheese and local foods: butter, beer, apple juice, eggs, sticky toffee puddings, shortbread.

It's great when people tell you that they've bought your cheese and they love it, and the number of people that say they've enjoyed the milk . . . You do feel that you've achieved something.

– *Would you say that you have a purpose in life?*

Yes, I was destined to be a farmer, and I feel that I have made a little bit of mark for women in agriculture. I couldn't have done all of this without my husband. If he hadn't looked after the girls, I wouldn't have been able to farm in the same way. I was very lucky to find him. He was also lucky to find me. But yes – you know – we all want to leave a little mark, don't we?

Gardener

(30s)

When I was younger, my mum gave me one of those old Victorian basins so that I could have my own mini garden. I went to uni and, as most people do, I forgot all about the outdoors.

I then went to work in marketing. The last company I worked for was not good to their workers. The company wanted me to give all my time to them. I hated it.

I ended up on mental health sick leave. They let me go the day I got back.

I spent a few months trying to decide what I wanted to do. My parents said, '*If you want to earn a few quid, come and do our garden*.'

Word spread and I became a gardener, and I love it.

My mum was a high-level IT consultant. She always said to me and my sister that she wanted us in the boardroom by thirty. There was a lot of pressure to go to university.

I've realized later in life that I don't feel like I was given the option of more vocational work when I was growing up. It's probably a class thing, and having that class bias against practical work is something I regret, because that stuff doesn't matter.

Yesterday, I spent three hours clearing a plant that my client didn't want. What was it called again? *Baby's tears*. Sounds horrific doesn't it? It's also called *Mind-your-own-business*. It'd spread like crazy, all over her garden. She put it in and didn't realize how it would spread, which is very common. I've had to do the same with wild strawberries. People just whack stuff down without realizing how it's going to look in a few years' time.

After the last frost of the year, the job involves a lot more planting, starting to mow, strimming, weeding. When I'm weeding that's usually when I'm really into a podcast. Sometimes weeding's mindful, calming. Other times it's, *I really wish I was doing something else, because I've been weeding for three days.*

This time of year, there's lots of leaf raking, which is the autumn version of weeding.

When I'm working, I'm just thinking about the one task that I have to do. I think, *I just have this task to do and then I can do another task.* It's not like marketing where you have a hundred things bouncing up at you.

Some clients have no gardening experience themselves. They say, '*Do what you need to do.*'

Others have more control. I've got one lady who's ninety-eight. She loves gardening, but can't garden herself any more, so I just let her tell me what to do. I call it *point-and-click.*

She sits there and watches me. If we're pruning a rose bush or a tree, '*Get that branch, that branch, that branch.*'

Some clients will give me a budget and say, '*Go and get me some plants.*'

That's much more creative. The first thing I'll do is ask them their favourite colours, then I'll make a mood board of plants with those colours throughout the seasons. They'll say what they like and don't like, and I'll go and get the plants and plant them.

I'm not really a garden designer. I can't draw what I want to happen, but I can visualize it when I'm standing in the space.

I look at the space and think, *that plant'll be 10cm high, but this one's 30cm. I don't want to put the small plant behind the big plant.* I find these things really hard to comprehend when I'm not standing there. It's probably something to do with the way my brain works.

There are stresses to it. I'm worried about the cost of living. We've had to rent out a room in our house. There's also the stress of *what's the weather going to do? I need to get this done today.*

But, on the other hand, you don't have any targets, it's not *data-driven* and you're outside as well, with all the health benefits of being in a green space: the vitamin D helps with your mood and your energy levels; the soil, when you disrupt it, releases a bacteria that they're now trialling as a medication for PTSD; and petrichor – the smell of rain after it's been hot – signals that the fertile season is here and seems to produce a happy hormone in us.

I don't know anyone who doesn't like that smell.

All of these things I get to experience . . .

It's a much calmer environment than the office. I haven't really had any problems with my mental health – *touch wood* – since I went into gardening. Before that I'd struggled for about ten years.

When I was in marketing, I bumped into a friend from school at a festival. We went for a drink. I said, '*What are you doing now?*'

She said, '*I'm working as a receptionist in a swimming pool.*'

I'd always thought that she'd do more than that and I said, '*Okay, what're you gonna do after that?*'

And she replied, '*I'm not going to do anything. I'm going to carry on as a receptionist.*'

I realized afterwards that I'd been judging people, without meaning to, for having jobs that are not seen as aspirational. That realization changed my view of working. I'm still aspirational, but in a different way. I'm still seeking the next step, but I aspire to different things.

– *What would you say you aspire to?*

To be happy. And to have a purpose in this world. To help people, help the planet, and to be outside [she laughs].

When I garden, I try to teach people that things don't need to look perfect, they just need to have life.

Roofer

(40s)

Where I lived in Spain, there were only two industries – tourism and construction. If you're not a hotel owner or a waiter, you're a builder or a labourer.

My dad was in real estate. He had lots of builder friends and contacts. And every time I was a naughty boy, my punishment was so many hours on a building site. Long story short, I was a little shit, so I was always on a building site.

The minute I left school, I went into building. And by the time I was nineteen or twenty, I had a group of us, me and five other guys.

I loved restoring, getting an old derelict house and making it beautiful. Mixing modern with old . . . I used to love that.

By the age of twenty-five I had a limited company with about twenty-odd people working for me.

And then by the age of thirty-five, I had about forty-five on the teams directly employed by me.

And then 2007 came. The recession hit.

At that moment, it was as good as it could get. We had a contract building five houses.

About halfway through the client pulled out, so we lost three houses overnight. That left pretty much half my team without work. And I felt really responsible, because they were desperate. I was very quickly down to my core team, which was about ten people.

I was at my doorstep handing out rice and noodles and milk to the

Moroccans that used to work for me. They were begging me for something.

A guy in our town walked into a cafe with a shotgun. He blew the bank manager's head off while he was having his coffee, because the manager wouldn't give this guy the money he asked for.

One of our lawyers jumped off a building.

I thought, *shit!* If lawyers are jumping off buildings, that's not good: normally when there's a recession they're making the money from bankruptcies.

It was chaos. And that's why I chose booze. I chose to put a big happy cloud over the whole thing and to just forget about it.

I lost my family. I lost my job. I was pretty much going down the drain. Have you seen *Leaving Las Vegas* with Nicolas Cage? No, well I was doing what he did in that – drinking myself to death.

There was a little footpath over a stream. It was summer. I was very, very drunk. I was in my hat and my motorbike leathers. I ended up stuffing myself under this footpath thing to get out of the sun. I could barely walk. But I remember being pulled out by two policemen and I was surrounded by locals looking down at me.

Someone thought they'd seen a body under the bridge. They thought I was dead. That's why there was a whole throng of people and cops and everything. They pulled me out and were like, '*What the fuck?*'

They thought I was a corpse, and that's pretty much how I felt.

I didn't think of ending it myself, but I just didn't care. I'd quite happily drive drunk on a mountain with no guardrails. It didn't matter to me whether I fell off a mountain or not.

It was like a passive suicide.

And then I met my wife. She was holidaying. Somehow, she fell in love with me instantly, which still to this day I have no idea how or why.

She said, '*Why don't you move to England?*'

And it was like a light went on in my in my head.

'*Wow. England. I never thought of that.*'
And I did move to England.

I went from turning over maybe €100,000 a month to working for £8 an hour: £8 an hour doing DIY stuff in England. It was humbling. I was still on the booze a lot. I was a raging alcoholic when I arrived. We got rid of that eventually. She weaned me off it.

It was interesting. A new arena, new materials, new techniques, new everything. I'm a grafter. I went from £8 an hour to £10 to £15 to £20. Then, once I'd finally made some connections and contacts and gotten other people working for me, I thought, *right, I'm gonna start a new building company.*

I started doing it and I thought, *you know what? No.*

I remembered that it's so incredibly stressful to be in charge of lots of people. It's not just the people, it's the whole family, their kids and their wives. They depend on you. I thought, *I don't know if I can do all that again.*

So instead, I spent a lot of years working for not much money. I liked fixing things and doing things.

I was fixing myself as I was doing all this work.

I discovered how to do some basic roofing and I also discovered that, in England, builders use scaffolding for anything. Anything at all. Ridiculous!

I'd repoint a chimney. I'd do it without scaffolding, because you don't need scaffolding for that. I'd charge £250 to repoint the thing and then I discovered that people were paying like £800 for scaffolding for this £200 job. I thought, *I'm onto something here.* I started advertising myself as a roofer or – well, not a roofer – but I fix leaks.

And I do not use scaffolding. That's my selling point. No scaffolding needed. I can still charge £500 pounds to repoint a chimney and I'm still saving the client money, but I'm making a lot – win–win.

There's one thing about my job that I love: finding leaks, the detective side.

A lot of people say, '*Oh, builder says the leaks caused by that*.'
I'll say, '*Er, really*?'

And then I'll always look somewhere else. There's normally more than one thing. I love finding the leak. Finding that smoking gun. I love that. I want to find the dribble. *There it is! there it is!*

The hardest thing for any business is to keep your workers. If they're good, you have to keep them, because they get poached.

One of the guys I have, I poached from someone else. It's a dog-eat-dog world out there.

It has taken ten years to find two guys. For one of them, I put an ad in Gumtree or somewhere saying, '*help needed – hard graft – don't call me unless you like these words*.'

People in England do not want to work. And they wonder why there's foreigners, because foreigners do want to work, and you guys just don't want to work.

This guy who answered that advert had a fright once. He had a harness on, and he had a roof ladder, but he wasn't clipped on. He slipped next to the roof ladder. As he was sliding down, he tried to grab it. The rungs were moving fast and bouncing his hands off. He managed to grab it just before he reached the end. And that made him skittish. I lost him for about a year-and-a-half.

After having a few businesses, I've realized that you need to include your workers in everything, and you need to be completely transparent.

The way we have it now, we all share a Google Calendar, and on the Google Calendar, I'll put in all the jobs that are coming up.

I'll also upload the quote that I've given the clients so the guys can see it. On the quote is a description of the work, there's a link to a photo gallery so you can see where the problems are, and there's a price.

They guys are all on 30 per cent of whatever the price is, and that's their wage, 30 per cent.

It's complete transparency. They're part of the team. They're part of the system and they get a lot of money as well. It stops them from even thinking about going off on their own, because they know when they see my quote they think, '*Shit, I couldn't do all that*.'

It's a very good system. It's working well.

Except now I need all week to do the paperwork. And I'm still way behind. I hate it. I've always hated it. I'm good on an Excel sheet. I'm good at organizing, but I can only do it for a limited time before I want to get out.

When I started my business in Spain, I was brave and young and very gung-ho with money. It was all very *flash the cash*. I remember once there was a wobbly table at a restaurant and I was like, '*I'll sort this out!*'

I got a big wad of cash, folded it, and used that.

I'm embarrassed to say it now.

I'm a lot more calm now. I think about things a lot more. A calm life. Lots of love. And I enjoy the simple things. The garden, friends, and good food. On weekends, the phone goes off.

Before it was all very much work, work, work. Family was like the appendage. Now it's the other way around. Work is the appendage.

CHAPTER THIRTEEN **CAREWORK**

Home carer

paramedic

Residential childcare worker

Home carer

(40s)

I'm from Zimbabwe originally. I arrived in the UK in 1999 when I was seventeen years old.

I was supposed to go to university to do nursing, but as I was going through the medical, I found out I was pregnant. I was a long way gone and I couldn't terminate it.

They rejected me, '*You have to give birth first.*'

When my daughter was born, I sent her back to Zimbabwe to live with my mum. I tried applying again, but I had trouble with my paperwork, and while I was waiting for it to be sorted out, I started doing care work, in nursing homes, as a home carer, as a carer for people with learning disabilities.

I was working everywhere.

The hardest job for a carer is working in a nursing home.

Say you work an early shift, right? From 7.30 a.m. until 3 p.m. You'll be given six or seven elderly patients. You have to give them breakfast, you have to wash them, and you have to get them ready for a 12 p.m. lunch. After they've finished lunch, they have to go to the toilet, and you have to handover. But to get all this done, you have to rush them.

On night shifts, you have six to ten residents, and you finish at 8 a.m.

The managers will say during handover, '*Oh, it'd be lovely if you wake about ten people in the morning to make it easier for the day staff.*'

We are told that you have to meet a target, so you have to do it.

By 8 a.m. you have to have ten patients up and dressed. That means you have to wake a ninety-year-old lady at 5.30 a.m., whether she likes it or not.

What I saw in the homes was that the patients who weren't vocal, the old and frail ones, were targeted.

If you go to an eighty-five year-old and say, '*Time to get up*', they'll say, '*No, I want to sleep*'.

So at 5.30 a.m., the carers will go to the frail ones, quickly change them into their dresses, put them on a chair. Some will be screaming at you, but you keep doing it.

I find it bizarre and wrong, very wrong.

I understand what they're trying to do, because day staff might call in sick (every morning, you have two or three people calling in sick), but it is punishing the old because they want to stay in bed.

Now, I work as a live-in carer. I prefer it to nursing homes. It's a little bit peaceful from a carer's point of view. I don't have six people to rush. There's no, *did I give medication to her this morning? Did I do this? Did I do that?*

I'm just looking after one person.

Sometimes it's difficult with the families.

I was working with one family and the son brought his family and friends to the house, seven people.

He said, '*Don't worry, we'll look after mum this afternoon*.'

I left for the afternoon and came back.

When I came back, they said to me, '*If you can just sort the kitchen out for us*.'

'*Uh, okay*.'

I went into the kitchen and – oh my stars – the whole kitchen was covered in dishes. A proper mess. I went back to them.

'*Excuse me, what would you like me to do in there?*'

'*Oh, do the dishes, tidy the kitchen, clean up. That's your job isn't it?*'

'No, that's not my job. I'm not your servant. I'm not your slave. I'm not your housekeeper. I'm your mother's carer. If you tell me that your mother has used these dishes, I'll go and do them. But if you used the dishes, I'm not doing them. You're adults, sitting around, drinking tea, chatting'.

I went to leave. They apologized.

These are the kind of things that come along when you're working as a live-in.

You also have to face the emotions of the family when doing palliative care. It's quite difficult. Some families don't visit. They avoid the house, but they want an update from you.

You say, 'Nothing's changed' or 'It's getting worse' or 'I don't know if he'll last the week'.

It's sad breaking that news but someone has to do it.

It's not just the families. The elderly are rude in their own way.

They say, 'Do your job because I'm paying you'.

I had to answer back to one gentleman who said this.

I said, 'If you think your money is that good, call the bank and get the bank manager to send your money here, see if it can do what I'm doing now. I want to see if that money is gonna help you'.

One job was seven hours away from my house. You're sent a patient profile by the agency and on this profile it said, 'This lady is so lovely. She'll chat to you'.

I arrived and the lady looked at me and she went, 'You're a negro'.

Trust me; she wasn't like the profile; she did not want to chat.

In the morning, I had to check her diary to see whether she had any appointments that day.

On the second day, I was checking her diary and she'd written, 'Oh my God. There's a negro in my house. I'm going to have to sleep with my eyes open'.

I called the agency and said, 'Guys, I don't care if she calls me names, but I'm no longer comfortable working for someone who doesn't want me in the house'.

The agency said, 'No, no, no. She's got dementia. That's how she is'.

On the third day, I wake up to bring her a cup of tea at 6 a.m. I knock on her door. There's no answer. There's nobody in her room. I check the whole house (it was massive) and there is no one anywhere.

I called her friend down the road.

She said, *'Don't worry, she's here. Don't take this to heart, but she said that she's afraid to be in the same house as a negro.'*

I called the agents, and they released me at 7 p.m. All day I was sitting in the house on my own.

I thought, *is my skin that bad? Do I look scary? Where did I go wrong?*

I could find no fault on my side. She was just that kind of person.

Mostly, in care, you just have to suck the lemon, to suck it up and work.

If you start raving, *'I don't want to go back there, she's this and that'*, then you'll end up being miserable yourself, because the live-in job is lonely work.

Carers are always on the bottom. As a live-in carer, you get £100 to £150 for a twenty-four-hour shift. But if I did a fourteen hour shift *not* as a live-in, I'd get paid £120.

Imagine how much they'd be paying me if I was paid £9.50 for each of the twenty-four hours. Yes, at night you are sleeping, but you are also on duty.

Back in the day, agencies used to send someone to assess a patient at home before they took the client on and put a price on the care.

They're not doing that any more. Now, they'll just phone the family, and the family will say, *'I've got my grandma here. She's ninety. She's all right. No, she doesn't wake up at night.'*

The family will tell the agency whatever they need to tell them to get the low care rates.

The agency will then send out the assignment and care plan to the carer.

The carer will go to the house and things are quite different to the plan. The patient's not sleeping. He's waking up four or five times a night. He's very vocal. He's violent, because he's got dementia.

As a carer you might have been told by the agency that it was a £750 a week job, but when you get there, they need a £900 to £1,000 a week service.

What happens? The patient will have new carers every day because no one wants to come back.

Agencies should stop being greedy.

They don't function without carers so they should treat us like human beings. They should assess clients properly and pay you accordingly. The carer doesn't get anything close to what the agency is charging for you.

But this is all a dream that will never come true.

When it comes to healthcare, it's always the NHS they sing about. Someone needs to stand up for carers. We're the ones who make the United Kingdom the oh-so-famous United Kingdom.

Now, most live-in carers are from South Africa. They're here to work. They don't have bills. They don't have rent. They just go from one job to another. They don't have children here.

It's killing us carers who live in the UK, with families and bills. If I say I don't want a job, the South African lady will take it. You convert the pounds to Rand and it's all right. But for me, the pay is not enough to pay my rent or the childminder for my son.

I'm one of those people who doesn't believe in benefits, and I've got my mum at home in Zimbabwe who needs me, so I can't afford not to work. But it's heartbreaking to leave my kids.

In Zimbabwe we look after our own. In 2015, my grandad was unwell. I travelled back home to look after him until he died.

I always find it difficult here when you ask someone where their mum is and they say, '*Oh, she's in the nursing home.*' It's strange.

If you put someone in a nursing home, at least check on them once or twice a week. Because, these nursing homes, if there's someone who's not being visited every day, that means there's no one who's going to nag the carers, '*How's my mum?*'

The ones who don't have relatives nagging are the ones that the carers wake up at 5 a.m.

It's not that they'll be abused or anything, but it's just that they won't have anyone in their corner.

When you don't visit someone, you put that person in a vulnerable position.

Paramedic

(30s)

I went out travelling to Canada, where I probably had the best eight months of my life. I was a bus conductor taking people on coaches to their hotels. It was a lot of drinking and skiing and snowboarding.

On days off, I'd sometimes think, *I should walk up this mountain.* I'd walk up it.

Sitting on top of a mountain is a good way to reflect.

I realized that I wasn't getting any younger and that I needed to take ownership of where I wanted to go in life. My dad had been an Assistant Chief Constable, third-in-command of a whole force. That was my benchmark for what a man does in the household. And I was pissing my life away on a ski hill.

Once, I was riding down one of the runs and I saw two ski patrollers go past me, really fast. The guy in front was in a tucked position, attached to a sled, focused on getting to the ambulance waiting at the bottom, and the other guy was kneeling in the sled doing chest compressions on what I thought was a real person.

That is awesome. I want to do that.

I didn't realize that it was a training exercise and that it was a mannequin, but seeing them was this kind of epiphany moment: *That is what I want to do.*

Now I work as a paramedic.

I live near where I work, so the local area is like a road map of carnage. Sometimes you're having a nice moment, having a coffee somewhere, and you suddenly think, *I did a job over there.*

The job is a real leveller. It lets you know that life is fragile.

That's become abundantly clear with my mum suddenly – like – going . . . my mum died of a heart attack.

I was on shift nearby when it happened. They brought me to the scene.

When I arrived, I was thinking as a paramedic. Rationally and logically.

As brutal as it sounds, I was thinking, *is she written off? Is this done? Do I need to start dealing with her death now? Or is there a little bit of hope that she might wake up and it all be fine?*

At the hospital, I was stood in A&E, and I could hear the LUCAS device, which is a chest compression device, banging away on her chest.

I could hear them calling out drugs that they want to give her. I was in the moment, *oh they've given her this drug*, but I kept on flicking back to, *that's my mother, that's my mum.*

My stepdad was hanging onto everything, 'She's at hospital. She's doing well.'

And I would think, *that means nothing.*

In my head, I had those jobs where you take a patient to hospital, and you know that they're not coming out. My mum was in that situation. She was super unstable. She was on a high adrenaline infusion just to keep her blood pressure up.

In fact, I'd stood at the foot-end of that exact resuscitation bay in that exact hospital, and I'd seen all this happen for other people. Back then I thought, *oof that's a bad day*, and then I'd gone for a coffee.

There's this disparity between the mask you wear at work and who you are in your home life. I was two people. I was the ambulance man with the thick skin that could go to these jobs and then say, *'Cool. I'm hungry. Let's go for some lunch.'* And I was the person I was outside of work.

Seeing this happen to my mum, those two people became one person.

At work, we talk about the *ritualization of resuscitation*. It's where you have a patient that's in cardiac arrest and it isn't going well. You go out and speak to the patient's family.

You say, '*We're aggressively treating them, giving them drugs, and managing their breathing, and they haven't responded to any of it. I'm going to go back into that room and we're going to carry on . . . but the heart isn't beating and they're not breathing for themselves. When I come speak to you again, I'll update you as to where we are. And if nothing changes, we're going to be withdrawing care at some point*.'

This is the family's warning shot. *It's not going in the right direction.* After a while, you come back and you say to the family, '*We've given them more drugs. They haven't responded. We're going to be withdrawing care in a moment but not yet. If you want to be there, I can take you in and you can hold their hand when we withdraw that care*.'

It's important for the family to be able to start their grief in the right way. Rather than us saying nothing to them and suddenly stopping the care with an '*Okay, they're dead*.'

When you finish your resuscitation, you begin your care for the family.

I used to do all of this. I would do and say the right things. But now I'm a lot more invested in it, in being with the family and helping them walk through the passing of a loved one. It's that sympathy. I have been there. And I am still there.

The other day we had a fifty-year-old cardiac arrest. It was 4 p.m. She was at work when she had her arrest. We did everything we could. It was a big job. Ten shocks from the defibrillator. That's a lot. When I was driving home, I thought *if she usually finishes work at 7 p.m., and if the police haven't yet been round, her family might not know yet*. Her family might still have been waiting for mum to come home from work, and I'm going home for dinner.

I dip my toe into someone's world, and I know what's about to happen.

But I've got enough of my own grief. I almost don't want their grief. I can be there for you. I can walk you through the process. I can be way more invested now than I ever was before, but it's someone else's bad day.

Your ambulance partner is valuable, especially if they're the right person. You can certainly work with the wrong person.

Once when I was still training, I went to a miscarriage call. My wife and I had just had a miscarriage ourselves. The call was for a young girl who'd been in hospital. She was miscarrying and the midwives were telling her, '*You've got to stay in the delivery suite*.' She insisted on going home and she delivered the dead foetus at home.

We get the call, and it came through as '*Birth Imminent*.'

We think we're going to deliver a baby, one of the best things you can do – there's a child near us who's named after me because I delivered it. Isn't that wonderful? – anyway, we went to this job. And the guy I was with was a bit of a cantankerous bugger, but he was the paramedic, and I was the ASW (Ambulance Support Worker, an apprentice paramedic).

He left me to do deal with the whole job by myself.

I'm in this tiny bathroom with this girl.

The foetus is in the toilet, in a disposable vomit bowl, which isn't the place you want it. The umbilical cord was still attached. She hadn't delivered the placenta, and she was bleeding a little bit, so she needed to go to hospital. I clamped and cut the cord.

She said, '*I don't want to see it*.' I was trying to put the foetus somewhere, not wanting to put it on the floor because that felt disrespectful. I remember looking at it and it looked like a person, a very small person, like one of those little aliens you used to get in those eggs, just like one of them.

'*I'm really sorry. There's nothing else I can say. I'm just really sorry. We're going to have to get you off to hospital*.'

We got her on a chair and got her to hospital.

It was a brutal job. But my partner didn't say a word. He didn't check in with me.

If I was to do a job like that now, I'd say, '*Fucking hell, that were a bad job weren't it? How you feeling? We're not getting another job, we're going back to base.*'

But I was a low-skilled member of staff and I thought, *well, maybe this is just part of the job.*

I remember him staring out of the window, playing on his phone.

I thought, *you prick.*

Then our despatch called us, '*I'm really sorry. That job sounded horrible. Are you guys all right?*'

'*No, I'm not all right.*'

'*Do you want to come off the road and get a cup of tea?*'

I said, '*No, I just want the next job.*'

I wanted to go to the next thing. I didn't want to go and sit at base with him not supporting me.

He'd heard me say that I wasn't okay, and he said '*Oh, y'all right?*'

I thought, *that's empty. You don't care.*

I turned to him and said, '*Yeh, I'm fine*', and we got on with the next job.

People like that are few and far between. Most people recognize that you need to be a bit softly-softly with these more abnormal jobs.

But the trouble is: We go to the abnormal. We go to the stuff that is not normal to see. That's the job. And it's okay to have the flash-backs and the sleepless nights and the nightmares and dreams for the next two weeks. That's a normal response to an abnormal stimulus.

It's normal so long as those flashbacks don't continue or become intrusive. If they do, then the mechanisms at work start kicking into life.

They'll take you off the road and support you with counselling. You'll speak to a nice person, '*Oh, that sounds terrible. See you in a couple of weeks.*'

It's better than nothing and it's nice that we have it, but all it does is flag that you might be at risk of depression or anxiety or PTSD.

Then work will tell you that you need to go and talk to your

GP. But how long does it take to get a mental health referral from a GP?

I did have some counselling after my mum's death. We did some stuff called EMDR (Eye Movement Desensitization Reprogramming). When the counsellor explained it to me, I thought, *this is the biggest load of bollocks I've ever heard.* But I went from '*Feelings of distress, out of ten?*' and I would have said '*Twenty*', to '*Two out of Ten*' after just five minutes of this reprogramming.

They get you to speak about the scenes and situations of that day. You become completely distressed and traumatized again. And then they do this eye movement thing, where you tap and blink at the same time. You're firing different pathways in your brain so that you can think around the situation.

Before I was thinking, '*Mum – Mum died – trauma*', rather than '*Mum – she took my kids on the hovercraft – she fell over on holiday and it was hilarious*'.

Now, I can access the sadness if I want to, but I can also think beyond it.

I don't know why we don't just have EMDR practitioners in the ambulance station all the time, ready to go.

– What does it feel like when a job has gone well?

It's like when you see a sports team and they're not obviously communicating with each other, but things are happening without instruction. Its effortless. They're operating on a different plane.

I'm going to cannulate. I reach for a drug. It's handed to me before I even ask.

But when you're working with someone that you don't trust, the effort goes up. You find yourself doing more because you can't trust them to do it. Your bandwidth narrows.

Years ago, we did a major incident training. It was an exercise that simulated a dirty bomb explosion. They had hundreds of actors pretending to be injured. We were the second ambulance on the scene.

We had actors trying to open the ambulance doors to get in. It was carnage. People screaming. People pretending to have had their legs blown off. Actors trying to get an Oscar for it.

Midway through the exercise, someone came round wearing a tabard, saying *'You need to eat something. Would you like a Snickers or a Mars Bar?'*

I couldn't answer. It was because all my decision-making bandwidth had been used up. And it was such a simple decision. Before, I'd have said, *'Both please.'*

Imagine what would happen if I was having to make a proper decision about something in that state.

– *What's the paperwork like?*

The paperwork has decreased since we've moved to an iPad, with a system that was designed with input from practitioners. It's beautiful. Really well designed. When you arrive on-scene it works chronologically:

Input patient details.

Primary survey (the initial assessment).

Secondary survey (a more detailed assessment).

If you're dealing with a stroke, you press *'Stroke'* and it will say, *'Have you done this? Have you done that?'*

You can use it to timestamp everything you do. Say I put a cannula in. I'll timestamp it as soon I do it rather than guessing the timings later on.

You arrive on the scene and you're like **tick, tick, tick, tick, tick**, **write a little blurb**, *'Okay, let's get you off to hospital.'*

And we have a business card that we give the police with the incident details on it. They can use that to access a PDF of all of our notes via a secure portal.

But at the minute, there's an outage and the iPads have been down. We've gone back to writing everything down.

We get the squeeze for our scene times to be quicker and for our hospital turnaround times to be quicker. The ambulance service wants you to do your best by each patient, to get on scene, to refer them to care pathways, to speak to the patient's GP or occupational therapist, to safeguard them. But all this stuff takes time. It might take an hour to get through to a GP, and that's an hour that you're not seeing the next person. Time is always tick tick ticking.

And yet, you try and do your best by each patient, you try to do all this stuff, but the service will chase you, *'Oh, you've been on-scene too long.'*

They'll never say those words, but you'll get a *'welfare check'* after forty-five minutes.

They'll say on the radio, *'Welfare check on scene.'*

I know it's a chase up, but I tend to go, *'I'm fine thanks. How are you?'*

Then they'll say, *'How long are you going to be?'*

Ah there we go, you want me off scene quicker.

You'll then be sitting in your performance review and your manager will tell you that your scene times and hospital times are a bit long. But, individually, each job is justified.

If you're taking a cardiac arrest in, say, you're not doing paperwork while the cardiac arrest is happening. You're caring for that person. So you have to start your paperwork after hospital handover. And that paperwork might be forty-five minutes to an hour, typing it all up, getting the batch numbers for the drugs.

So, if all of these jobs are justified, why are you telling me that my hospital times are too high?

It's because we're trying to look at qualitative things in a quantitative way. And that's because it's the targets, figures and numbers that bring in the money for the ambulance service.

Residential childcare worker

(30s)

As soon as you walk in, you see that it's just a normal house. A big house with five bedrooms. The kids can unlock the front door whenever they want. This is a nightmare because of absconding, but you can't keep them here against their will.

As you go in, on the left you've got a games and music room, with a piano, games consoles, and a PC if they want to record music. On the right you've got the kitchen and dining area and a relaxation room. Upstairs, there's bedrooms and toilets.

Residential care used to be very institutionalized, but we're trying to be more homely. The kids get involved in pretty much everything, even the wallpaper. You do think, *who chose that?*, but the kids liked it, so we put it in.

Changeover starts at 7.30 a.m. until 8 a.m. Count the money, the meds, do your health and safety checks. Find out what's happened with the kids during the night. And then get the kids up for school.

Some kids go to mainstream schools, others go to additional support schools. One girl needs four-hundred wake-up calls because she does not want to get out of bed. Some refuse to go to school. Give them as many chances you can. If they refuse to go, you usually find that something's happened with their family the night before.

Psychologists say that there's a four-day fallout whenever there's an incident. Let's say a kid's been involved in a fight, they'll be a bit iffy for four days no matter what.

The kids often can't get up in the morning. Most of the abuse that has happened to these kids happened at night-time. So they don't like being in their bedroom. It's not a nice place for them. They refuse to go to sleep. They sit on their phone for hours. They watch TV shows. It's understandable, but it has a knock-on effect.

At 8.30 a.m. we leave for school. You can have interesting conversations with the kids when you take them to and from school. It's one-to-one time.

And picking them up from school is the highlight of the shift. You have weird and wonderful conversations. The other day, one of the girls was telling me about her day. She's gone from an additional support school to a mainstream school, which is really good.

She then stopped talking for a couple of minutes as she just looked outside.

Then all of a sudden she screamed, '*I want to go skiing!*'

I was like '*What's wrong with you!?*'

And from then on we'd always refer back to *Going Skiing*.

Once the kids are dropped off, you come back to the house and run errands, shopping, picking up prescriptions. Some of the kids are only in school until 12 p.m., so they'll need picking up.

If they've got a sour face on the journey back, then usually something's happened at school. I try to work with them. I've got a habit of acting daft. It's what I'm known for. If you're daft and stupid, kids don't feel like you're a threat or that you're judging them, so they can be themselves around you.

I'll say, '*When I was at school, I done this and that.*'

The kids'll say, '*Really?*'

I want to make them feel like they can make mistakes. If you act daft and stupid, then you can ask questions and find out stuff that social workers need to know.

I think everybody's too serious in youth work.

There's a phrase that flew about, '*If this was my kid, they wouldn't get away with that.*' But it's not your kid. This is somebody else's kid, who's been through trauma and who can't help what they're doing because they're not quite wired right.

These are kids that are fight or flight, and it's often flight, often trying to get away.

People say, 'These kids don't understand sarcasm. They don't understand jokes. Don't do that sort of thing with them.'

But I've always done it. The girl that screamed about skiing, the other staff find her one of the most difficult children to work with. But she's easy. She never used to understand sarcasm and now she does sarcasm with me.

At 4 p.m. the kids come home and do their own thing. Some of them will put their laundry on. One of the staff, her husband is a sports coach. He takes the kids out to kick a ball around. We're trying to encourage them to understand that, just because they're in a home, it doesn't mean they can't do anything.

After that, the staff will cook dinner and we'll try and get them to settle in the lounge.

Night shift starts at 9 p.m. One staff member will give the night shift handover, explaining what's happened during the day.

Sometimes I'd come in for a night shift and all the staff would be around talking to me. I'd think, *Who's looking after the kids?* The kids would've had a good day, but then they'd get annoyed because all the staff have left them watching a film, so they'd start kicking off.

I've also noticed that if the kids have had a really good day with you, they don't want you to leave; if you were a parent, you wouldn't leave.

I don't know how many times I was supposed to leave and finish work at 10 p.m., only to get away at 3 a.m.

On the night shift, you try to make sure they're in their beds for 11.30 p.m. They tend to have their TV on and their lights on to drown out noises and thoughts and that. Generally, they'll be asleep at about midnight. But that's a good day.

A bad day is restraints. I won't restrain unless it's a last resort. I always get pulled up by management when I don't restrain until after I've been hit a few times: '*You shouldn't get hit at all*.'

You try to give the kid a chance. The restraints aren't designed to harm them. I always say, '*I don't want to touch you but I also don't want to be touched.*'

They can't help themselves, because they need to lash out.

One of the kids we looked after, the psychologist said that they needed a minimum of two hours of restraint. So you're holding them against their will for two hours every single time.

Sometimes you're in three or four restraints a night. We wait until they're calm before we let them up. You do aftercare as well: you go and get them a drink.

There are seventeen staff members and five kids. I remember a new staff member coming in. He was on his phone at the start of a night shift.

I said to him, '*This is what I do on nights. I'll do handover and then I'll go and spend some time with the kids to make sure that they're okay and that they've had a good day. If they're in their room, I'll knock on their door and see if they want to see us and I'll try to spend a bit of time with them, and try to come out alive if they decide they want to chat my ears off.*'

He said, '*Oh I'm not going up to them. They'll come down here if they want anything.*'

I said, '*No, they won't. These kids won't come down and see you. You're a new face.*'

They won't care about you if you don't care about them. Some of these kids have been in fourteen, fifteen care homes.

There've been many times when I've said, '*Do you want anything to eat or drink. I'm making hot chocolates. There's a hot chocolate downstairs if you want it.*'

They'll say, '*Fuck off.*'

But you can bet that half an hour later, they're coming down the stairs to have a hot chocolate when they've not left their room for days. And that's all because you've shown interest in them.

* * *

When the kids leave us, it's usually because sadly we can't keep them any more, because they're a risk to themselves.

We're a private company. We get the kids that the council don't want, the difficult kids. They're usually violent or suicidal, self-harming or sexually exploited. And when it gets to a certain stage, we can't have them any more. You feel like you've let them down.

For the other ones who leave and go to live on their own, they still have support. For example, I'm in a group chat with one of the leavers so he can message us. I always see him as our success. He sold drugs for his dad. He was a very troubled boy, but now he's in work and he's got a flat near us, so he can come back and see us. He's got a girlfriend, a dog, and his provisional licence.

The other day he wanted to put some blinds up in his new flat. I showed him how to do it.

It's left to us to try and teach him things.

His girlfriend messaged me once to say that she was afraid of his temper.

I tried to explain to him. '*Yes, your girlfriend wants to spend time with you, and maybe she nags at you, but you don't need to be angry about it.*'

I also played daft and said to him, '*Ah the missus keeps moaning at me. She says she doesn't get to see me, and she wants to cuddle all the time. So I just take myself out of the room and give myself a couple of minutes peace and quiet before coming back in.*'

Nobody's taught him this stuff. It's a constant battle to support him. And he's someone that's meant to have left. But how does he learn without us?

There's another child that feels really bad about herself. She'd say, '*Nobody loves me. Nobody cares about me.*' We had a long conversation about how you can have different levels of love. How you can love a partner, a dog, your kids.

I said to her, '*There's a love that I've got for you that's as much as I have for my own kids.*' It's different of course, more like the love of a carer than a parent. But it means that this job isn't a job, there's something else lying underneath it, an underlying thing . . .

The kids know that I've two boys. But the way I talk about my kids is that I've got them with me and that I go home and see them.

But I've not seen them in three years.

I think I substitute, not intentionally, but I do substitute . . . I make a big deal over these kids in the home because I know they've been in care and they haven't had the best start in life, but I do think I've become paternal to them. They're like my own kids.

My manager knew what was happening with my own kids. When I told her, she said, *'I'm so sorry. Just be aware that the kids in our home love you. They want to spend time with you. They see you as their own.'*

But I felt like crap because I could look after these kids in the home, but I couldn't look after my own.

They say that residential youth workers have a shelf life of three years. Three years before you burn out. It's probably the hardest goddamn job on the planet. It's draining. The restraints. The stress. The worry. A kid absconds and you're sitting there worrying about them. It takes over your entire life.

You're supposed to have downtime and switch your phone off. But you can't help yourself. My manager's the same. When you know that so-and-so is seeing her gran that day, you'll drop a colleague a text to say, *'Wish them a good day from me.'*

Their wee personalities take over your entire life.

– Earlier, you said that there was an 'underlying thing' in this job. What do you mean by that?

The underlying thing is that you need to care. People get into this job just to do the job, but that doesn't mean they care. I genuinely care about these kids. And I think you have to be that devoted because you're their ambassador. They've not got anyone else. If you don't care about them and don't want to have that kind of relationship with them, then why the fuck are you in the job?

CHAPTER FOURTEEN **TEAMWORK**

Supermarket worker

floorhand

Advertising copywriter

MOT tester

Supermarket worker

(late teens)

I'm approaching the end of my second year in retail. I started when I was sixteen. When I started, it was £9.36 an hour, which didn't change depending on how old you were, so it was really good money for me. At the time, the minimum wage for under-eighteens was £4.62.

I think it's one of the best working environments I've heard of, because everyone gets on really well. But the working environment has been deteriorating. It's become all about efficiency, about squeezing you to get the most out of you that they can.

For example, I work in fresh produce and our department used to have sixty hours a week unspent on wages. So it should have had sixty more hours of people working there through the week. But instead of hiring a couple of people, they just got rid of the hours and I now do what used to be – five years ago – two or three people's jobs.

I work five days a week in retail and five days a week at college. The amount of hours I'm doing now is to the detriment of my education. A typical day will be getting into college at 8 a.m. and finishing at the supermarket at 9.30 p.m.

I'm knackered.

If I didn't work, I'd have seven solid days to revise. I'm not going to lie, when I get home from work, tired after a long day, I am not revising.

On Sunday, say, I'm on fresh produce by myself all day. I work

6.30 a.m. to 4 p.m. and I get up around 5 a.m. to set off at 5.45 a.m. I'll get there ten minutes before I start.

We're one of the few supermarkets that still have people who are in all night working, so when I start work, I'll do handover from them.

If the stock delivery hasn't been done, I'll finish that. Sometimes I come in and I'll have ten pallets to unload in two hours. It's just not possible to get all the stock worked and ready on the shelves in that time.

After that, you make sure that the quality of your section is of a high standard before we open at 9.30 a.m.

We call it *brickwalling*. You make sure that the shelves look like a brick wall, with no gaps in the produce and no mess.

Then, before we open and throughout the day, you do process stuff.

Quality checks to make sure that all of the products out are of good quality, with no broken packaging or rotten food or anything like that.

Gap scanning, where you scan gaps on the shop floor and investigate the reasons for the gap.

Markdowns, marking down the price of products with customers trying to reach over you and snatch things from you like they're in the wild.

Availability reports, which is a report that tells you how long a product has been sat in the back when it could have been out on the shop floor and selling.

Binning reports, which are like stock audits in the warehouse.

Sense checks, which is where we use a scanner to check the deliveries to see if anything's missing.

Point of sale, which is re-doing all the signage saying '*Offer*' and '*Price Match*'.

Rotation checks, where we make sure that the oldest products are selling on the top of the shelf and the newest products are right at the bottom so they can't be sold.

In your mind, you have to be twelve steps ahead otherwise you'll get moved onto something else. If a manager comes up to you to say, '*Right, if you're done on your department, move over there*', you need to be able to say, 'Well I'm doing this, then I've got this then this then this to do.'

If I've started at 6.30 a.m., I'll take my break at around 10.30 a.m. when it's quiet. Even though I'm free to take my breaks whenever I want, I've been told that I should take them to fit around the business.

I'll go upstairs off the shop floor and away from customers. There's a big room with chairs and tables and a kitchen and tellies and things.

They used to have a hatch where they'd serve you subsidized fresh food. You'd pay a quid and get a full Sunday dinner, but they've cut that because it cost too much money.

I'll go back down to the floor at 11 a.m., which is when it picks up on a Sunday.

I'll have a tidy, make sure the shelves are full, organize the flowers maybe. We make a lot of money on flowers.

And then I'll be working stock: picking products out the back, getting the stock out onto the shop floor, and keeping standards as high as I can. I'm a bit of a perfectionist so my standard can be too high. It's like with exams at school, no matter how well I'd do – if I got 99/100, an A* – I'd be annoyed because I'd lost that one mark.

The stereotype is that supermarket work is just tins of beans on a shelf.

When I'm at college on a Monday morning, one of my friends will say, 'Why are you so tired. You were only stacking shelves at the weekend.'

I'll say, 'You don't even know. You don't even know.'

And I'll tell him about the million things that I have to do.

– When do you feel most alive?

When I'm working the stock, *quick quick quick*. Three pallets to do in an hour and off you go, *constant constant*.

When you get home, it's nice to know that you've grafted, that you've given it everything, and that the person who comes in next is going to appreciate what you've done because you've taken it off their shoulders.

In our supermarket, it's us and them. The management sit on a table down one side of the break room. Then all the colleagues sit on these big tables on the other side.

Sometimes a manager walks in, and a colleague will say, '*Are you gonna sit over here or over there with the rest of the gentry.*'

That's how it feels sometimes, but it's not that bad. We just joke about it. A lot of people, the older people, compare supermarket work to school, what with the gossiping and the managers being like teachers.

The managers say, '*Come on, get working.*'

Everyone has a good laugh. The other day, I was walking through the shop floor with this one colleague that I'm quite good mates with. We got asked by a customer for a product, a massive sack of pet food.

'*Sure, we'll go in the back and get it.*'

I started walking, he started walking a bit faster and then he raced through one door to get the product and I raced through another.

We came back through the different doors. The customer looked one way and saw me running to them with the pet food. They looked the other way and saw him running with another bag of it as well. I got there first, slung it in the basket, **boof**.

'*Get in.*'

We're not meant to do this stuff because it's a bit informal, but you can't help it.

When I first started, I was positive about the work, open-minded, but everyone at the supermarket started saying to me, '*That'll soon change.*'

A lot of my colleagues could talk for hours about the job and how much they hate it.

Certain colleagues openly admit, '*Ah, I don't really give a shit any more. I don't pay attention to stock rotation.*'

The younger people like that don't stick around, but you also get it with the older colleagues. It's very difficult to get rid of someone who's been there sixteen years.

Generally, there's a negative view of the work '*It's not what it used to be.*'

To be fair, my view of the job has changed to some degree since I started. We're treated more like a number than we used to be. For example, in my first year we got a £400 bonus, which for part-time work was good. This year, it'll work out at £40. And next year, they're not doing a bonus for us at all. The reason they gave was that they've given us pay increases instead. However, when you look at inflation, that doesn't really make sense to me.

— What do you want to do after you leave school?

I've got unconditional offers from some unis but I don't want to go to university. I'm not interested in the debt, and I prefer working. I'm looking at doing an accountancy apprenticeship down south, which is where most of the jobs are.

Why do I want to be an accountant? Because I'd never be out of a job and I'm money motivated [he laughs]. Accountants retire really early. It's a practical decision. I want to earn a good wage and to be on the property ladder. I want to be moving up in the world.

I know that if I graft it'll get me somewhere at least. As long as I'm trying and trying.

He later turned down his unconditional university offers and joined the management apprenticeship scheme at the supermarket.

Floorhand

(30s)

I always struggled in school. I have dyslexia and I struggled with the reading side of things. When I was told to just sit there and read and read and read, oh I'd go insane. But when it came to maths, dimensions, sizes, I could read a drawing better than I could read a book.

I could picture what I needed to do in my head. One of the technology teachers identified this. He'd say, '*I've got a few things I need helping with over lunch*.'

The techie department brought in a welder in my final year, and we started doing metal work. I had a natural knack for using the welder and my teacher said, '*Have you ever thought about becoming an apprentice fabricator?*'

So I ended up doing that. I finished the apprenticeship as a machinist toolhand in a stamping firm, producing electronic components for cars. That was me all the way up to 2020 when lockdown happened.

Covid showed us the true colours of the company I was working for. I thought it was a first-name-basis kind of place, but you were turned into a number when lockdown hit. You were put on furlough – pushed away to the back – and you weren't updated on what was going on.

At this stage, I had a few friends offshore. They told me what I needed to do get my offshore tickets. I got them during lockdown. It was like a boot camp. Then I was put on a waiting list for ages. Getting into the industry was very hard. It's all about who you know.

Growing up, I had a friend who lived in Aberdeen. You'd go past the docks and see these big supply ships and rigs out there. These great big pieces of designed equipment that can go out to sea and sit there and work all day. Offshore has always been in this part of the world. A lot of the people on the rigs are from this area. It's close-knit.

I got offshore last year. My first trip was over Christmas.

It was my very first time on a helicopter.

You check in like a normal airport.

You go through security.

You're made to turn your phone off. For the next forty minutes, you sit in silence for the safety briefing. You put on your life suits. They're tight suits, the worst scenario of your life if you're claustrophobic. You get the life jacket on, earplugs in, and then you're escorted to the helicopter with its blades already spinning.

Nobody talks for the hour it takes to get to the rig. Then you go down to the recreation room, and they brief you on what's going on, whether you're on day shift or nights. You go down and change and then you're straight out onto the rig floor.

I had Christmas Day on my first time out there. As much as I missed my family, I felt welcomed on the rig. After that trip, I got asked to come back. And then a trip or so after that I got a full contract with the company I'm with now. There's about one-hundred-and-forty people on-board our rig, spread over day shift and night shift.

Our rotation is two weeks of nights, one week of days. Twelve hours on, twelve hours off for twenty-one days. I'll get up at 4 p.m. and go to the gym, get showered, have my breakfast/dinner at 5.30 p.m., and go through to the boot room, where we'll get suited up. Then we'll have a start-of-shift briefing where the tool pusher (the overseer of drilling operations) and the barge engineer (the person responsible for the day-to-day running off the rig) tell you what's been happening on the decks and what operations we're doing for our third-party clients. The holes we're drilling are for these clients, so they're the ones in charge of what goes in the hole and what comes out. We're just their puppets.

As a drill crew, what's our priority? The hole. Anything that happens in and around the hole is our priority. We've got to make sure it's secure.

Night and day it's the same thing. There's always equipment on the move, stuff being brought up on cranes, and there's always oil production on the go. When the third-party clients say, '*Right, we're at a standstill because we need to talk to the office on land*', we do maintenance: we'll grease up the top drives, do inspections.

Some operations take ten hours. Your brain can go numb with the repetitiveness, but you need the situational awareness to do the job, so we'll keep switching out into different roles every couple of hours.

The big tooling and the heavy machinery, it's what I've done before in my career, and it made me stand out when the opening came up to join the drill crew.

Some of the work we do is outbound of the rig. You're on the side of the rig, harnessed up, life jacket strapped on, personal locator beacons on. And we'll lift a one-hundred-tonne-plus blowout preventer off from the live hole of the well. We'll lift that whole thing clean off the riser, which is connected to the seabed, and we'll place this one-hundred tonnes of solid steel on a stump that sits outside of the rig's parameters.

You've got a hundred tonnes of steel hanging onto joists and you're the one that has to be down the side of it, guiding it onto this stump. It sounds dangerous, but because of the protocols and safety precautions in place, and because you know that you've got three or four sets of eyes on you, it's no more dangerous than sitting at your desk typing.

Our rig has been fully converted to cyber: on a cyber rig, all the lifting is automatic. They've taken man out of the line of fire.

Working in a crew, it's working with a bunch of guys that are trying to reach the exact same goal: everyone wants to get home safely. There's also no point in having an argument with anyone because you've got work together for twenty-one-days' solid. There's a sense of brotherhood.

Our supervisor is a young guy for his position, but he's on the ball. He's ex-armed forces. I look up to him because of his work ethic. He likes to make sure everyone's in a good mood. If someone's not right, he can see it and he'll say, '*Right, something's up. You can get the easier job today.*'

The assistant supervisor, he's a supervisor so he needs to stand back, but he's come from the floor and he always wants to come back to the floor. He has that itch to get involved. And I love that. '*You come with me, and we'll go do this.*'

The other guys are younger than me, but they've been doing it for three or four years, and they're on the ball all the time. They make me think, *okay, that's gonna be me later down the line.* Everyone bounces off each other and everyone makes sure that the guy next to them is safe. And that's what I love about the job.

What I bring to the table is my mechanical background. If something breaks in the middle of a process, I'll jump in, '*I know how to fix this.*'

It's a good feeling to know that you're the go-to guy when it comes to needing stuff fixed. I feel like I'm quite an important part of the wheel that's turning on this rig.

There's nothing natural about what you're on, a solid steel structure jacked up ninety feet into the air.

But the nature is around you. You get whales, seals. I once saw a seal having its dinner. It'd found a fish, and it was eating away at it.

And the sun rising out there is the most beautiful thing I've seen in my life.

You get days where the water is calm . . . it's the most peaceful place.

But then you get days with 40mph winds, twelve-meter swells, and you think, *Oh my God, why am I out here?*

But when you're out there, there's nothing around you. You get picked up by the helicopter and you fly away, nothing but a small piece in a big ocean.

It's been hard for the missus. She goes from me being home all the time to pick her up from work to me being away for three weeks. She's got family around her, but it's been a hard change. I've got to accept the fact that I'll miss birthdays, Christmases, this and that.

But if it's something you enjoy doing, then you've got to do it.

I'm earning more than double what I was earning on-shore. I feel financially happy, you know what I mean? I'm not worrying.

If I was twenty-two, earning this rate, I couldn't tell you what I'd do. But nowadays I'm not a big drinker. I'm married and we want to get a house. We've got to save up.

Advertising copywriter

(30s)

At school, I couldn't shut up in class.

We had this one teacher who mispronounced words. He said, '*of cawwse . . . becawwse*'. That's just how he spoke. And I had like an urge inside me to mimic him. An itch that you cannot not scratch. It's ADHD, right? But I wasn't diagnosed at the time. I just blurted stuff out. It felt so involuntary.

I still have that itch now. I've always found it difficult to focus and concentrate on one thing and get one thing done. I'm always on to the next thing. And I think that's reflected in my career as well. I jump around and get very antsy.

I've had a few different businesses. Middle-Eastern brunch pop ups, chocolate milk delivered in glass bottles to your door.

I worked for a chocolate company as the head of sales. I was driving round the country with a box of chocolates selling them to posh hotels and restaurants.

My CV was once described as looking like '*a playground*', which I took as a compliment, but the interviewer meant as an insult.

I just love experiencing different things and different environments. I call it '*falling forwards*', or '*falling with style*' as Buzz Lightyear says.

The chocolate company didn't work out and they went into administration, so I lost my job there. It was at the same time as I'd split up with my girlfriend.

I was twenty-five. I moved back into my mum's place. I was really struggling. I've always been quite emotionally volatile.

But out of strife and failure comes something new, and the phoenix rises [he grins].

I'd heard of this uni course for advertising. I got in.

As soon as I started ad school, I was like *this is who I'm supposed to be. These are my people. This is the kind of work I want to be doing.*

In advertising, you work in pairs, a copywriter and an art director. I've been partnered up with my art director since ad school. I do the words, he does the pictures.

Back in the day, the copywriter would type up the ads and the art director would screen print his work onto it, a real collaborative and physical process.

Now the work is much more digital, but the partnership model has survived, despite the fact that – for the agency – it's fucking bad value for money, right? If one of us asks for a raise, it's doubled!

But I'm so glad it's endured. It's been great to have someone to work with.

– Is it like having a work spouse?

It's exactly like that, in the language you use, in how you have to keep an open dialogue between the pair of you, always being honest.

It can be delicate and tense but it's rewarding. They say that there's often a *chucker-upper* and a *siever* in any creative team.

I think I'm the chucker-upper.

Then he sieves, '*That's bullshit. That's bullshit. That's bullshit.*'

You don't know when you're gonna have a great idea. It could be in the client brief when you're fresh to it or it could be like, *fuck I'm stressing. I've got nothing to show the client. I don't like any of my work.*

Then: *boom.*

It's such an inexact science.

When I have the idea, I voice note my art director . . . and he doesn't reply [he laughs].

To come up with ideas you have to learn how your brain works and be quite self-aware.

Everyone's different. My place is in the pool when I'm swimming. That's the only place where my brain is truly quiet. And that's when a lot of my ideas come. I love the freedom of being weightless and I think better in motion. I have a notebook that I take in my gym bag because of how often stuff comes to me.

It isn't always good, but some of it has been. In fact, some of the funniest ideas I've had, I've had underwater.

A unique, brilliant idea is in most people. The question is, are they in an environment where they can come up with it? Do they have the freedom, the space, the lack of stress, enough sleep to have it?

It's all about feeding your subconscious just by doing weird things and experiencing life and all it has to offer. Go out to museums, see weird films you wouldn't ordinarily see, go to a bingo hall, go to the races, go to the dogs.

In the modern world of advertising, data is tearing creativity apart.

I can't remember who said this: *'it's much harder to make something difficult sound simple than it is to make something simple sound difficult.'* And what's happening a lot of the time is that simple things are being said in very difficult ways through jargon and data.

The outcome of some piece of research that's done for the brief will be: *people are on their phones more.*

I could have told you that! Just look around; but we're too busy looking down at the data to look up.

Bill Bernbach, one of the great ad men, said, *'Humans have been evolving for 100,000 years, they're not going to change now.'*

We still want the same things, we want to be happy, successful, loved. We still aspire to be better. We want to chill out and be in our pyjamas and not speak to anyone.

We've always wanted the same things.

But I think a lot of modern ways of collecting and using data exist just so we can avoid thinking about the existence of these universal wants, because if we did think about them, if we acknowledged that advertising really was so simple, then it would put a lot of people out of a job.

There are these rules going around the industry these days. For example: *you've got to show the brand logo in the first two seconds*. This is based off of the insight that people click off ads after two seconds. But to me, it's such a good example of where data has fucked with our heads.

What if people are clicking off early because they're seeing brand logos? When they're on Instagram, they're not here to look at your brand; they're here to look at their mates on holiday.

It's a really good example of how data is deluding the industry. It's the appearance of logic.

If I see a coffee shop logo in the first two seconds and then I piss off, it's not going to make it more likely that I go to that coffee shop. It means that I'm probably annoyed at the brand.

Instead, what if we show them some fucking great entertainment in the first two seconds that grips their attention? And then we show the logo in the last two seconds of the ad and – look – we've kept their attention the whole time!

If you think about the way that advertising has changed from the eighties to the nineties to the noughties, the number of channels that you can advertise on has increased a hundred-fold or more.

The days of doing one TV ad, a few print ads, and some direct mail, and that's your year for a client, they're over. Now it's a full spread. Facebook this, D2C that, B2C, B2B, print, out of home, digital, above the line, below the line . . . it's endless, the environment now.[11]

This has contributed to the decline in advertising being this glamorous thing. It's nothing like *Mad Men*. As a copywriter now, you're

11 'D2C' stands for 'direct to consumer'; 'B2C' is 'business to consumer'; and 'B2B' is 'business to business'.

testing this message on this audience, that message on that audience. And to do this creative work in an excel spreadsheet is a nightmare.

Fundamentally, you can't even test the value of a great new idea because it doesn't exist yet. Maybe you can look at similar case studies, but you can't test it.

All the great ad campaigns, you can see the genius of the copywriter and the art director. You can see that they've not come from testing multiple ideas.

You've got nothing to hide behind if there's just one idea.

There's one really famous ad for Rolls Royce. *'At 60 miles an hour, the only thing you'll hear in the new Rolls Royce is the clock.'*

Good, right? It tingles. That didn't come from data; that came from going to the factory and speaking to someone who makes the car. That's human beings making a beautiful insight, making a wonderful headline.

Maybe there are great pieces of work that a fucking robot made or whatever but I'm yet to see them.

No, great advertising is when someone says the truth in an interesting way.

MOT tester

(30s)

I'm from a broken home. I attended five different primary schools. Two different high schools. I'd be with my mum for a while but then I'd feel bad for my dad, so I'd go live with my dad for a while, then I'd feel bad about mum, and back I'd go.

It was horrible.

When I was at high school, my stepdad was strict. No make-up, no short skirts. I didn't have what the other kids had, and I used to get bullied for it.

My dad said, *'If you come live with me, you can dye your hair, you can have all these clothes, you can go out with your mates.'*

I wanted to be like everyone else, and so for the wrong reasons I went to live with him. I should have known. He let me down so many times. It was six kids and two adults in a two-bedroom council house. I used to just go out and do what I could.

I found myself being out more than I was in. The people I was with had no prospects. None of them wanted to do anything. Their families were all on the dole. There were reasons they couldn't work.

Then I fell in with the car lot.

We used to go driving around with all the boy racers. It was modified cars – Honda Integras, Toyota Celicas, Citroën Saxos, and Golfs – with remaps and superchargers, all to change the brake horsepower. This got me on the online car forums as well.

From the age of fourteen, I was out with the car lot most nights. I got to know a lot of people. My friendship group went from the people

I was at school with to these twenty-somethings. I met a bloke. He was thirty. We became close friends. I used to look forward to each night when after he'd finished work, he'd come and pick me up from my house and we'd cruise around before sitting in a retail park chatting away to people. It was an escape from the chaos, and I miss those days.

My dad decided he was going to move away. I didn't want to leave everything behind and move with him. So I ended up moving in with my boyfriend at the time. I was sixteen. I was at home with his stepmum, looking after his siblings. It was a dirty house. You'd wipe your feet on the way out. I wasn't happy but I had no other option. There was no help for me. '*There's another kid. Chuck her on jobseeker's and leave her to it.*'

I wanted more than that, but I couldn't have it because of the position I found myself in.

The council gave us a flat and that was when my boyfriend changed completely. He was going about behind my back. Then there was the physical abuse that I endured. The neighbours were ringing the police all the time. He was paranoid, telling me what I could and couldn't wear, who I could speak to, and cutting me off from everybody. Then he got rid of me. Dumped me and tried to keep my son, who was only two-months old.

I tried to get social services involved. Social weren't interested. Even though I was his mum and he needed me, I ended up sleeping on a friend's sofa with access to my child once a week if I was lucky. Then one day my ex turned around and said, '*You can have him back. He's not mine.*'

I thought, *really?* He was with a new girl who wasn't happy that he had a kid in-tow.

I ended up getting a council house with my son. The first night, other than my son's cot, I didn't have anything. But for once in my life, I had quiet.

To be able to sit down in the living room and there not to be shouting, it was something I'd never had.

Naturally, I was on the dole. I'd do what I could for my son, picking up things cheap. It didn't matter what I'd got so long as he had everything he needed.

There's not a lot you can do once you're stuck on income support with a baby. You can't get childcare 'til two, so I was screwed there. There wasn't much I could do other than wait it out until I could get free childcare and I could go work in a McDonald's or what have you. I'd have done it. Anything that I needed to do.

When I'd got my own house, I started to go out more and meet people down the car park. I had a friend come pick us up. My son in his car seat. I remember seeing this guy, Mark, working on a Mini in these burgundy overalls. Massive curly hair. He was there with two kids. I was in awe. I thought, *how nice that this dad's down here with his two kids. Why can't my son have a dad like that?*

A week later, we went up to the airport. There's a lane that goes up to the runway. We all used to park up and chat and watch planes coming in and out. Every time I'd be lighting a fag up, he'd be there with his lighter straight away. We were chatting for ages. He told me about his marriage and why it had broken down. I said that I understood. A week later, I persuaded him to go out with me. He came round, we sat on the sofa talking and talking and he never went home.

He worked at an engine reconditioning firm. He'd be doing anything from complete engine rebuilds to cylinder head-skimming, valve and piston ring replacements, all that kind of stuff.

His boss decided to retire. Mark panicked, '*This is all I know. It's all I've ever done.*'

We decided to borrow money off Mark's mum, buy his boss out and do engine reconditioning on a mobile basis. It was scary, because I'd never worked. I was like, *what do I do?* I had to learn on the job how to do invoices, how to book jobs in, how to speak to people in a professional manner.

A few people that knew Mark started telling other people that he'd gone mobile. Before we knew it, people were recommending us. We decided to get the business registered, get a website up and running, get onto Facebook and on the mechanic forums.

Four years after going mobile, we got our own workshop. People were asking if we could accommodate MOTs. So we had all the ground-work done in the garage, got permission to change the usage, got the MOT ramp and all the testing equipment. I had to do a manager's course, because I couldn't run an MOT place without doing it.

Mark then said, *'You need to go and get your MOT tester's licence as well.'*

'What? This wasn't part of the plan.'

I had a bit of mechanical knowledge. I used to help him do the head gaskets and engine services. Even when I was forty-weeks preg-nant, I was under the bonnet of a car, bump over the engine bay, putting cylinder heads back on.

On the course, it was me and six other lads. I got 96 per cent on the exam. I was pleased with that, because I'd left school with nothing, and I only knew what Mark had taught me over the years.

The garage has grown since then. It's busy.

The work is exhausting. We get phone calls in the middle of the night, *'Do you do recoveries?'*

'No.'

I've had to put my phone on silent.

Using my mobile number when we started out was the biggest mistake we made [she laughs].

I'm up at 6 a.m. to get the kids up and ready for school. I get to work at around 9 a.m. I'll go through what we need to do that day. We've got a self-employed mechanic and MOT tester who works with us, and another one that we employ.

I'll go through it with them, *'Right, this needs doing today. We've got this car coming towards the end of the week.'*

Then the MOTs will come in and we'll begin to do those.

You do the pre-checks: go round and make sure that the doors open and shut, make sure the oil and coolant levels aren't low, and that there's enough fuel.

We go online and log the vehicle's details.

We print out the inspection sheet, put the car on the inspection ramp, and you start your test.

Bonnet checks, interiors, check, seatbelts.

It's like hundreds of points.

The on-ramp points. Shaker plates. Turn plates. Steering. Suspension. Emissions tests.

The older cars struggle to meet the emissions tests, so we have to get them stonking hot. If I've got an old car, I know that if I just tested it once it'd fail, but if I persist with it, it'll pass. I'll be persistent. I'll take twenty minutes to do an emissions test, raising the revs, getting the catalytic converter really hot, and everything falls into place. All green.

I suffer with anxiety and that inspection ramp does not help in the slightest. Can you imagine someone as small as me with a Class 7 transit van above my head? I'm having to use the shakers. The whole ramp's shaking above my head. I'm waiting for the ramp to flatten me into the concrete. I can't get the fear out of my head.

Some MOTs take me an hour-and-twenty. But you can also have an MOT done in thirty minutes. Teslas, especially, there's plastic trays that cover the underneath of the car. You can't check brake lines or steering and suspension because they're behind a plastic panel. You just advise, '*Factory-fitted trims. Can't physically check*.'

I'm not comfortable with it. How can you check the safety of the vehicle if you can't see whether the brake lines are rotten?

During the tests, we've got a viewing camera so that customers can sit in the office and watch. And once I've finished and logged the MOT, I take the customer underneath the ramp and show them what I've advised. If there's a slight play on the steering, I'll show them. It puts their mind at rest.

I've cost myself thousands over the years because we've had customers come in and say, '*I want this doing. I've been told it needs this and this*.'

I'll put the car on the ramp, and I'll see that it's scrap and not worth spending the money on. I'll say to them, *'Look, if it was my car, I wouldn't put money into this.'*

I'd rather cost myself work by being honest than think, *great, I've got two grands' worth of work here.* You don't know if that person's got nothing. I've been there. I've had nothing.

When you've finished your test, you staple together your emissions test print out, roller brake test printout, your inspection sheet, and your pass/fail certificate. Then you file it.

Mark struggles with paperwork. I try to find his parts receipts, whatever I can, and give them to the accountant, but the accountant will say, *'We're missing like eight months of paperwork',* but I don't know what he's done with it. I just file what I've got.

When the time comes that we're audited, then I'll say, *'Just fine me if there's stuff missing. I can't give you what I don't have.'*

With running a garage, you have to have *ABC . . .* all the way to *Z* in place. I didn't know all this when I started.

I didn't even know that I had to have a fire risk assessment until last year when the fire service rang me, *'We're coming to do your fire risk assessment audit.'*

I was like, *oh shit.* Straight onto Amazon to buy fire extinguishers and blankets. I built a COSHH cupboard and shoved all the flammables in there. I got a checklist and went through it. When they came round for the assessment, I said, *'I won't lie to you. I didn't know I had to do this.'* They were laughing saying, *'This is amazing.'*

If I'm doing something wrong, don't belittle me or treat me like I'm stupid, just teach me and I'll work on it.

Being a mechanic is a very masculine job. If you're a woman in the motor trade, people just think you're a secretary. The amount of times people that don't know us have to come to the garage and walked straight past me, up to one of the lads.

'All right, boss, just want to pick your brains about something.'

I get phone calls, *'Can I speak to the MOT tester.'*

'Yes, she's speaking.'

'No, the mechanic.'

'Yes, speaking.'

'What, you're a mechanic?'

But I like that my job is different. One of our customers, her daughter's just left school, and she wants to be a mechanic because of me. You can't put a price on that.

I'm the only one in my family that works. My older brother's on the dole but works on the side, putting it in his pocket. I've reported him several times, but nothing ever comes of it.

I have to declare everything I own and pay tax on it. Why should the likes of him buy quad bikes and recovery trucks and go on all these holidays, when I can't do that? But yeah, I'm the only one who works. And I was the one everyone expected to just pop kids out and be on the dole.

I'm proud of myself. We're contributing to society. We're keeping people safe. We're providing for our family. We don't owe anybody anything.

I was stuck in a rut until I was given an opportunity. I took it and I was scared, and I've screwed it up a load of times, but I've got here.

CHAPTER FIFTEEN **BOSSWORK**

Headteacher of Pupil Referral Unit

restaurant manager

customer service manager

executive assistant

Headteacher of Pupil Referral Unit

(50s)

I do this job because this job has meaning for me. And the job has meaning for me because I had a really shit childhood. I came out of it with trauma and attachment issues, utterly lost.

I did 150,000 jobs. Garage forecourts, stacking shelves, a bricklayer's apprenticeship, working on construction sites, all sorts. My life seemed utterly meaningless.

There was an adult in my life who'd persuaded me to go to university. It didn't change anything. I carried on living a very chaotic lifestyle, but it did mean that I had my degree, and that when an opportunity came up to go into education, I could do it.

Ten years after I'd done my degree, someone said, *'Why don't you become a teacher?'*

I opened up my local newspaper and it said, *'Graduate Teacher Required'.*

I rang the school, went down the next week, and they gave me the job.

The young people that I enjoyed working with back then were those who were struggling to stay in mainstream education, because they didn't fit mainstream and mainstream didn't fit them.

One year we did an end of year assembly for Year 11. Three or four students came up to me and said, *'If it wasn't for you, we wouldn't have made it through'.*

It was very emotional, a powerful moment. I thought, *I want that every day.* And I got to thinking, *well, if I go and work with young people who've not been successful in mainstream, then I'll have that feeling every day.*

And how wrong I was [he laughs]. That was thirteen, fourteen years ago. But I do love my work. It gives meaning to my existence.

I left mainstream at Christmas and moved into a Pupil Referral Unit in January. It was a complete shock, because I went from being a head-of-year figure, walking into assemblies with three-hundred children, and I'd walk in and they'd just go quiet because *'It's sir.'*

From that situation, I started the new position, and I was called an *'Effing C'* twenty times a day.

I had to relearn how to engage with these young people. You have to build a relationship with them. They have to trust you. If you can do that, then you can start to lead them to the water.

Often the lives of these young people can be very chaotic. There are no structures, no routines. They're with us for about six-and-a-half hours a day. The other eighteen hours a day are spent out in society.

When they arrive in the mornings, we welcome them to the school. We say, *'It's good to have you here',* not *'How are you?'* because they might not be very well.

Then they come into the building and there's another welcoming team saying, *'We're really pleased you're here.'*

The young people then hand their phones in.

The next part of the routine is breakfast. If you were one of these young people, it'd be highly likely that you wouldn't have had any breakfast, so we're going to feed you and meet that basic need. The staff are going to sit down and eat with you.

These are gentle rules, societal norms, norms of sitting down to eat and being able to have conversations with people.

Following that, we go into what we call *coaching sessions*, which is like a form tutor group. For fifteen minutes we'll discuss current affairs and give assemblies. It puts you into a classroom, sitting down in chairs at a desk.

And at the end of that you go to period one, regulated and calm.

* * *

I myself have a very strict routine. I get up at 5 a.m., seven days a week.

I do a series of physiotherapy exercises, then Yoga Nidra. It's lying down yoga and it's the most spectacular thing. It's a highly meditative deep rest, but you remain conscious throughout. It's a glorious feeling when you finish.

Afterwards, I'll have breakfast, take the dog for a walk, put on my suit, make a cup of tea for myself and my wife. My son is usually downstairs, and I might join him for a bit of scrambled egg. And then I'm good. Everything's perfect. My family knows I love them. I know they love me.

I get in my car, and I'm centred. I listen to spa music. The drive is forty-five minutes of good thinking time and planning time.

I'll arrive in the office at 7.30 a.m. I'll walk into the office and say 'Alexa, play home spa music.'

I'll work for forty-five minutes, dealing with the few emails that have come in overnight and writing my list for both the senior leadership team briefing at 8.45 a.m. and the staff briefing at 9 a.m.

The young people start arriving at 9.15 a.m. onwards. Then during the day, I'm ticking things off this beautiful wall planner. It's staffing work, infrastructure work, budget work, HR issues, occasionally teaching.

I try to leave here at 5 p.m., which means I get time to sit down and eat with the family. If I need to work after dinner, my wife understands. I try not to do too much at the weekend, but I get up at 5 a.m. on Saturday and Sunday morning so I can do two hours of work on both of those days.

As a head, you can feel that you don't have the depth of personal relationships that you used to have as a classroom teacher. I didn't come into education to manage staff. But I'm still out and about a lot. I make sure I'm there to greet the children in the morning, and I can still feel when a school is just *pulsing*.

You can feel it in the staffroom. You can hear it in the buzz of conversations. You can see it in the young people being engaged in their work, when you walk into a classroom, and you hear absolute silence from young people who never used to be able to do that.

It's an atmosphere in the building and in the people. It's like when you walk into a church and you feel a certain way. I'm getting goosebumps just talking about it . . .

— *When do you feel most alive at work?*

When someone says, '*Thank you.*'

— *How often does that happen?*

Never. But if someone says to you as a head, '*That was a good decision.*' That's what it's all about. I've made a difference.

We have different criteria for success here. If someone's attendance is 10 per cent when they come to us and 50 per cent when they leave, that's awful attendance, but it's multiple times better than it was.

Or if someone can have conversations without swearing when they couldn't before, that's a massive success. They can now be part of a much wider society than they could before.

But we only have them until they're sixteen. Then they have to go out into the big wide world. And half of the children that leave Pupil Referral Units fall out of their placements. If we got 100 per cent of our young people into college, 50 per cent would drop out. It's a horrific situation.

— *What's changed over the course of your career?*

There is a growing understanding in education that children aren't just naughty. There's a rationale behind the behaviour, and even if you can't see what that rationale is, it's still there.

I don't think children have changed over the course of my career. Children are children. But the environment into which they're born has changed. There are significant parts of our country where things have gotten worse. Take criminal exploitation. We have people in our society who deliberately target young people to exploit them criminally and even worse. It is an absolute moral outrage. And that did not happen a generation ago to the extent that it's happening now. It is constant for us. Every day.

I also think a lot more is asked of schools and teachers than it ever used to be.

We have young people here who don't have clothes and don't have food to eat. You can't say, '*I can't help you*', so you have to go beyond what you're funded for, towards social care. For example, we're building a clothing storehouse, so that the young people have a pair of shoes they can wear to school, a winter coat, hygiene products. That's the level of need we've got to meet. It's got nothing to do with teaching you about World War Two, but, without it, how can you learn?

Pupil Referral Units are beacons, absolute beacons. We are part of the frontline along with other public servants, all fighting the good fight.

But there are some young people we can't reach, young people who are extremely vulnerable, many of them engaged in criminal activities.

It's awful. You fight really hard, but sometimes the damage has been done and the influences around them are too great for you to overcome in the short window of time you have.

I have a former pupil in jail at the minute. He was a lovely lad, but very troubled. I remember I went for a walk with him and his mum down by the river. We had a proper conversation, and everyone was crying. I thought, *maybe we'll get somewhere*. But it wasn't enough. The negative influences around him were too great for him to extricate himself. He was a really good lad, but he's not coming out of prison for a long time, and if he comes out, he'll probably go back in again. And that's a tragedy.

Do I stay up at night worrying about what he's done? No.

Does he come to mind every now and again? Yes, he does. And I think I could still do more for him.

I should probably go and see him in prison. I haven't done that. I should probably do that . . .

Teaching is genuinely exhausting. It's a very hard gig. I've worked on building sites and that's physically exhausting, but there's a mental fatigue in teaching. You're not just working with your mind, you're also working with your heart. You give up yourself to the role and that drains a person.

Through all of this, my routines are my sea wall. Because I'd gotten myself into so much trouble in my twenties, I had to get myself sorted out. I ended up doing a twelve-step programme. It made a difference. It gives you a routine, a structure. Then and now the routines keep the waves out. It takes a really big swell to come over the top and overwhelm my week.

– *What are those swells?*

At the moment, unless someone gives me a lot of money in the next twenty-four hours, we're looking at large-scale redundancies. It's a huge financial crisis. I came into this school and on the surface there was a surplus. This was not true at all. The operating model of the school may not survive.

I wouldn't be here if I wasn't the right person to do this job.

I'm here because I have the skills and abilities to solve this difficult problem.

We will work our way through it.

Restaurant manager

(30s)

Hungary was under communism up until the Russian collapse in 1989. My parents grew up in that regime, and they say it takes three generations for imprinted habits to die out.

When I was a kid, my parents were in their late twenties – young guys, really.

In the nineties there was this false sense of freedom for them. You were allowed to do whatever you wanted, but the freedom was false. There was an inner gate in their minds. A gate that only lets out as much as you know you should let out, always looking behind your back; because this was how communism was.

And I've always had this struggle with freedom my whole life. There's a desire in me to work hard to fulfil those things that society wants me to do. And there's a desire in me to just fuck off and live off-grid. I've never put that straight in my head. I still don't know what I'm doing.

The reason I stayed in hospitality was because I couldn't figure out for shit what I wanted. I was good at it. I am good at it, and I enjoy it, but I've never really known what to do.

– Why did you decide to leave Hungary and come to the UK?

My ex-boyfriend's brother worked in the Scillies.

He said, '*Why don't you just come out for a summer to learn a bit of English and get some money*.'

Looking back, the pay wasn't that great, but it was great compared to Hungarian wages, let alone with the accommodation, the food – easy life!

We signed a seasonal contract. My ex was washing dishes, and I was in housekeeping. Four years went by, and I never left.

I came to my first manager role when I was twenty-five. I applied for the head housekeeper position, and he called me in the office and said, '*Have you thought of the head waitress position?*'

I was doing waitressing part time at this point.

I said, '*This is not the position I applied for.*'

'*No, but we think you can do it.*'

And he put that faith in me.

At that point loads of my colleagues were older than me. They'd been there since the building was built, two-hundred years' old and working in the same job as waiters and waitresses. Yet they chose me. I had ambition. They had no ambition.

I struggled. I tried to implement new things, but I lost authority. I tried to befriend my colleagues. I tried to take back control. But all these old people – old as in *mindset* – they didn't want to change, and if you don't have the help from senior management, then you've lost.

Looking back, the main power was still with the guy above me. I was his puppet, the hated one.

I then broke up with my boyfriend, and I thought, *okay, let's go to the mainland*. Since then, I've worked in nearly all the places around here.

I've made this mistake again and again: when you're doing well, they make you a manager, and it's the greatest scam I've ever seen in hospitality.

Let's say you're on £10 an hour as a supervisor. Next week, you're made a manager because you're doing *A Great Job*.

You are expected to arrive early, leave last, fill in the gaps in the rota when your staff are ill.

Your phone is going to be ringing,
'*It's your shift.*'
'*It's your responsibility.*'
'*Rota.*'
'*Orders.*'
'*Rota.*'
'*Orders.*'
And they'll offer you a salary based on £10 an hour with a forty-five-hour working week. You'll see the number written down,
'*£22,000.*'
You think, *that's pretty good.*

As a number it looks a lot better than the £10 an hour or whatever wage you were on.

But if you break it down, you're going to end up coming home with £6.50 an hour, because you're going to work sixty hours a week and no one's going to pay you for the extra.

A couple of years down the line, the managers realize, *dude, they robbed me – daylight robbery! – I'm working sixty hours a week but no one's paying me because I'm not paid hourly any more.*

If you're smart enough, you turn it down and stay as a supervisor, or you ask for more money.

I've been in places where people come back after they were made manager somewhere.

Screwed-with, burnt-out people.

They'd quit or had a break and they come back as waiters, waitresses with no responsibility, nothing . . .

But it's the whole industry. You don't get appreciation.

There's a big demand for workforce at the moment. Maybe that will make the hospitality industry pay more. It's demanding, hard work – physical work as well. The wages are low, the hours are bad. There's no life in it.

During lockdown, people went to deliver for Tesco, and they realized that – for the same money, if not more – they could pick and choose what shifts they want to work, get double money on the weekends, do nine-to-five, see their partner and kids. When they realized all that, they never went back to hospitality. I don't blame them.

I think this would be a good time for hospitality to realize that we need to pay these fuckers if we want them to stay. We need to not look at hospitality as a summer job or an '*I don't know what to do*' job. We need to make it a profession.

Do you know how many times I'm asked, '*So when are you going to get a real job?*'

'*Good one, mate!*'

I once did some management training, and they gave us these questionnaires. *What sort of manager are you?*

I was the full-on dictatorship type. That type's more present in a military setting, where there's someone who says the command and you do it, no questions asked, because it needs to be done. There's no, '*What do you think, Private Ryan, shall we just bomb those people? Or shall we just ask them why they're coming towards us with those guns?*'

No, there's no time for that.

Let's say that we're in a cafe as busy as the one we're sitting in.

People are waiting at the door. But look, the table behind me is empty and needs to be cleared and reset for the next people coming in. If you don't see it yourself – and it is your job as a waitress to see it yourself – and act on it straight away, I'm going to tell you, '*This is what you need to do.*'

I'm not putting it up for a discussion. No huffing and puffing, no eye rolling, just go and do it. If I had time, I'd do it myself. But you're on your phone. You're doing nothing. You're talking about your Saturday night with the other girls. *No, go and do it.*

My life is boring. I *do* want to hear what these twenty-somethings are doing on their Saturday night. *Hell yeah fill me in.* But not during service.

Service is literally two hours. Shut the hell up and do the job. After that, we all sit down for a beer. We all chat. *Two bloody hours.* There are quieter spells when you can polish cutlery and have a good chinwag but not when there is demand.

I've heard from people that I'm blunt or straight-up rude. It really hurt me, because I am not rude, no way. Blunt, maybe. But I'm not nasty.

It really, really hurt me. And I was digging inside myself to find the root of that for a very long time. My accent doesn't help. It sounds a lot harsher than I intend it to be.

Some people say, '*Oh wow, you're so angry.*'

I'm not angry. If I'm talking passionately, intensely about something, people do interpret it as anger. They just think I'm just being a dick.

Men are a lot easier to crack. If you're nicey nicey to a man, and you just brush their egos, they'll do anything you want. This is how I've done it.

I'm not gonna lie, I can make them work.

I say, '*Look at you, looking good today.*'

And look who dives into the salad straight away.

This is what you do when you work front of house, you read people.

The girls are tougher. You can't do this trick on them. If you say, '*Just been to the hairdressers?*'

'*Yeah, so?*'

The jealousy, all this emotional stuff . . . I've found it a lot harder with women.

Where I grew up, if you wanted money, you worked hard, you shut the fuck up, you did what you were told, and that's it. You power through life with this mentality.

It's what I wanted from my employees. Growing up and having this imprinted in you, it's a very difficult thing to let go of, to find different approaches for people. It took a lot of learning to figure out that not everyone is *shut-up-and-do-it.*

I've changed now.

* * *

After so long in hospitality, I wanted a good work–life balance and I wish people in hospitality could have what I have.

We're a small restaurant. It's the two of us, the chef (who is also the owner) and myself.

– What's your relationship with the chef like?

I had a meal at his restaurant, and I was not satisfied with the service. I thought, *it's such a small place, it could be so good.*

I texted him, '*Can I pop in for a coffee.*'

I said, '*Do you have a restaurant manager here?*'

'*I've got two staff and I cannot afford a restaurant manager.*'

I said, '*Come onnn.*'

A couple of days later, he got back to me and said, '*Yeah okay let's give it a go.*'

In all honesty, neither of us had the greatest of reputations. Everyone told me not to work with him. Loads of people told him not to work with me.

It's because we are very similar. I'm from Eastern Europe. He's Scottish. Work has to be done. And there are no excuses. It has to be done.

It's a demanding service. There is no room for you being away with the fairies. And me as a restaurant manager, I'm demanding. Him as a head chef, he demands. When we started to work together, it was a great click. Because it's the two of us, there's nothing lost in communication.

– Talk me through service.

We do fourteen covers max, all in one sitting.

I go in at 5 p.m. I lay the tables. I'd normally have cleaned everything the night before. Then I finish polishing the cutlery. I do a little run around to check if my wine's up from the store. We've got a set menu with wine pairings, so I have to see if all those wines are ready to go – check the temperature – check that the fridge is working.

I then make myself a coffee and go through emails.

Service starts at 7 p.m. People start to arrive. They get seated, they get the menu presented, and they choose their drinks. At the moment, it's four courses. Each course, the chef goes out and talks about the food, what he does and why he does what he does.

Then we start the evening. The customers are getting food, I'm getting new cutlery and matching the wines with each course. And when they're all done, and the puddings are cleared, they can stay around and have little chit chats, coffees, or another drink.

What we do now is because of the pandemic.

Before the pandemic, people arrived every half hour. It was still a set menu, but because of the different start times everyone was on different courses. I was also going to the tables and telling them about the menu dish by dish. This meant that it was a longer service, often 'til midnight. But it was like a well-oiled machine. We had a guy in the kitchen who did the washing up, and I had a girl who helped run the service.

When we had to space out tables because of social distancing, we had to get rid of half of the tables. After we had reduced the numbers, we ran it as we used to for the first few nights. But the first table were sitting on their own, with no atmosphere whatsoever. And catering for fourteen people over the course of six hours, it wasn't enough to cover the cost of the utility bills.

I said, '*Why don't we try to get them all in the at the same time, like a supper club?*'

I then said to the chef, '*What if you go out and talk about your dishes?*'

Chefs, they hide in the kitchen for good reason. They don't like the psyche of *Ta Da!*

I said '*Go, they'll love it.*'

As he started to talk to people – he's passionate, he's amazing – people started to get it. *This is great!* We call the restaurant a little theatre.

We started charging people when they booked. It's a set menu, so we advertise it now as a ticket for the evening, like a concert ticket.

If you need to cancel, that's all right, you sell your ticket – as you would with a concert ticket for Metallica. Because you can't be ringing up James Hatfield saying *'sorry, I can't come to your gig'.*

No, you sell it to your mate or on the internet.

Covid forced us to think outside the box. It's a shorter service for the chef. He's got kids and now he's got time to be with the family.

Hospitality is normally so demanding. You've got no life, no life. We are lucky that we've found a way.

Customer service manager

(50s)

I've worked for my company for twenty-four years.

I studied electrical engineering. I went to work for a company of fifteen people that did design work. They were writing software that helped you design the wiring in cars. The first day I had to build my own desk. That gives you an idea of how small the company was.

I started doing customer support, helping customers who were having problems using the software. They would come to us and ask, *How do I stop the software from choosing the wrong terminals inside the wire connector? How can I make it so that it puts the right amount of tape on the wiring harness? How can I calculate the length of copper used?* If you put seventy-eight kilograms of copper into a vehicle for its wiring and you're able to reduce that by 5 per cent, that's a massive difference for the hundred-thousand vehicles produced a year, a major saving. Our software helps with that.

I used to look at our customer's wiring designs and say, '*Why are you routing the wire from the dashboard over the headliner into the boot of the vehicle? Why don't you drop it down along the passenger side of the vehicle and then into the boot? You'd save half a metre of copper wire.*'

We were bought out by a larger company that we'd been taking market share from. When we moved over to them, it was a big culture shock. We'd gone from being quite penny-pinching and self-sufficient to flying everywhere. I went travelling all over the world.

I enjoyed it, but I did miss some of the growing up that my kids did. That was a big . . . not a mistake, because the kids wouldn't have half the stuff they have now if it wasn't for me doing that, but I probably would have changed that if I could.

One of my work colleagues, when she was younger, she used to get up in the morning, feed the kids, take them to nursery, leave them at nursery, go pick them up when she'd finished work, feed them, bath them, put them to bed, and she'd never get to do anything with them but that. I thought, *this is crazy*. But I couldn't say anything, because I was in flippin' Detroit with teams designing vehicles while my wife was doing all the housework and taking them to see sheep in the field.

A few years later, the larger company that bought us out was bought out by a huge corporation. We went from 4,500 people to 30,000. There are five of us still left from the original company. There were more but they've retired.

One of them said, *'I'm retiring because I know that we'll be on the fourth generation of the software. My knowledge isn't great enough any more to allow it to progress.'*

And I'm getting to that stage as well. We're moving to cloud-based systems. My knowledge isn't there. I can understand the tool, but I can't do the infrastructure. I'd be the wrong person to lead in this area. We have to bring people in to make the tool go forward.

I still have pride in the tool. Even now, it's changed so much from when it was originally designed, but I still have pride in it. It solves the same problem: electronics in cars.

I would quite happily battle with a customer and say, *'No, you're wrong. The software isn't wrong. There's logic behind it.'*

A lot of people would just back down but I will defend that product. I've had to defend it in court, and I would defend that product over anything, because I know what it's capable of doing. I know what cost savings it's capable of producing.

It's the love of the product that's kept me here. It's a comfort blanket. And I know that when we move over to cloud-based software I will be out of my comfort zone.

I do still help customers with their design work, and at times I say, '*Why are you doing that? Everybody does that. Why not change the process?*'

Cars now they're practically all the same, just different shells. A Volkswagen Sharan is the same vehicle as a Ford Galaxy. Skoda, VW, Audi, they're all the same company with the same vehicles for all three, but under different names.

And this is because, if you look at most companies now, they struggle to find true design engineers, people who have the ability to think outside the box and think, *what about if I did that?*

For instance, my son is doing mechanical engineering.

I asked him, '*Where do you see yourself in three or four years?*'

One of the first things he came back with was '*The banking industry.*'

'*Why the hell are you doing a degree in mechanical engineering?*'

'*In finance: one, the money's better; and two, they'll snatch up mechanical and electrical engineers.*'

I said, '*Why not go and work for British nuclear fuels or whatever they're called nowadays, or for BAE designing dreadnought submarines and the new generation of Typhoons.*'

And he says, '*Yeah, but is it gonna be exciting?*'

Do you see what I mean? We're losing the culture of engineering design.

– What does tomorrow look like?

Tomorrow, I'll have my first meeting at eight o'clock in the morning with the Japanese support team to discuss issues with a customer.

At nine o'clock, I have a meeting with our development team to discuss which defects should be addressed in our next service pack.

At ten o'clock, I have a meeting with another team to discuss another area of defects that should be addressed in another service pack.

At 10.30 a.m., I have a meeting to discuss how we can improve the team and sort out some process issues.

Then I've got nothing until 3 p.m. when my US team come online, and I've then got three one-to-ones.

Then I have a mini team meeting with five of my team who deal with high-value customers.

My final meeting is with a customer at six o'clock to discuss how we can deploy staff internally.

I spend more of my time in meetings than doing work.

Executive assistant

(50s)

I blagged my way into my first PA job. It was to be the PA for a quality control director at a seatbelt manufacturing firm. I hadn't studied business skills at school, and I couldn't copy type then, but I felt very confident, and I said to the interviewer, '*Yep, I can do this, I can do that. No problem*.'

Afterwards, I thought, *oh my gosh, what have I done?* They had no idea that I'd blagged my way in until I told my boss when I left a couple of years later.

He said, '*Well, you do a good blag*.'

Later on in my career, I worked for a fast-food logistics company. At first, I worked for one of the vice-presidents. I got involved in everything he did. I took all his dictation when he was responding to emails. I did all his diary management, organizing and attending high-level meetings and appointments. There was nothing going on in the business that I wasn't aware of.

Towards the end of my time there, I worked for someone who was very difficult to work with.

He'd never had a PA before. He didn't like the feeling of me knowing where he was and what he was doing. But when you're a PA it's your job to know where your boss is, to know what he's doing, to know when he's free.

The big bosses in the States would call, wanting him. They'd ask what he was doing and how they could reach him, but I never knew from one day to the next where he was.

He left this trail of destruction behind him.

People would approach me, '*Steve didn't turn up for the meeting; do you know where is?*'

I'd say, '*I know where he should be. Let me see if I can get a hold of him for you.*'

Or they'd say, '*He cancelled this meeting but it needs to go ahead.*'

'*I wasn't aware he'd cancelled that, sorry. Let me look into it.*'

I was having to pick up everything, because he wouldn't communicate.

All he needed to do was to talk to me and say, '*Right, this is what I need to do today.*'

I got the sense that he just didn't want me knowing where he was or what he was doing. Maybe he found me to be an irritant. The relationship was difficult.

I'd say to him, '*Look, let me help you. You do your job and leave your diary to me.*'

And he'd say, '*I know I'm difficult to work for because I shoot from the hip, so if I'm rude, don't ever take anything I say to heart.*'

'*I need communication from you. For me to make you shine, you need to let me do my job.*'

'*Yeah okay, I'll try.*'

But he just couldn't do it. He wouldn't let me get close to him. With my previous bosses, I'd had access to all their emails, everything. I said to him at the start, '*You don't have to give me access, but it really helps me to know what's going on.*' He was reluctant to do that.

At this time, I was responsible for organizing the visits of global vice-presidents to UK distribution centres. From the minute their jet landed, I would look after them, all of their meetings, all of their meals, all of their transport – everything.

Once, a vice-president from the US wanted to come over and visit a distribution centre on a bank holiday, a busy time for us. I pushed back a couple of times and mentioned it to one of the UK directors, who also tried to move the visit, but the American VP insisted.

So I contacted the manager of the distribution centre, who

happened to be my boss's daughter and I said to her, *'We've got this VP coming from the States. I know it's a busy time, but can she spend some time with your team?'*

She said, *'That's absolutely fine.'*

My boss asked if I had everything in hand with the visit. I was like, *'Nothing to report. It's all in hand.'* But I sent him the itinerary and he lost it.

'Why have you organized a visit on a bank holiday? That's totally incompetent. And why have you tried to pull the wool over my eyes?'

And it went on. His tone was very rude. I'd never experienced this. I was doing my job, the job I'd done for ten years to everybody's satisfaction.

I was fuming. I shared it with one of the PAs who I shared an office with.

She said, *'Wow, that is well out of order. What's he on about?'*

I emailed him back in a very polite way: *'I've think we've got a miscommunication here. I provided all this information to you. And I checked with the teams, who were all happy.'*

He didn't respond for a while.

I went back to him again, *'To be honest, nobody has ever questioned my integrity my whole career. I'm not going to tolerate that now. I'd like to have a face-to-face meeting with you to discuss this so we can clear the air.'*

He replied saying, *'Oh no, it's all fine.'*

He never discussed it with me in-person. He never apologized for being rude. He never said anything more about it.

On his last day at the company, he came up to me and said, *'I'm really sorry for being so difficult to work for.'*

But I'd lost my respect for him by then. I think he was out of his depth. He'd been promoted into this role, but he wasn't ready. He would never accept that he was in the wrong. He would never apologize. It was the only time in my career that I've had any issue with anyone.

When I left that company, I remember reposting something on

LinkedIn about '*how best to use your PA*'. It was well-written, all about how it should be a real partnership. Every time I read it, I thought of him.

After I posted it, he liked it. That made me laugh. I thought, *that was about you!*

At the moment, I'm working as a PA to the CEO of a private hospital. He's very respectful and we're very open with each other. I know exactly where he is, what he's doing, and what he wants.

I can read him.

He said to me once, '*You know exactly what I need before I ask. Nobody has ever been able to do that before*'.

I have access to his diary, and everything is organized via me. He doesn't touch anything at all in his calendar. I'm also his eyes and ears, so I'll go around getting feedback from the various teams, *what's going on where, who's not happy with what*. And I'll share that information with him without saying who's said what.

He involves me in everything, and it makes me feel alive. He'll ask my opinion and often he'll take my advice. Though he'll never say in front of people, '*My assistant suggested this*'.

Instead, he'll just say, '*So I've decided to this*', and I'll think, *okay, he's taken on board what I've said*.

– *Does it bother you that it's his glory?*

Not at all. I get paid well. I get overtime.

And I know that he appreciates me so much. At staff forums, he'll regularly say of me, '*She's the boss*'.

It makes me feel good, right? He needs me and he can't do without me.

It's also my job to make him shine, to make him look like the most organized person in the room. For example, I'll give him prompts when we have online or hybrid meetings. At a staff forum the other day, I was messaging my boss on Teams things like, '*Don't forget to do a leaving message for Sue*'.

I'll see his head move just towards the message on the screen and he'll say, '*And the last thing I was going to say was about Sue . . .*'

It doesn't look obvious at all. He keeps so cool when he does it. One of my colleagues was sitting next to me at the meeting and she said, '*This is hilarious. Now I know how he works!*'

We trust each other. That's the important thing. We trust each other.

Lots of companies furloughed or sacked their PAs during the pandemic. They said, '*We don't need them any more. We're going to do our own admin.*'

There was a perception that PAs just made coffee for visitors and did a bit of typing. But the pandemic was a wake-up call. People have found that they are now doing so much more work themselves – diary management, expenses, travel.

Sacking the PAs was a classic example of companies not knowing what a job involves. How can you ever know what my job involves unless you do it?

CHAPTER SIXTEEN **PAPERWORK**

Job Centre work coach

IT director

minister

local government worker

Job Centre work coach

(50s)

My working life began in 1981 after I left school. I wanted to get into engineering, but at that time there was a recession. It was difficult.

I applied for a job in the Civil Service, and I was offered a job in the Manpower Services Commission.

It was a steady job working on something called the Community Programme. The government paid long-term unemployed people a trade union wage to do real work.

That scheme fell away, and it was replaced by schemes that gave you your benefits plus an extra £10 for being part of a job training scheme. These schemes became known as Employment Training, ET, or *'Extra Tenner'* as far as the punters were concerned.

One of the managers there said, *'If you want to get on in the Civil Service, the best course of action would be for you to go and work out in the field in a job centre.'*

So I applied for a transfer and spent many years at various Job Centres around the North East.

Out of the blue, I once got an opportunity to become a job club leader. It's the job that I've enjoyed doing the most in my career.

We would run training and coaching sessions for jobseekers. Anything from *how to write a letter* to *how to do well at a job interview*. We'd spend all morning and afternoon with people. You really got to know them. It was unlike being a benefits claims adviser, where there's always an element of mistrust from the other side of your desk.

You shared in their triumphs and disappointments. Sometimes

you'd see grown men cry, men who'd had their hopes pinned on getting a job, who'd thought they'd done well in an interview, and who'd then get a rejection letter. You'd pick them up and put your arm around them.

Eventually, the job clubs got contracted out to the private sector and I ended up going back to the benefits office environment again.

When Labour got into government in 1997, I took on a role as a New Deal adviser for the over twenty-fives.[12] The government spent most of the money trying to help eighteen-to twenty-four-year-olds. The over twenty-fives were a bit of an afterthought, so there wasn't a lot of money, but I was given carte blanche to go out and try things.

We had a subsidy of about £1,500 a month that we could offer employers who took on a jobseeker. And with this subsidy, I helped a lot of people into work who'd either never worked at all, or who'd been long-term out of work.

For instance, one man in his late twenties – David I think his name was – not only did he have no work experience, but he was absolutely filthy. I drove him to one of the training providers and there he made significant improvements in his appearance and personal hygiene. I wouldn't say he was immaculate, but he got to the level where he was employable. He was offered work by a fruit and vegetable supplier.

It's very rewarding to know that you've made a difference in somebody's life.

It's a moving thing.

At one Job Centre I worked at, I had a manager who was a dreadful man. I felt like he was trying to impede my career. If something went wrong, he would be quite abusive to me. He burdened me with extra work. It didn't really suit me to be working late when I had a wife and two young children.

12 Labour's 'New Deal' was a collection of policies intended to reduce youth unemployment.

I tried to apply for a promotion and he told me that he didn't think I was suited to it. Then, when I got a transfer to a different Job Centre, he told my new manager that he and I had almost come to blows. It was a pack of lies. He was trying to poison the well. I raised it with the area manager and made a formal complaint, which was upheld.

The relationship with my new boss became strained. She was intimidated by my old manager. My home life also became difficult because of the strain that all this put on my marriage.

I started to suffer from depression. My marriage eventually broke down and I became estranged from my children.

It was hard for me to do my job. I was working as an employment counsellor where you spend your time taking on other people's problems.

I had an extended period off work, and I felt myself sliding into a bit of an oblivion. After I got back, I was suffering badly with anxiety, I wasn't sleeping, and I was taking all sorts of medication.

As it happened, one of the managers took an interest in me and helped me get my life back on track. She put me onto a pilot scheme at the Job Centre called *Route Back*. It was for people who'd been absent from work for a long time. There were three groups in the pilot. One group got all the help. The second got some of the help. And the third was a control group that got no help at all.

Happily, I ended up in the group that got all of the help. The main thing I got from it was cognitive behavioural therapy. It helped me to get my head around why I was depressed.

– It must have been strange to be taking part in one of these programmes having spent twenty years delivering them.

Well, it taught me a great deal. You're never immune to life's pressures. I'm now very aware of this when I deal with people at the Job Centre; I see people who are broken, and I have real empathy for them.

But my career stalled at this time and since then I've never really pushed myself to succeed.

I'm pretty sure I could have done a job in a higher grade. But I shied away. I was conscious of what I'd been through. I was estranged from the children and the Child Support Agency (CSA) were making my life difficult. They would try to moralize with me, '*You must pay for your children*', without understanding the complexity of the situation. I had money that would have covered child support payments tied up in endowment policies, but my ex-wife took two years to sign them over to me.

I was struggling to get by. Eventually, my case got transferred to a different CSA office and they were much more reasonable.

It becomes very hard to motivate yourself at work when the very organization that you work for, the Department for Work and Pensions, is making your life difficult.[13] And so I coasted for a good period of time.

I can understand why the customers at the Job Centre feel so disenchanted with government departments.

I'm a work coach at the moment, and I'm not particularly enamoured with the job.

In the years gone by, when I was a job leader, I felt like I was making a difference to people's lives. Going back to the days of the New Deal, I was left to get on with it. '*Here's the guidance, read it, get on with it.*'

Now, I feel like a box ticker.

We're given insufficient time to interview people. We have ten-minute appointments. And because we're at a temporary site, you have to pay people travel expenses to come to us. It takes ten minutes to copy their travel tickets, to fill in the reimbursement paperwork, and to set up a payment on the system.

After you've finished that, you then outline the agenda for the

13 The Child Support Agency exists within the Department of Work and Pensions.

appointment. And when that's done, there's no time left to look at job vacancies or opportunities.

Ten minutes isn't enough.

There's also a *failure to attend* process, where we have to send out a message to someone that doesn't turn up for a mandatory appointment. I should just be able to click a button on the system that sends a message to the customer saying, '*You didn't attend your appointment. We notified you of the appointment on this date. Will you please let us know why you didn't attend.*'

But no, I've got to cut and paste the information, populate a form, and then manually send it to the customer. You can easily spend half an hour doing this, which stops you preparing for the next day. The IT we use is not fit for purpose.

There are other things that never seem to get factored into the job. Replying to messages on the IT system from customers who aren't happy about something. Re-arranging appointments for customers who can't attend. Customers who've run out of money and need a food parcel delivered.

At one time, we were given discretion to say, '*Right, this person is job-ready. They can be left to get on with it without us having to see them and challenge them.*'

Now, we have to do weekly appointments with customers who are in the first thirty weeks of unemployment. It's a one-size-fits-all process. If we weren't having to see these people who don't need us, we'd be able to give more help to those that do need it. There's no logic to it.

We don't do what we used to do in terms of training or adding real value to people's lives. Now, DWP is more or less a gateway organization, where any training is delivered by private sector organizations.

When I joined the Manpower Services Commission, they used to run skill centres, huge buildings where you could go and learn how to become a bricklayer, an electrician, a plumber. Over the years all of that has been hived off to the private sector and it hasn't really been done with the same level of quality or investment.

If they put me in charge of DWP, I'd sack the board and bang their heads together. They have no idea what goes on at the coalface. They keep adding and adding and adding to the processes that we have to include in the interviews with jobseekers. But the interviews have to stay at ten minutes.

You can't do it. You can't get a quart in a pint pot. It just doesn't happen.

This micromanagement, this duplication of work, it's entirely unrewarding. I've lost a lot of job satisfaction . . .

I'm painting quite a grim picture, aren't I?

I intend to retire at fifty-nine. I'm within forty-eight weeks of retiring.

– Do you regret not having had a career in engineering?

It would probably have been more lucrative, and I probably would have been better suited to it. But having said that, I went through a very difficult period in my life, and I spent a long period coasting in my job, not doing it with that bit of extra pizzazz, all of which was a reflection of my mental state at the time.

If I was in another career, I could have been out of work for a very long time, and I don't know how I would have coped with that.

I could have left DWP when I was down, but I knew that I wasn't right mentally, and I would have always worried that I wouldn't get through a probationary period. Yes, you could argue that the job has contributed to the pressures that caused me to be depressed, but it's also helped me through those times.

Despite all this, I do think work is rewarding. We want satisfaction and adequate financial reward, and we want to feel valued. That's the essence of it.

IT director

(40s)

My dad is one of seven and his dad was one of thirteen. They came from the Fens. My dad has always regretted the fact that he never got a higher education when he was younger.

He always told me and my brother as we were growing up, '*Work hard at school and the rest of life will be easier. You'll be a pencil pusher rather than digging holes and ditches in the road*.'

I'm the director of IT at a company that does clinical trials on behalf of clinical research organizations. The company has exploded in the last few years because of the pandemic. We expected to recruit fifty people in 2020, and we recruited one-hundred-and-fifty.

A lot of my time is spent responding to messages in Microsoft Teams, in Outlook, in Jira, in Salesforce, in SAP concur, and most of the rest of the time is spent in meetings.

We seem to spend an inordinate amount of time discussing how we're going to do things and then re-discussing, re-discussing, and re-discussing, before we say, '*Okay, we're going to do that*.'

One of the first things I found when I joined this company was that everything ended up being escalated to the boss.

'*Oh, I can't answer that, let me ask my boss . . . Oh, I can't answer that, let me ask my boss*.'

And up it goes, up and up and up.

Eventually, an answer comes down the chain but by that point we've wasted so much time. If we understand what the problem is, we should start making changes immediately rather than waiting for approvals of approvals and reviews of reviews.

I was just on a project call. Yet again the dates for the project have slipped. We're now delivering the project in Q3 of this year, because they've changed the scope again.

It's like, *come on! Why are we changing the scope again?* Let's deliver to the original scope and then we can extend it with another project afterwards. It's annoying that we can't start fixing things without waiting for people to agree that we can fix them.

It's so much easier to work through problems when you're all in the same room together.

Six months ago, a support ticket came in and got escalated up to me. I was in the office and a couple of other people were around.

I got up from my desk and went and had a chat with one person, *'Can you do this?'*

I then had a chat with someone else, *'Would it be all right if we did this? Are you happy with that?'*

'Right. Let's do it.'

We fixed the problem in about ten minutes. The adrenaline of racing from one person's desk to another, it gave me a real buzz. We talked about it afterwards and I said that it would have taken us twice long just to set up an initial call. You ping someone on Teams,

'Are you free?'

You ping someone else,

'Can we have a call?'

You can end spending an hour just talking.

Those times when it works quickly are few and far between.

Minister

(50s)

I was born and raised in a staunch loyalist, paramilitary community. I was sent to a Protestant Sunday School from about five years old where I was taught Bible stories that have always stayed with me. But – do you know? – I always found the church service boring.

A couple of times, I thought to myself, *what a brilliant job it'd be to be that man up there at the pulpit, because he only works one day a week and gets paid for it.*

When I was around the age of twenty-four, I went to something called *The Walk of a Thousand Men.* It was a group of men who evangelized the gospel. Some of these men were former Hell's Angels, some had been in jail for murder. They were giving their various testimonies of how they came to faith in Jesus Christ, and something struck me that night. All I can say is that I made a decision to follow Christ. I wanted to be like him in character and I wanted to be a disciple.

I had to let go of various habits and I had to let go of good friends. I could never have walked as a Christian while running with them. It was painful, but I had to come away from them or else I would still have been in the nightclubs – at the time we were into the rave scene, with its various temptations.

Coming up into my thirties, I had gotten involved in prayer ministry and I had been asked to take leadership positions in my church. I had become an electrician by trade, and I was on a good salary as a technical sales engineer. I had a company car and a pension. I believed the Lord had blessed me. But the only way I can describe it, Charlie, is that I felt a holy discontent. There was something missing: you're working, you're making money, you're providing, but there was a lack of fulfilment.

I ended up talking it through with my minister. I said, *'Look, have I sinned somewhere and not confessed?'*

After several conversations, he said to me, *'It may be that you're being called to the ministry.'*

I laughed and said, *'No way.'*

There was about a year and a half of this discontent, where I felt that God had given me gifts that I wasn't fully exercising because I wasn't in a position to do so, gifts of teaching and preaching.

It got to the point where the unrest within me got so bad that I remember putting my hands up and saying, *'Lord, if this is what you want for me, you've got me. I'm going to go for it, and if a door opens, a door opens.'*

The doors seemed to open. I was ordained. I met my wife at seminary college. She's an ordained minister too.

I remember the day I left my job to go to college. I walked out with one of those printing paper boxes, that was my desk. I then walked home to the house I was selling . . . It was very scary, but at the same time I felt that it was a new adventure. And when I started college, I had a sense that this was where God wanted me to be. I can only describe it as a peace.

I was forty years old when I left.

I felt a bit like Moses, who was eighty when he was called back to Egypt. One of my fears was, *what if this decision has been me, and God's not involved at all.* But it was money that was the big fear. Although I had no home to pay for – because you're staying in college – I still had to fuel a car and fuel myself. I also had a son, who had to be put through schooling and so forth. But in the three years at college, until I was given a church and a stipend, I never went without.

Today, my wife is the minister for two churches and I'm the minister for two churches. We don't share the pastoral concerns of our congregations with each other, and you're always going separate ways when you've both got two churches, but we sense that God has told us to work as a team.

I still look back at my old life, but I don't regret becoming a minister. There are times in ministry where you sit in your study wondering *what on earth am I doing.*

I've had burnout. I've had churches and congregations that have been extremely difficult because of the church politics . . . but, for me, I cannot not do what I do.

– How does it compare to your former life?

When I was an electrician, we would first-fix a house, putting the conduits and the cables in, and then we'd come back to the house when it'd been plastered, and we'd set it out with all the sockets and the light switches. One of us would go and sort out the consumer unit and all the fuses.

We'd work together on these houses with good craic and good banter on the building site.

Afterwards, there was a feeling of beauty when you would later drive past a building site. You'd point to the houses and say, '*I wired those houses.*' There was a satisfaction when you'd see that couples and families had moved in, the lights were on, the Christmas tree lights were on. You felt a sense of completion, a sense of achievement.

After I came into the ministry, I struggled with the fact you may never see the results of your work.

Ministry is like planting seeds. You may be moved to a different church and never see the full bloom. Let me give you an example. We've been working with other church denominations on setting up a well-being centre for people with mental health issues and their carers. But my wife and I are moving churches later this year, so I may never see the results of that work, that centre in full bloom.

You have to learn that sometimes God uses us to plant and uses someone else to reap.

And you have to learn that it's not your work as such, but it's God's work.

– Tell me about your working week.

This week has been quiet but next week I could have three funerals, two Sunday services in the morning and a Sunday service in the evening.

In a week like that – or around Christmas and Easter time – you have to fall back on sermons that you've given elsewhere, in another part of the country. You refresh them and edit them of course.

In the early years of ministry, I would have felt guilt reusing sermons, but you have to or else you'd never be able to close your eyes.

On a Wednesday or Thursday, you have the Bible study courses. The day before, you write the material for them.

On Thursday, I'll do some writing for the sermon, and I'll visit the prayer groups that we run.

Friday morning, I'd have another look at the sermon. Friday afternoon is the time my wife and I have off. Unless there's a funeral or an emergency, we'll go for a coffee and have a nice meal.

On Saturday, you finish off your sermon, cut the grass, and wash the car.

On Sunday, I have two services in the morning and various healing services at night.

On a Sunday if you're preaching and there's a hush, that's when you hope things are going well. It can mean one of two things: either you're being too dogmatic, and you've shocked the congregation; or there's a weight to what God is saying for you.

Oh and sprinkled throughout the week, you'll have the phone calls.

'What do you want me to do with the £1,000 that needs to go here.'

Ministry is vastly different to thirty, forty years ago. We're always available, always available.

And if I don't reply to a message quickly enough, people think you're ignoring them.

An awful lot of ministry today is like being an administrator, a pastoral administrator. I have qualms about that . . . The stipend I receive is money set aside for me to provide spiritual care, for me to pastor the flock. And I think there's a difference between pastoring the flock and managing the flock.

I get less and less time to study the bible for myself because of all the managing, and sometimes the conflict management, that I have to do.

Where I am now, there's no administrator. But in my previous church, I had a lady who belonged to the congregation who had years of experience as an administrator in the police service. She was paid to be the church administrator. It freed me up so much. It gave me the freedom to get little discipleship groups going, to do school assemblies, to get into the community.

The work is all-consuming and, even though it's a noble consumption, you discover as you go along that there is more to life than ministry work.

During Covid, it was like the BBC in our study. My wife and I were putting together videos and editing services. We wanted our respective congregations to receive comfort at a time of crisis.

But when I reflect back, I think I could have done a service just once a week and I could have spent time with the Lord reflecting in an imposed sabbatical.

I spoke to a nurse the other day about her experience during Covid.

She said, '*Because of our vocations, we are people who cannot just walk out when the bell rings at five o'clock. And we are in a society that will keep taking and taking and taking, but it will not give.*'

And in the ministry, though we are called by God, we are still human beings like everybody else. We cannot be 24/7. There has to come a point where we say, '*I have given. Now I need to step back.*'

Local government worker

(50s)

I did a master's degree in planning. At the time, I thought I was going to go down the academic route and become a lecturer. That didn't go according to plan. I couldn't get any funding.

I hung around the university. They were too polite to tell me to go.

I ended up working in a bookshop for five years. It meant that I could still look around the university, still attend seminars, still talk to people.

A new source of PhD funding emerged. I tried again to get a job in academia. I remember going into this room, quite a big room, and sitting on a chair. I remember there being at least six people on the interview panel, but I've no idea whether this is true or not. It felt intimidating. It was a nightmare. I didn't get the job.

For a brief period, I worked in the constituency office of an MP. I then saw a job at the council in *Committee Services*. I thought it would be six months of maternity cover. Instead, I spent sixteen years at the council doing all sorts of governance type things.

The job was a home for the waifs and strays. When people left the council who were responsible for a governance function, they'd say, '*Where shall we put the function?*'

Then they would give it to me to look after. I did *Member Conduct, Council Constitution, Freedom of Information, Data Protection, Local Government Ombudsman complaints, Community Grants*. At times it was quite lonely. It wasn't the sort of job where people would be happy to hear from you.

If you pick up the phone to someone and say, *'I've got a really tricky Freedom of Information Act request'*, they wouldn't say, *'Oh, that's great. Lovely to hear from you.'*

We'd have full Council meetings every six to eight weeks. All of the councillors would get an agenda. The agenda was a big thing. Agenda day was always on a Friday.

On Friday afternoon, they'd be a group of us in a room with each of the agenda items, piles of documents interleaved. We'd go round the table, picking up items, stapling them, enveloping, taking them out to the post room. There were some hairy moments, but it was a job well done. You could point to a physical object – and the agenda wasn't an insubstantial object – and say, *'We made this'*, which was a big thing for people who spent most of their time typing.

The job had built up and built up and built up and it'd got too big. I was a manager of a team of seven.

I ended up having a bit of a mental health crisis.

I said, *'I can't do this any more.'*

It just so happened that someone in the team left, so I stepped down into their role and did that for two years. It was a relief. It was the same job that I'd had when I'd started at the council. It was familiar, comfortable, and just what I needed while I got better.

Someone from planning at the council then told me that they had some vacancies coming up.

I was ultimately successful and I'm now a planner.

I do enjoy it. I was right when I had those initial thoughts, all those years ago, that planning was something I'd quite like to do. I was right back then. Even though I'd since thought that the opportunity to do something like this had passed.

My wife and I both get the same train there and back. The train on the way in is just after 8 a.m. The train back is at 5.40 p.m. My main role is to prepare the Local Plan and to support the delivery of this plan.

Planning applications are determined by the extent to which they comply with the Local Plan. It deals with how many homes we need to provide and the best places to put them. And when development does take place, the plan addresses with how we make sure that it's the most appropriate form of development: *what should the houses look like? How will the development deal with environmental issues? If, for example, you've got a hundred new homes, where are the two-hundred new children going to go to school?*

It's intellectually challenging and it's also important, because people care deeply about these things and once things are built, they tend to stay for a long time.

Local authorities are supposed to update their Local Plans every five years, although generally speaking, not that many manage to do it that quickly. Some have plans that are decades old.

There's a five-year cycle of getting the plan together. What you're doing varies quite a bit in that time.

Within the five-year arc, there are three smaller stages. The first stage is producing a document for public consultation. That public consultation is then analysed. Then you do a better document and another public consultation.

A lot of this work is behind a computer. With Google Streetview and advances in mapping technology, what previously might have required a site visit doesn't any more.

After that, the second stage is three weeks of public inquiry, where all you do is turn up in front of the inspectors in the public hearing sessions. We've just had this and we're waiting for the inspectors to give feedback.

The final stage is for the council to adopt the plan as the policy of the local planning authority, which is a full council decision.

Each of those stages is a significant milestone. But, if you compare parts of this process to those Friday afternoons making council agendas that I mentioned – where you could tell when they were finished because you'd put them in an envelope and post them – then you'll find that sometimes you can't actually tell when a stage is finished.

Take the public inquiry, for instance, it officially ended with the inspectors saying, '*Thank you, we've heard everything we want to hear. You'll get a letter at some point.*'

Unofficially, the feedback was quite positive, but in terms of that tangible ending, there isn't anything you can point to.

– Do you have a theory about what good planning looks like?

What frustrates people about planning is that what gets developed isn't as good as they were told it would be. People stop trusting the system to deliver when the new houses or the new primary school don't look like the glossy pictures they were shown.

The focus is always on, *where are these houses going to go?* and there's sometimes not enough time to think about how we can make those homes – and the development that goes with them – the best that they can be.

Unfortunately, the outcome of people saying, '*Oh, it's not quite right*', is that they think we need to put more steps in at the beginning to make sure that those issues are addressed in future.

And so, planning comes to involve more processes and becomes more bureaucratic.

If you were to compare today with six years' ago, in terms of both the amount of documents and the length of documents that are submitted in support of planning applications, you'd find that people are submitting so much more today. Whether those documents deal with the original issue that the extra process was brought into deal with . . . well, that's another question.

Say you're doing highway modelling to work out the impact of a new development. If it gets to a point where the only person that can understand it is the highway engineer hired as a consultant to produce the report, then the system is over-complicated.

Elected councillors in the plans committee should be able to make a decision on a given application, so it has to be capable of being understood by them.

Maybe it's not a good parallel, but it's like those complex fraud cases where the tribunal has to be assisted by experts. Is the defendant getting a fair trial? How can there be a fair trial if the tribunal doesn't understand what the defendant has been charged with?

The art of planning is to say, right, there are a number of competing interests here. These interests are represented by evidence. My role is to weigh those interests and to balance that evidence to come to a reasoned decision, with the policy framework in the background to guide me. That is as much an art as a science. Throwing more process and more science at it doesn't fundamentally change this ultimate role.

— When you look back at your career, are you content with how it's gone?

I am.

None of my career has been particularly planned.

One of the questions that I would dread at an interview is, *'where do you see yourself in five years' time?'*

Because that's just . . . that's just . . .

I'm not particularly ambitious. I don't have goals. I don't have everything mapped out. I don't want to have achieved *this or that*. I want to do a wide variety of tasks while having the comfort of staying within a familiar organization. I'm not a big fan of change, certainly not change for change's sake.

CHAPTER SEVENTEEN **CITY WORK**

Derivatives trader

lawyer

management consultant

cleaner

Derivatives trader

(20s)

The desk that I work for is a market maker. It's a trading desk that makes markets in certain derivatives, quoting a bid and an offer in the derivatives universe.

The derivatives trade in the market, and their price will go up and down. I take a view for the desk on whether we want to be buying or selling.

I've been doing it coming up to six years now. There's definitely an element of imposter syndrome, I suppose, which just relates to being a young analyst in the market when most of the people I'm interacting with have been doing this for ten, twenty, thirty years.

Every trade I sanction I'm taking the other side as someone with infinitely more experience and knowledge to me. And that is both hugely scary and a strange, strange feeling.

You can see at the end of the day what your profit and loss is.

It's an assessment of your value to the firm every day for the whole team to see. It has its own particular psychological dynamic that takes some getting used to. I suppose not dissimilar to other jobs where it's very clear how much you brought in at the end of the year, but we get it on an hourly or daily basis, too.

You can open up the risk systems and see what everyone's made. And you know that you're all competing for the same bonus pool. And you also know that if another trader on the team gets paid more, you're going to get paid less . . .

Last week, I had a situation where I was facing potentially a huge

– absolutely huge – loss. I had one day of last week where I was shaking and vomiting all day, in total terror at what might happen. I think I slept for about five hours between Monday and Friday just because of the stress.

I'd say that this has happened to me twice in my six years of doing this.

Normally, it doesn't feel great if you post a loss, but I'm pretty disengaged from it to be honest.

I don't know if this useful for you because I don't know how good a barometer I am for the rest of the industry, in that I'm totally not invested in this career or interested in it all . . .

I got into the City because, when there's a world that you don't understand, it's exciting learning something new. And there's a huge amount to learn coming into derivatives, which are significantly more complex than equity markets. It is quite interesting and exciting, initially.

But, for me, I struggle to see the point of my job. I think it doesn't really need to be done. It basically serves only to make myself and my company's shareholders richer.

I'm totally checked-out to be honest.

– Why?

It's a convergence of factors.

It's a lack of meaning lack of purpose. Possibly it's because I know how to do it all now and I can do it reasonably well.

It's quite a tough job to do if you're not really excited by it. You have to have an immense amount of self-discipline, because I'm literally just told at the beginning of every year, '*Go off and make this amount of P&L.*'

And that's sort of it. It's then up to me to go out and find opportunities, to look at the products I want to. I never really have anyone breathing down my neck asking for things. I don't have any deadlines. I'm a free agent, doing my own thing. And if you're not really enthralled by what you're doing, I think some people can struggle with that sort of work environment.

But I'd say it all comes back to just the issue of a lack of meaning or purpose.

I get in every morning at six-thirty, but I'm out the door by six every day. It's quite cushy honestly. Those hours, compared to friends of mine who are lawyers, they're not bad. The return on effort is truly . . . I could do this for the rest of my life. The pay is very good. It makes the way that I feel about it worse. You feel like, *you've got such a sweet deal, why can't you enjoy it?*

Bonuses are getting paid tomorrow. The only feeling that I have around that is a feeling of comfort that I haven't totally wasted my time, because whatever happens I can tell myself that this was a sensible thing to be doing. How else would I have bought a house?

The money helps.

I wouldn't be doing it without that.

But I want to be doing something that effects some change. There's something really deep in us that wants to feel like there is something that comes out of all these hours that we're working. Like a child who beams when she pushes a toy along the floor, when she discovers cause and effect. There is something in us, isn't there?

My job at the moment is buying and selling. I buy stuff low, I sell it high. And I think I'd want to do any sort of career where I felt like I was actually being useful or creating something.

In my fourth year working in finance, the range in my cohort in terms of what people were paid was anything from £200,000 to £1.4 million – at twenty-five-years old.

The people that are at the higher end of that spectrum, the traders, have lost all sense.

They don't think at all when they spend. They're paying huge amounts for flats and going out for expensive dinners and crazy holidays.

But on the whole, I'd say most of the people in my graduate class are still living in a relatively normal way.

The money really takes you by surprise, but it's remarkable how quickly you get used to it.

Every year, we have comp day. It's a huge thing. Everyone's got to wear a tie, or nice shoes if you're a girl.

You get taken into a room one-by-one by the head of your team. They hand you a piece of paper that tells you what your bonus is going to be.

I remember my first bonus and just being thrilled, thinking, *this is such a fantastic sum of money.* The head of the trading desk came over.

He said, '*You were the only person that smiled today when I gave them their number.*'

Then my unofficial mentor took me aside into a room. He was visibly annoyed.

He said, '*Don't you ever do that again. You must never, ever, look anything but mildly displeased or irritated when you get your number, even if it's beyond your wildest expectations.*'

They rank your response in terms of how pleased you seem. It's the cardinal sin to seem pleased, because that's something they take into consideration for next year.

It's quite a strange thing to start in the same graduate class and, within a year, we're all getting paid differently.

You go for a coffee with your best mate on comp day. She's done the exact same – possibly fewer – hours than you every week over the past year. There's not been a visible difference in your contributions to the business, but for some reason, she's getting 50k more than you. That's incredibly frustrating when you're young. It's a lot of money.

As you get older, the numbers get bigger. It's an anger, a feeling like you've been undervalued, a feeling like, *this number is my value.*

Ultimately, we are in an industry where it is all about the exchange and valuing of different securities. We come to view ourselves like that. We have a value to the firm. And there is a number that a competitor will pay us. And if our employer pays us less, people see that as a real cost to themselves.

Lawyer

(50s)

We don't have to get in too early, but I don't finish until the early hours of the morning.

I could have a look and see when my last email was . . . The last email is typically sent at 2.30 a.m., and then the first email would typically be sent at 8.30 a.m.

The hours are quite long. It's not solid until 2 a.m., but it's still work. I don't know how common that is, because we're all products of our own environment.

Everyone's got different priorities, I suppose. From a work point of view, I'm quite lucky. My kids are at boarding school, so they're cared for most of the time. I can devote a lot more time to work than other people can.

If you've got, say, a relationship and someone's going to leave you if you don't speak to them, then that's not great. Or the people that have children at home: I think that's also quite challenging. When my children were growing up, they had a full-time nanny, so again you're able to shift that weight.

At the moment, I feel that I'm not in great shape. Not in terms of being unfit, I'm just not mentally as robust. Things upset me which wouldn't ordinarily upset me. Things get to me which wouldn't get to me. I'm tired and I'm more likely to snap. It's like a toddler who's tired.

I know that people in the office have started to notice.

That's a worry because, of course, you have that worry that the more junior people look at you and think, *God forbid, please don't let me end up like that.* So you've got to try and do something about it.

As a client, I wouldn't want somebody who's had four hours sleep looking at my contract; I try to do things that aren't necessarily so critical late at night. Training. Updates on changes to the law.

. . . I think you can do these hours for about three months before you start to flag. As soon as junior people are back from holiday, I tell them to book another one for three months' time.

But I don't know when I'll next be able to take a holiday.

On a personal level, I find I can cope with most working patterns, as long as people work hard.

We are paid an extortionate amount of money, and we lose track of that so easily. There was a something on a legal gossip site the other week. It was a quote from someone that said, *'I'm twenty-six. I have no discernible experience and I can't iron a shirt and I earn a hundred grand.'*

And that is true!

In the great scheme of things that is an enormous sum of money. With that kind of money, unfortunately, you've just got to work for it. It doesn't come for free. You do have to work.

One of the associates goes to the gym every evening. Great. That's fine. He'll be out of the office between 6 p.m. and 8 p.m. every night. It's blocked out on his calendar.

He's always back in the office afterwards, and then he'll work through 'til midnight. That's just his working pattern. He does work hard.

To me, there's no difference between that and somebody saying, *'I want to get home for my child's bathtime.'* To others, getting home for bathtime is seen as okay, but *'I want to go to the gym'* is seen as self-indulgent, which I think is very unfair.

I learn every day from the younger people in the office.

They're ferociously ambitious in a way that perhaps I didn't expect, because I had this preconceived idea with young people that they're always bleating on about social ills.

They're tough. They're not snowflakes. They're tough.

In a sense, actually standing up for things and saying, *'No, I'm not going to put up with that'* is tough. Rather than just taking it and saying, *'Okay yes, shout at me. I don't mind'.*

They're fairly unafraid to ask direct questions that perhaps I wouldn't have asked.

They will ask you *'Well, what do you do with your children?'*

There's a big push towards diversity, which I think is a good thing. But ultimately who do we get? Quite often white, male, privately educated. And why is that? Well, it makes our lives easier, because broadly speaking I can put them in front of a client – no problem. He will know how to behave, and he will know how to be socially gracious. He will know just how to conduct himself, and when to shut up. And in all fairness, a lot of the young women will know these things too.

When it comes to more socially diverse candidates, that's much more difficult, because they need that little bit more support. It doesn't mean that they lack the ability or intelligence, but they haven't grown up with the same advantages that make these things easy for someone like the privately educated white man. It's much harder.

And I have to say – we're inevitably going to go a bit into Covid – one of the things that I feel is potentially very damaging is that those very people, that sort of candidate perhaps not from the most advantaged background, was just the kind of person that needed to be in the office, just to see how to conduct yourself in a business environment. They won't have got that. They will lose out. What will that mean for them in the future? I don't know.

In the workplace, we have people who have spent essentially their whole training contract online. We're going to have people who have spent their first year online. You do not learn in the same way. These people are going to be behind. Technically, they'll be behind. And we can push and push to catch them up. But when will we realize, actually realize, that these people are behind? I don't know, because there's an awful lot that can disguise it. People say, '*My hours are really good*.' Well, of course they are. If you've got a printer at home that prints about three pages a minute, and you're told to put a binder together, you can sit there all that time, but are you learning anything? No.

. . . This is a generalization, but my impression is that if you're passionate about working from home, then you are probably a hard worker, but there's also a 20 to 30 per cent chance that you're basically a skiver. If you come into the office, I'm 100 per cent sure that you're a hard worker. Therefore, my bias is towards people wanting to come into the office.

And being in the office is actually kind of fun. There's a definite feeling of support, a real sense of working together, a desire to get the work done, shared jokes, that kind of thing.

You lose that when we work from home.

You lose the relationship that you have with your colleagues, and you lose the ability to train someone properly. You can't train someone over Zoom any more than you can bring up a child via Zoom. You just can't do it.

I suppose it's a variation of imposter syndrome, but I get very surprised when people tell me I'm intimidating, because my own image of myself is definitely not that. When people say they're scared of me, I say, '*Why?*'

I don't know why people are scared of me. I guess it must be a seniority thing, or there are some things I do know, and I know very quickly. They say, '*How did she know all that?*'

But it's just experience. When you've looked at the things I've looked at . . . I've just had more time to look at them than they have.

Even now I still get nervous that I won't know stuff. Even now I massively over-prepare for meetings.

I don't want to look stupid.

*   *   *

What do I feel judged for? I feel judged for only taking three months of maternity leave. I was going to take six, but it was so brutal. I can't describe it. I came back after three, so I felt judged for that.

I hated it. I was rubbish at it. I couldn't bear it.

I also felt judged for sending my children to boarding school at eight.

– Had you been a man do you think you would have been judged for those things?

No, no . . .

– What's it all for?

I do it for my children, so they won't have to.

– What would you like them to do?

Something that makes them really happy, that brings them joy.

– Law?

No, not just because it's an awful job, but because they're ill-suited to it.

– Will you keep working for ever?

Yes, I can't imagine not working.

It's a bit of a worry because the retired partners do tend to drop down dead – a quick end to retirement. I'd definitely like to keep my hand in.

I wouldn't mind working for the government at the end of my career.

I did think of travelling a bit. When I was younger, I was never into backpacking and not knowing where your next shower was coming from. But I wouldn't mind travelling when I'm a bit older. Beyond that, I don't know. It's really terrifying.

Maybe I will just be one of those ancient partners shuffling through the corridors.

I don't make time to think about these things. This is always the trade-off. When people at the firm say, '*Oh, I can't do this or that*', you can. You are choosing not to. I choose this. This is a choice.

This is what I signed up for.

Management consultant

(20s)

I studied engineering at university. I tried working in industry, but you end up becoming very specialized. It's very difficult to diversify.

I opted to look for something more varied. The two options open to me were investment banking or management consulting.

– Why were there only two options?

It was a money thing and a location thing. I wanted to be in London. Plus, compared to the average starting salary, I felt like these were a good starting point.

The company I now work for is an end-to-end technology consultancy.

If a client has a problem that they want solving – either with a specific technology or via outsourcing an application to do the job for them – then we can provide that whole service.

We say to the client, *'Here is the technology you should be using. Here are the people who are experts in it. Here are the change management people who'll help you enforce the new software on your company. And here are the support services, the help desk services'.*

It's at a massive scale.

At the start, the consultancy feels like an ocean.

I did a project at an oil major. It was a data analysis role. The client was building a dashboard to monitor their customer service interactions under certain contracts. For example, it would measure how many orders were completed on time.

My role was to figure out what calculations would reflect the company's customer service metrics, and then to find the data for these calculations.

There were two other people from my company and eight independent contractors on the project.

My superior was a senior manager in the consultancy. In the three or four months I spent on that project, I met her twice.

The managers are spread across a billion things. If our company has won a bid for work and said to the client, '*We have this person who's an expert in blah, blah, blah*', then that person has to put some amount of time – for example, 2 per cent of their time – into the project. One thirty-minute call per month.

This happens to an exponential level, everyone's doing it.

And so you don't get enough time from the managers, and so you don't get enough support.

I felt like I was alone during this project.

I felt like my work wasn't being seen. I was doing all this work for the client, and I'd just deliver it. I don't know if the client was happy or not, because there was no bridge between us and them.

I wasn't happy with the role. I fought to leave it.

But an annoying thing about consulting is that there's a lot of politics in leaving roles. There are sensitivities.

Sensitivities around having once committed to that role.

Sensitivities around burning bridges.

You can't say, '*This role isn't teaching me anything any more. It's not interesting to me*', but that's ultimately the truth.

They say, '*Join a multinational consultancy and the world's your oyster. You can get involved in so many things*'.

But in reality, when you want to explore these things, there are many hoops you have to jump through. You have to be very careful about who is on your side, and careful that others know about your work and performance.

It gets a little bit frustrating to have to evidence yourself constantly.

You always have to demonstrate your '*worth*' in order to check boxes. You feel like you have to – what's the word? – '*self-praise*'.

– Are you comfortable doing that?

Not at all. I'd rather receive praise quietly than have to say, '*Everyone, look at what I've done. How great is this?*'

During Covid, you didn't bump into people any more. There was an added pressure. You had to *really* shout about any positive feedback you received.

I received a piece of positive feedback from my client. It was out of the blue. I didn't ask for it. I shared it with my pastoral supervisor, because they're meant to keep a record. He then shared it with every single person you could think of. Actually, it circulated twice.

I feel like I shouldn't have to do this all the time for you to trust that I'm doing good work, or for you to believe that I'm doing what's expected of me. I find it awkward.

But to a certain extent the company pushes you to have this nature, this nature of shameless self-promotion. You have to tell people that you're amazing, because in an environment where you have all these big characters trying to show off over the tiniest of achievements, it's those loud voices who succeed. In this atmosphere, you have to compete.

Since the office re-opened, I've been back a handful of times. The first time I went back, I was completely put off. One of the partners who leads our area was there. I felt like everyone was really kiss-arsey. I couldn't believe people were just blowing off meetings, or throwing to the side any work in front of them, just because *so-and-so* just stepped into the room or *so-and-so* was nearby.

I felt like, *I'm not here to suck up to anyone, and I'm not here to make silly small talk with someone with whom I have no mutual interest, other than that she might promote me one day.*

* * *

I fought my case to my managers that I wasn't being well supported in the oil major role. I said that I was still early on in my career and that I wanted to explore different options.

I switched roles to another team working on a client's data governance: *How do they access data? How do they make sure that the data is trustworthy?*

That team was really high-performing. Their ethos was *always deliver or over-deliver before deadlines*. It was quite stressful. The partner was great, but she was very picky with absolutely everything. In the words you used, for example. Sometimes I'd think, '*Well, I'm saying the same thing, you're just saying it in different words*.'

With hindsight, perhaps you appreciate that there was a specific reason behind her pickiness, but it often ate into our evenings.

We'd always start by 8 a.m. We were working with teams across the world, so we wanted to maximize the times for calls. We'd usually have calls from 8 a.m. until minimum 6 p.m. Back-to-back calls and workshops.

Every single thirty-minute slot in your life had to have a structured agenda with materials prepared: *what do you plan to present to the client? Why should they care about what you're telling them?*

'*Here is my agenda. Here is what I want you to get out of today's meeting*.'

It was good, but it was strict.

Work would extend into your evening if there were things expected of you by the next day.

Other people would be up from 7 a.m. staying up until 9 or 10 p.m. to finish work off. I wasn't really prepared to do that, to be honest.

I started getting in the habit of blocking my calendar out for an hour or two per day: *this is the time I need to finish this deliverable, or to write this article*. My team could only see the free and busy times on my calendar. If someone added a meeting in that time, I'd say, '*No, I can't make it. I've got a clash*.'

– Were you expected to always be available?

It's a funny question, because it's implicit.

People email you at weird hours of the day. *'Let me know as soon as possible'*, they'd say.

But in their email signature, they'd have, *'I work flexibly. I'm not awaiting your reply blah blah blah'.*

Explicitly the company says, *'Work your hours. Set your boundaries'.*

But you get these emails, and you get deadlines that make you think, *how am I meant to meet that deadline? When am I meant to do the work?*

And when they talk about harassment, the company talks about *zero tolerance.* I was in an intra-company training call where they give you these hypothetical scenarios to discuss. One scenario was about how a woman had just been promoted in the consultancy and then a client says something derogatory, implying that she'd only been promoted because she's a woman.

In the training call, we were discussing whether anyone had been in similar situations. I shared a story about how I was running a workshop for a client. and I was the only female in the room.

One specific guy in the workshop kept making derogatory comments about women, saying something about his wife. I can't remember what it was, but it was *she-stays-in-the-kitchen* type of thinking. I kept quiet, but one of the other guys said something, defending me, *'She's an engineer actually blah blah blah'.*

I was telling this story in the training call, and I said, *'I don't know. Maybe it did bother me. Maybe I should have said something immediately'.*

And then I had comments from people more senior than me, saying, *'It's tricky because he's a client, and you don't want to cause any friction that could potentially cause detriment to any future contract blah blah blah'.*

They say *'Zero Tolerance'* and *'Bring Your Whole Self to Work'*, but then they say, *'The client is paying for us. You don't want to get on his bad side'.*

I think many other people would have found that offensive, to be honest. I shrugged it off. I thought, *okay, well I understand now that the company's number one priority is not us, but money – cool.*

Working on the high-performing data team felt really stressful. I felt like, *I'm ready to quit.* I applied for several jobs, and I got an offer in fact, but I stepped back and thought about it more pragmatically.

I thought, *I'm still building skills. It's still a really good name on my CV. I've also got the option to leave. Why don't I just keep going to make sure I've exploited consulting as much as I can . . .*

Sometimes in the peak of lockdown, I'd just burst into tears, and I've had days where I've woken up feeling like, *oh my gosh, I just can't stand switching on this laptop and going through the motions all over again.*

But I'm at a plateau now, I'm not nosediving.

I've learned that as long as I get my work done, my time is still my time. Before, I felt like a corporate slave, tied to my desk 9 a.m. 'til 6 p.m., even if there was no work, always available in case anything came up. I've definitely moved away from that.

Now, I think, *well, no one is observing my every move, and they're still satisfied with what I'm doing. Maybe I'll work 7 a.m. until 11 a.m. tomorrow, catch up with someone, come back at 4 p.m. and work the rest of my hours.*

The autonomy is important.

– It's a backwards situation: to be able to function in the job, you have to not care.

That's very true. I have a friend in the company who is the complete opposite. She cares way too much about work, to the extent that it causes her trouble sleeping. She's been promoted ahead of me, but in the grand scheme of things it's not worth sacrificing your happiness for.

I've come to accept that work is work to a certain extent.

Only the lucky few are completely passionate, in awe of the work they do, waking up absolutely thrilled. For the lucky rest of us, work is work, and as long as the benefits I'm getting, and the balance I have, isn't encroaching on my personal life – not affecting my mental health, and not taking me away from my friends and family too much – then that's good enough.

I do feel quite strongly that management consultants are replaceable. We're just cogs in the wheel. I want to do something where I feel like less of a cog and more like a valued individual.

Cleaner

(30s)

My English isn't so good. I don't have lots of vocabulary. But I'll tell you my story here in London.

I arrived many years ago. I came illegally from Brazil to marry my ex-husband, who was Brazilian as well.

I was eighteen when I came. He was nearly thirty. We met on a website, because he was already in the UK. He asked if I wanted to come. I met him when I arrived. He told me all about how things work here for illegal people. I said, '*Okay, fine.*'

I started to clean houses, because they don't ask for documents. I was eighteen so I didn't think about anything. I didn't think, *what could I do with my future?*

We have a big community here. You feel like you're in Brazil in London. It's everything you can imagine. I have my Brazilian church. We have lots of Brazilian shops. We have hairdressers. Lawyers. Builders. Drivers. Everything.

It's also very funny, because here in London you have the opportunity to live with Brazilians from different places – Brazil is very big – and we've realized how different we all are. But this Brazilian community is why my English isn't so good, because between ourselves we're always talking Portuguese.

I never went to an English school because I was illegal. The English I speak, I learned by myself with clients.

Being illegal made lots of things much harder for me. I couldn't travel. It was illegal for me to study. But I did have a bank account and the GP never asked any questions. Now, it's difficult to have these things, because immigration is closing the gaps.

I had a fear that immigration would knock on the door. But it was much worse for my husband who was working in construction. I worked in houses. It'd be impossible for immigration to knock on the door and say, '*Hello*'.

But in the construction industry, there were lots of times when he ran away when he heard, '*Immigration's coming*'.

It's funny now, but it was terrifying then. They want to stop your life here. I had lots of friends who were caught by immigration. It was like a death. They disappear from your life without saying goodbye.

After many years, I got my visa. We got one for my son when he was seven. And then I applied. We had to pay £8,000. Then we had to wait and wait and wait.

I got a message from my lawyer, '*Immigration have approved your visa*'.

I started to cry, and I rang all my friends. I was not believing that it'd happened to me. The visa makes things totally different. It changes my life.

But I was happy with my life before – that's the truth.

When I got my visa, everyone started to say, '*Oh, now you can stop working as a cleaner*'.

Being a cleaner is a problem for lots of people, because it's working with dirt. People think it's not nice. But I like being a cleaner. I work inside someone's house. It's something that's very intimate. And when the house is a mess, I make everything straight and everything nice. It feels good.

I listen to Brazilian music when I'm cleaning, which makes me feel close to Brazil.

You have time to think about things, time to sort things out in your head, and I have time to put my headphones on and talk to my best friend every day. We know everything about each other's life. But sometimes I have to message her, '*The client's here, don't call!*'

My first job was for a Portuguese man as a housekeeper and a nanny. He used to pay me £7 an hour. But he used to use me too much. His wife was English, and she thought about me more.

She would say to him, '*She's done for the day.*'

But he was always saying, '*No, she can go and do this.*'

The woman used to travel a lot and when she was away, I had to come to his house every day and work from 7 a.m. until 9 p.m. He used to pay me £50 per day. I used to come and help with breakfast for the kids. He'd take them to school. And I would clean the house, cook, and wait for the kids to come home. I'd do baths and then put the kids to sleep.

He'd say, '*Can you come in every day?*'

I'd say yes because I always thought about the money weekly, rather than per hour. But he was nice to me, because I wasn't a good cleaner then [she laughs].

When I stopped working for him, I started work in a company run by a Brazilian.

I had to get up at 5 a.m. I lived at one end of London, and I had to get to the other end, where this company would pick us up in a minibus and take us to a posh town near where we'd clean houses. I'd work nine hours, for £5 an hour. He'd charge us out at £8.50. He'd check the money we got from the client. There were twelve girls, so he got £3.50 an hour. I'm sorry to say that there was nothing on paper, it was untaxed.

– *What did you used to talk about when you were in the minibus?*

We used to complain [she laughs]. Complain about our boss who drove the van. But it was fun. Hard but fun at the same time.

They used to tell us to wait outside the houses when we were done, because they didn't want us to have a relationship with the client. So we'd wait for the minibus outside. Sometimes it was raining. We weren't paid for the waiting.

During the week, I had no free time. I used to wake up at 5 a.m.

and I'd get back at 8.30 p.m. At the weekend, I used to go to church in the evening.

— *Did you ever look to leave?*

No, I never thought about that. I knew my life was this, you know? I didn't have any other choice. If I wanted to stay in this country as an illegal, then I had to do this cleaning. And from the cleaning, I was going to have enough money to pay my bills, to survive here, and to send money to Brazil.

Cleaning was like a safe place for people like me, without documents. My clients never asked me if I'm illegal. They were happy to have me. So I never thought about leaving. But I was tired. Very tired.

Every Tuesday I worked for one lady called Mrs Taylor. All the girls in the van were complaining about her. She was eighty years old.

Even my boss said, '*I'm gonna take you to a new client, but she's very difficult.*'

I said, '*Okay.*'

Mrs Taylor lived in the middle of nowhere, she was rich, and she was English, English, English. Every week she had a new cleaner. But I like old people and I like to talk.

She said, '*Ah, you are Brazilian.*'

She would ask about my life. She was very bossy, '*Do this. Do that.*'

I would say, '*Sorry, sorry, sorry.*'

That's the first word you learn here, '*Sorry*'. She was the first person that made me cry at work. I cried in front of her. I didn't clean something properly.

She said, '*Come here. Look at this. It's dirty.*'

I started to cry. It was the way that she talked to me.

She said, '*I don't want tears. I want work.*'

I thought, *oh my God I want my mum.* The way she was talking to me it was like. *You are the cleaner. I am the client. You have to do what I want.* And she was right, but it was the way she talked to me.

Week by week she was changing. I started to get to know her.

It was her birthday, and I don't know how I knew, but I brought flowers for her. She used to have a sunroom, where the wall was glass, and it was full of flowers. She used to have champagne there. Her house was beautiful. I bought an orchid for her.

She said, '*You shouldn't buy anything for me.*'

But after that, I started to get love.

She started to talk about my boss, '*Don't say anything to him, but he's like this . . .*'

I'd think, *yes, he is like that.* She also helped me a lot with my English. This friendship was like a secret. If my boss knew, he'd change the house I worked in.

I just knew she was going to like me. I have patience with old people. I have the patience to understand them. I put in my mind, *I'm gonna win.*

She used to say, '*Can you get me something?*'

And I was quick. I used to run through her house to get it.

She'd say, '*Oh, you are great!*'

She started to love me like a granddaughter.

But I was tired. One day, my ex-husband was talking to me, and I started to sleep.

He rang me the next day to say, '*I don't want you working for this company any more. It's too much for you. It's too tiring. You can find something in London.*'

After a few weeks, I came to Mrs Taylor, '*I have something to say to you.*'

She said, '*You're going to leave me, aren't you?*'

I said, '*Yes*'

She said, '*Don't worry*' and she then asked, '*Do you want to clean my flat in London? No one lives in it.*'

Another Brazilian girl used to clean the flat, but she was going back to Brazil.

I said, '*Okay, that's fine.*'

I told my boss that I was leaving him and that he could let my clients know. My boss told Mrs Taylor that I was going back to

Brazil. She said to me, '*Can you believe he said you're going back to Brazil?*'

Then I started to work for Mrs Taylor directly, cleaning her flat. I started to clean her daughter's house three times a week as well. Then Mrs Taylor told her neighbour that I was cleaning for her in London, and the neighbour asked if I would clean for her parents who also lived there. And then I started cleaning for the neighbour's siblings, then for their children, then for the children's friends.

And then I have millions of clients – not millions, I know – but I have friends who recommend me to friends who recommend me to friends.

And it all started with Mrs Taylor.

I now have two girls working for me. With new clients, I pretend I'm a big company. I say, '*Let me check if I have some girls in your area*' but I only have two girls.

When I clean, I receive between £17 and £20 an hour. I don't ask for £20, my clients give me that. I charge the girls out at £15 and they get £12.

The business is still not legal at the moment, because I've only just got my visa, so I'm sorting my life out, getting my documents and taxes together. I've had to save money to pay for the visa. I know that's no excuse. But with the visa I can now finish this cycle of my life.

When Covid came, most of my clients texted me to say that they were going to carry on paying me as normal until it was all over.

One of my clients said to me, '*If I have my job, you have your job.*'

I felt so grateful. *Oh my God.* If I start to cry it's because it's something that touched my heart, because I didn't have a contract with any of the clients. They had no obligation with me. My furlough was God.

I never imagined that I would know so many rich people in this world. Before Mrs Taylor, I'd cleaned houses for rich people and most of them treated me like a cleaner. Mrs Taylor, she was rich rich rich but she called me by name.

I got married again last year and we exchanged letters. She sent me some money for the wedding. I used to ring her, and she used to ring me.

Last winter she passed away. I cried like someone in my family had died. She was part of my life for so many years. I was invited to her funeral. I know my place, I'm just a cleaner, but I also know that I had more life with her than many of the people I saw at that funeral.

Next week is the last time I'll clean her London flat. I know I'm going to cry. I found out I was pregnant in that flat. And I used to take my son with me to the flat when I worked.

I'm grateful for everything that Mrs Taylor brought to my life and I'm grateful for everything that cleaning has brought to my life.

We Brazilians come here because of money. One British pound is now six Real. We work so that we can send money back to Brazil. I've built a house for my parents and given them some savings as well. And I have to say one thing to you English: I love your country. I'm very grateful for everything. When the Queen died, I cried.

I'm very grateful. I came here at such a young age. I'm in my thirties now. My whole adult life is here. Everything I have now is because of England. God Save the King. I couldn't have this life in Brazil. I'm from a very simple family there. The money, the food, the flat I have now, I couldn't have in Brazil. My son was born here. All my life is here now.

We are chasing your dreams – can I say it like that?

CHAPTER EIGHTEEN **WITHOUT WORK**

Unemployed due to disability

retiree and ex-commercial account manager

musician

Unemployed due to disability

(40s)

I have a master's degree in electronic engineering. I was a principal enterprise architect at a telecoms company. In 2008, I went freelance to work as an enterprise architect consultant.

In 2010, I was on a kayaking trip south in the Hebrides. We stopped on an island for lunch, and I went for a climb.

As I was climbing, a rock fell apart underneath me, and I fell ten to twenty feet into shallow water. Fortunately, my friend spotted me, dragged me out of the water, and called the coast guard. They flew me out to Stornaway, and then onto Glasgow.

I spent nearly two years in a brain injury rehabilitation centre. I went in on a bed and came out with a walking frame and splints. I've got rid of the walking frame and splints, but I still don't walk very quickly.

I also have a number of other problems. For example, my memory is rubbish.

Since my accident, I've done bits and pieces of work, but mainly I go to drop-in centres for disabled and mentally ill people, and to a group run by one of the local churches. That group's for ex-alcoholics, but they'll let anybody in. At the church group, there's free teas and coffees, a pool table and card games.

I've had two jobs since my accident. One was as a customer service agent for a company that provided IT support to supermarket customers. That was forty hours a week. After three months, I took three weeks off due to tiredness. I spoke to them about whether I could come back part-time, but they said that I could only do that when I'd been there six months. I decided to leave.

Towards the end of January last year, I got a part-time job at an optician. It was mostly scanning and summarizing consultation letters. Unfortunately, I left after five months because they decided that they couldn't afford to pay me. So I'm currently looking for work again.

After I graduated, I found looking for work easy. These days, I'm struggling. I get a few interviews, but I get the impression that I'm getting interviews because I'm disabled and not because they actually want me.

I recently had an interview for a job as an IT support agent. It would have been twenty hours a week, which is on the upper limit for what I can do. After the first set of interviews, they decided that they didn't want to take my application any further forward, which was a bit of a shame, but never mind.

I've had a few interviews like that but unfortunately, I can't remember where or when.

On Mondays I go to a church group from 10 a.m. At 12.30 p.m., I go to the drop-in centre for disabled people for lunch. At 2 p.m. I go to another drop-in centre for mentally ill people. At 3.30 p.m. I'll join everyone leaving the centre at a cafe.

On Tuesday, I go to a drop-in centre at 12.30 p.m., have some lunch, and get a lift to go shopping in the afternoon.

Wednesday is a church group day. I'm there from 10 a.m. until 4 p.m.

Thursday morning, I have a video call with a neurological support group charity. I can't remember who they are. I leave that call at 12 p.m. so I can go to a drop-in centre for lunch and the afternoon.

Friday, I'll go down to the cafe for lunch.

Saturday, if I can get a lift, I'll go to the cafe for lunch.

On Sunday, nothing's open and there's not a lot to do so I twiddle my thumbs.

I used to have a Motability car, but I crashed it, and it was the fifth claim I'd had so they wouldn't replace it. I'm going to use part of mum's estate to buy a car. She died a year ago. For the time being, I'm stuck with public transport, taxis, and lifts from friends. The problem is that the bus times are not very convenient or frequent. I can get one into town at 12.40 p.m., but I have to get a taxi or walk home, and I don't walk quickly or far.

— Do you feel valued?

Probably not at the moment. Before my accident, I guess I felt valued. After my accident, probably not. But I'm not sure it bothers me, because I deal with what's happening here and now.

I have very little memory of what's going on the past or what's going to come up in the future. I live very much in the moment and watch what happens. Hopefully, what will happen is that I keep getting Universal Credit and PIP, which keep me funded at the moment.

— Has your perception of yourself changed since your accident?

I'm not sure my perception of myself has changed, but I think other people's perception of me has changed. My ex-wife reckons I've changed quite a lot.

Unfortunately, the problem is I can't remember what I used to be like.

— What would success look like in your life now?

It would probably involve getting another part-time job. That's my main challenge at the moment, finding something to do that's going to help me contribute to society and bring a little bit more income in. Quite what that job will be, I've no idea, but it needs to be twenty hours or less, because I don't think I could cope with any more.

– If you had a magic wand, what one or two changes would you make to your life to make things easier for you?

The first thing I'd do: I wouldn't have gone for a climb when I was kayaking.

Other than that, I think my main objectives are getting a job and having my mum's money coming through so I can get a car.

– Are there any times in the week when you feel particularly alive or happy?

Not particularly, no. It's very much the same. It's just a matter of getting by and doing things day by day.

Retiree and ex-commercial account manager

(60s)

I had a great job as a commercial account manager for a multinational food and beverage corporation. I ended up managing customer accounts that turned over a hundred million. Quite substantial.

I used to leave the house at 5.30 a.m. and get back at around 7.45 p.m. It was a long day. On top of that there was a lot of international travel.

What I got out of work was just doing a damn good job, and knowing that at the end of the day, *I've done a damn good job.*

That mindset has changed. People don't have the same view, the view that *to progress I have to deliver day in day out.*

The mindset now is: *I've come here to develop my career and I expect that to happen and for you to help me.*

They don't ask themselves, *Am I really delivering?* And so the routes of progression have become so different. I started as a salesman, became an area manager, a regional manager, a national account manager. Now, you see on LinkedIn the number of people changing companies each month.

– What changed over the course of your career?

The individual has had to become so much more self-sufficient at work. And this is driven by technology. When I first started in work, you'd have secretaries and administrators and all these people who picked up jobs for you.

This allowed you to do what you needed to do. If you were a customer manager, you'd be spending time with customers rather than preparing sales presentations.

Now, putting the presentation together is down to the individual. You have a bit more control, but it makes you poor at planning. When you were relying on someone else, you had to fit it in with their diary. Now, you do it the night before, and it's not quite the same quality, and not quite the same amount of thought has gone into it.

There came a point when I was getting on fifty. I had become expensive to employ. There was a restructuring, and within these restructurings you always see the older people falling out of the company. That was me.

I ended up with a really good redundancy package.

I walked straight into another job on the same money doing consulting work.

We had some fantastic years growing the business. Then Covid struck. All the face-to-face delivery stopped, companies withdrew consulting spend. It was a tough period. Even when we started to recover, you could no longer go out and train people face-to-face in the same way.

I had ten years of experience facilitating training. I could do it standing on my head. Then suddenly you're stuck behind a screen . . .

I'd had a retirement plan for a little while. Initially, it was to retire at fifty-six, but a divorce and a remarriage messed that up completely.

Part of the decision to retire was knowing that we weren't going to return to that world of face-to-face contact and travel. Do I want to be stuck in this study for three or four days a week, three or four days in front of a screen?

I didn't need to do that, so I decided that I'd just retire.

The mortgage was paid off last year. The children have virtually left home, we've just got one at home. There are no real commitments. I've managed to accumulate enough wealth to be reasonably comfortable. The money is sat there.

We've got a net wealth of about a million-and-a-half, and if the worst comes to the worst, we'll sell the house. The financial advisers are saying, '*Look, draw your money down. It's there to be spent on doing what you want to do. Don't just sit and look at it.*'

You can get a bit obsessed with the number.

Since Covid a lot of the ritual of retirement has gone. We'd spent so much time working at home that retirement wasn't dramatically different from work.

It would have been more of a shock had I been commuting for years and years and then suddenly you commute in on a Friday and don't on the Monday.

The most pressured part of retirement was that I had applied for a golf club membership and there was a waiting list. I desperately wanted to make sure that I got the membership.

I was chasing them and chasing them.

I kept saying, '*What's going on here?*'

After all that, I picked up my membership the day of my retirement.

The plan for retirement was to spend more time playing golf. I wanted to take it seriously.

Before I left the consulting job, we were talking about our objectives for the year. I had short-term plans about handover, but the other goal was to get my handicap down by four shots.

I now play golf three or four times a week. I've not missed work one bit.

There's a camaraderie in golf. I've spent some time discovering who my golfing partners are as people, their jobs and lives. We'll talk about politics (we all think a bit alike), but ultimately 60 per cent of the conversation will be about golf. It's incredibly competitive. When you first start playing with these guys, you realize on the quiet that there's an edge to it all.

One of the guys who plays golf sold his business at forty-five and always he said he was going to buy another business. He never did and he's been retired since he was forty-five, happy as can be.

It's not like he's got a stack of things going on in his life. He plays golf, a lot of golf, talks golf, watches golf, plays golf. But outside of that, he doesn't do a massive amount.

I met a guy on the chipping green a few weeks ago who had recently resigned from his job. He had decided he was going to become a professional golfer, hitting balls every day of the week. And he's playing off a four handicap.

I get the sentiment. It's about self-improvement. What can I do to make myself better?

– *Are there moments when you have time to reflect?*

Yeah, I do. Sometimes I think, do you know what I'm just going to watch the cricket for a couple of hours. And I'll put time aside to do that.

When my wife retires, things will change again. At the moment, I do what I want to do.

She does play golf, but she doesn't quite get women's golf and doesn't want to be part of a women's golf society. She'd just as rather play with men. But there are men who think that think that playing golf with women is a pain. So I think this will be a bit of a challenge, and we'll have to work our way through that.

My wife and I need to sit down and go, '*Okay, what do we want to do in retirement? Where do we want to go? Let's put a few goals in place.*'

It's almost going back to that work mindset. Even if it's just: *replace the fence in the garden.* It's still using the structure, the thinking and the mindset of work, but applying it differently, not to commercial targets, but to less important goals. '*Okay, I've got my handicap down to fourteen, twelve is the next goal.*'

It's a weird life stage. Really, you've got no pressure to achieve anything, or to be ambitious about anything. You've got no stresses and pressures. A period of contentment.

Though grandchildren will come along and that will change things again.

Musician

(50s)

I'm not working. I haven't really worked for a long time. I play jazz music – jazz piano, jazz guitar. I've been doing intense practice routines every day for over ten years. My intention is to be a full-time professional jazz musician.

Before the lockdown, I had various bookings at different places, open mics. And now they've just started to come back and I'm taking every opportunity.

Years ago, I qualified as a barrister in the nineties. I did that for a bit. Once you're qualified as a barrister, you are a barrister, you're just called a *'non-practising barrister'*. It's an official term. I read it in a book.

I've got a different lifestyle to everybody else, and it's emerged like that.

I've been living in this town for years. And ever since, it's been music practice *and* getting to know a lot of people in town. That's my lifestyle, like that. It's not a quantified work in as much as you get a living wage for doing something. It's work on a different angle.

I stick to a strict routine. In the morning, I get up and do everything you have to do, breakfast and all that. Then I do two hours of music practice. Then I have an early lunch. Then I come out to the cafe in the afternoon. And then I do another four hours of practice. It's a strict, timetabled thing.

I come alive when I'm playing. I'm performing – like how I'm talking now – in front of people. That's why I chose to be a barrister.

I did criminal law. Did it for a couple of years. And I love the concept of getting on your feet, talking in front of people. It just gives me energy. So it's the same with the music. It gives me energy.

If I can make a living doing that and travel around to play music – that's my ambition, to travel around the world – that'd be the ideal, most wonderful thing, you know?

I do the open mics and you meet a lot of people at the open mics. I met one man last night for the first time. He told me he used to be a session guitarist. He went to music college for jazz, funk, guitar and things like that. In his twenties, he went around the whole world as a session musician. He said he was doing up to two-hundred-and-eighty days a year touring. He said that it got a bit much. But to me that'd be fantastic. I would love to be in hotels and be there for a reason.

There's a phrase, '*If you do something you love, you never have to work again.*'

It's true, isn't it? If I could play music professionally and sustain an income from it, then that . . . that will be just the ideal situation. Every day it would be a joy to do it.

Jazz to me is a wonderful subject because it deals in musical harmony. It's a fantastically mathematical subject is music. The symmetry of the mathematics is beautiful, especially in jazz harmony. You take notes or chords, and you alter them and it's all got a mathematics to it.

And I believe I've come up with my own style after studying for a long time and listening to a lot of music. To get recognition for that would be a wonderful thing to happen.

I'm very driven because I feel now is the time – the age I'm at – to really go for it.

And success for me would be to get my music to the highest standard possible, and then let it unfold. Music unfolds and life as well . . . life as well.

Like I'm sitting here now, and this interview has happened today. And I don't know what's going to happen tomorrow.

Conclusion: one lesson on bureaucracy and four brief lessons on happiness

Earl Wiener, 'Law 29: Whenever you solve a problem you usually create one. You can only hope that the one you created is less critical than the one you eliminated.'[14]

Earl Wiener began his career as an air force pilot. He ended it as a professor of management science at the University of Miami. Wiener gave over much of his academic life to the study of pilots and their role in aviation safety. His research took him back into the cockpit. He would sit behind pilots as they flew, watching and taking notes. He was particularly interested in the relationship between the pilot and the aircraft's computers. For Wiener, this *human–machine system*, as he called it, was precarious. A system to be kept in careful balance. Rely too much on the pilot's judgement and you would invite human error. Rely too much on the machine, on the powerful autopilots, and

14 'Wiener's Laws', *Aviation Week*, 28 July 2013. Accessed 24 June 2024, https://aviationweek.com/wieners-laws.With thanks to Tim Harford for drawing Wiener's laws to my attention: Harford, Tim 'When your smartphone tries to be too smart', Financial Times, 3 May 2024. Accessed 24 June 2024, https://www.ft.com/content/178ab808–21ff-4ac2-a81f-f831326c22d4.

you would create machine-reliant pilots, less able to fly without assistance should the panicked need arise.

After years of pilot-watching, Wiener came up with several 'laws' of aviation safety. The 29th law – *whenever you solve a problem you usually create one* – is a law of unintended consequences. It applies to pilots who become too reliant on magic computer systems. It also applies beyond the cockpit to almost every other form of work. If there is any lesson hiding in this book, it is Wiener's: the sharpest problems in today's workplaces are created by yesterday's solutions.

To see Wiener's law in action, look at the childminder, the teacher, the midwife, the construction site manager, the accountant, and the many others who spoke with some despair about the growing amount of administrative work involved in their jobs.

I've had a few people in recent months ask me questions about being a registered childminder. One was a slightly older lady that asked me about how to get registered. I says to her, *'I don't mean this awful, but if I was starting out I wouldn't enter the industry, simply because of the paperwork'.*

Every time you mark a bunch of papers, you input data, *data data data*.

We need complete contemporaneous documentation. As things happen, we need to write them down. It's really time-consuming. There's a saying, *If you don't write it down, you might as well not have done it.'* Even things like massaging someone's back. You write down, *'Massage given with consent. Patient reports good relief from pain'.*

I've got sixteen-hundred unread emails in my inbox . . . They're a massive, massive problem. You can't have a conversation with a guy on site without recording it in an email.

It's checklists like you wouldn't believe. That's what kills you.

Each of these administrative tasks enters the world as a solution to a problem, born with the best of intentions. A hospital asks its midwives to make a note of every massage they give because the hospital trust is worried about being sued; thorough notes will help its defence.

It is the same with construction companies. Afraid of litigation and blame, main contractors ask site managers to make a careful record of everything that happens on site, and of every conversation with subcontractors – all the promises made, and excuses given.

Headteachers, too, ask their staff to keep thorough records – lesson plans, seating plans, marking data. For them, the concern is not so much litigation as a bad Ofsted report, published online for the world to see and pass judgement on.

When organizations – both public and private – worry about things going wrong, their first impulse is to make people write things down. The more thorough the record keeping, the better they can ward off the things that scare them. Risks appear to be avoided. Problems appear to be nipped in the bud. But Wiener's law holds: *whenever you solve a problem, you usually create one.*

The note-taking takes the midwife away from the woman in front of her. It is as if the paperwork is another patient, making constant demands on her time and attention. '*It's non-stop. I try not to make it a barrier between me and the woman*'.

The construction site manager, meanwhile, suffers by having to spend every spare hour bailing out his inbox. '*It's like an addiction. Sometimes I'll be there at 10 p.m. replying to emails, because they come in at such a rate. The wife goes mad*'. His peers are sunk by the workload: '*I've seen so many people that get swallowed up by it. You see it in people's faces, they're gone*'.

Teachers say similar things. Good teachers do everything they can to teach according to best practice. They write careful lesson plans tailored to every ability. But they don't have the time to meet these standards. They work longer and longer hours, until they burn out and leave the profession. What was it that the soldier who became a primary school teacher said? *'It was far less stressful in Afghanistan.'*

There is an irony to all this. Organizations ask their staff to keep more records because they are worried about the risk of public and expensive failures, such as being sued or subject to a bad Ofsted report. In turn, the record-keeping takes staff away from their actual work and makes them so miserable that they begin to leave. And what happens? The failures that each organization sought to avoid become more likely: the most conscientious teachers leave and the standard of teaching falls; the midwives have less time to spend with each patient and make mistakes; the site manager spends more time responding to emails than managing the construction crew, making litigation-worthy delays more likely. To put Wiener's law another way: the medicine may well cure the disease but it often kills the patient.

Once you start to look for it, you see Wiener's 29th law everywhere.

Take email, Slack, and Teams. These technologies have made work faster, but they have also made chatting about work faster, allowing us to fit much more chatting about work into the working day, as this IT director found:

A lot of my time is spent responding to messages in Microsoft Teams, in Outlook, in Jira, in Salesforce, in SAP concur, and most of the rest of the time is spent in meetings . . . We seem to spend an inordinate amount of time discussing how we're going to do things and then re-discussing, re-discussing, and re-discussing, before we say, 'Okay, we're going to do that.'

The time saved by the technology is swallowed up by the change it causes in our behaviour. You see this time-swallowing effect in other technologies, too:

In the modern world of advertising, data is tearing creativity apart . . . what's happening a lot of the time is that simple things are being said in very difficult ways through jargon and data . . . The outcome of some piece of research that's done for the brief will be: people are on their phones more. I could have told you that! Just look around. But we're too busy looking down at the data to look up.

If you were to compare today with six years' ago, in terms of both the amount of documents and the length of documents that are submitted in support of planning applications, you'd find that people are submitting so much more today.

There's a lot of paperwork. Things you did routinely but never wrote down now take five pages on a computer. Things that were done because it made common sense you now have to write a ten-page report on.

Each describe, at least implicitly, a technological change. Ad agencies are bringing in data analysts to make use of new data collection and processing software. The people who advise on planning applications – lawyers, traffic-management experts – are writing documents on computers. Hospitals are putting computers on the wards.

In theory, each of these changes should speed up and improve the work that has to be done. Nurses can file and access patient notes more quickly. Planning advisers can work on applications with all of the benefits of modern productivity software – collaborating on documents, copying over past work, inputting new data into existing models, sharing files instantly, and so on. And ad agencies have more information open to them when making decisions.

But the world of theory is not the world of practice. Practice is Wiener's world, stalked by unintended consequences and whack-a-mole problems. And in practice, these technological changes have little time-saving effect because, once again, human behaviour adjusts to the new technical realities. In this case, the more that technology allows us to process and store information, the more information that we say we need in order to make decisions and to act.

Ad agencies won't commit to an idea unless it is supported by hours and hours of data analysis and testing. In the planning world, long applications become the new normal, applications with hundreds of pages of supporting documents, with impenetrable expert reports that claim to model every aspect of reality. And in hospital wards, management come to expect more detailed notes.

In this way, the time freed up by new technology exists only for a brief moment – a moment when our jobs feel easier – before the saved time is once again swallowed up by an inevitable rise in expectations. Perhaps the work involved in meeting these raised expectations is worth it. Perhaps the adverts are more persuasive, the planning decisions fairer, or the hospital systems more secure. But looking at Britain's sclerotic productivity and state capacity, that is certainly not always the case.

What should we make of the record-keeping of the anxious organization and the illusory time-saving promises of technology? The lesson seems to be that we should never under-estimate humanity's ability to generate plausible-sounding tasks for itself.

In the final analysis, these tasks are often unrelated to the effective provision of goods and services. But the more that our work has become about solving the abstract problems of the post-industrial services economy, the harder it has become to judge its usefulness. The worker building kitchen units can tell when he is finished (*'I have a big pile of metal on the floor and by the end of the day I've built a big frame and put sockets on it'*). But there is no comparable standard for questions like, *'Are we sufficiently protected from litigation risk?'* or *'Is this pitch deck good enough?'* or *'How can we better measure employee productivity?'* When it comes to answering those questions, so long as the organization can afford it, there will always be more work to be done, more information to be collected, more tasks to be conjured out of thin air.

One lesson about bureaucracy and paperwork is more than enough. It's like standing behind a two-stroke engine. Too much of it and your head starts to fog up. We read books about work to learn how to become happier and more fulfilled, to imagine how our careers and lives might be different. What do the interviewees I spoke to say about that? Let's end with four brief lessons on work and happiness – as told to me by sixty-eight British workers.

Lesson one: Care, but do not care too much

Learning how to care less is an important skill. We are rarely taught it. It doesn't come up much in our appraisals or on LinkedIn. Instead, it is something learned in moments of crisis, a response to situations that seem impossible.

In the medical professions, for example, staff withhold something to stop themselves from feeling the weight of other people's sadness:

> . . . you also have to have a wall. You learn how to build that wall. You learn how – not to build a wall exactly – but how to leave things behind, or else you'd be drowned.

Or consider the teacher and the management consultant who both decided to change their relationship with work rather than leave their jobs:

> Before, I was constantly working, working, working . . . I began to teach in a way that would mean I didn't have to be sat at home marking books the entire time.

> Before, I felt like a corporate slave, tied to my desk 9 a.m. 'til 6 p.m., even if there was no work . . . Now, I think, well, no one is observing my every move, and they're still satisfied with what I'm doing.

Maybe I'll work 7 a.m. until 11 a.m. tomorrow, catch up with someone, come back at 4 p.m. and work the rest of my hours.

In this way, caring less sometimes allows you to care for longer.

Lesson two: Careers are driven by crisis

Among the interviewees, there were vanishingly few examples of someone changing careers on the back of a thought-out plan. Instead, once we begin in a particular direction, though we might move jobs several times, we are unlikely to change careers without being urged on by a chance event of some kind.

> When I was a carer, I ended up having a breakdown and having six months off work . . . My doctor told me that when I went back to work, I should go back and do something that I love. I thought, *well if I did cleaning, and worked for myself then I can pick and choose when I want to work.*

> My dream job would have been to be a nurse in the RAF . . . But I had to put those plans to one side when I was twenty. I had a bad accident at work. I was working in a residential care home and one of the residents hit me on the back with a walking stick and knocked me down.

This means that our most significant career decisions are made at moments of fear and uncertainty; when we are eighteen or twenty-one, picking a career on a whim, applying for the same jobs as our parents or the people we play football with; or when we are older but just as scared, trying to figure out how to make work fit with the fact that a family member needs more care. Given such circumstances, we should not judge ourselves too harshly for the decisions that we make.

It also means that we are less in control of our lives and careers than we imagine. We can fight that reality, and blame ourselves for not having done more to find a better career, or we can accept the situation that we find ourselves in. The interviewees who looked at their life with a measure of acceptance were some of the happiest people I spoke to, like this joiner:

[I] don't want a fleet of ten vans. I don't want to be on a million pounds a year. I don't want to be any higher than I am. I'm happy. Everything's balanced nicely, work, social life, family, gym, and still time for other things. I know that what balances can easily topple over, but if that happens, I'll deal with it . . . Whatever is meant to happen is meant to happen. I try to let life run its course. I try not to mess around with it too much.

Lesson three: Seek out the good task

A job is a collection of tasks that we spend all day doing. That statement is not only obvious, it is also so trite that we dismiss it out of hand. Instead, when we think about what a good job looks like, too often we focus on everything but the tasks involved: we think about salary, working hours, qualifications, subject matter, what the people are like, and the status that the job carries in society. Those all matter, often deeply, but they do not matter as much as the tasks the job requires. It is the difference in those tasks that leaves the cleaner and the delivery rider happier than the derivatives trader ('*I'm totally checked-out to be honest*').

Picking through the interviews, an idea emerges: a good task is one with a clear and immediate result.

> I get a real sense of fulfilment when I look back at a room I've cleaned. I think, *oh yeah, lovely.*

> Being a software engineer is an honest job in some ways. You write code and the code either works or doesn't work. There's no bullshit.

By the same token, if the outcome of a task is slow to come or uncertain, then that task can start to feel thankless, as the management consultant found:

> I felt like my work wasn't being seen. I was doing all this work for the client, and I'd just deliver it. I don't know if they were happy

or not, because there was no bridge between us and them.

The good task is also one that you aren't forced to rush:

By 8 a.m. you have to have ten patients up and dressed. That means you have to wake a ninety-year-old lady at 5.30 a.m., whether she likes it or not.

And it must involve some element of skill. More particularly, the good task is the sort of task where, if someone were to watch you to do it, they might say afterwards, 'That was good work.' Of course, it can only be *good work* if someone else might have done it less well – if, in other words, there is skill at play. It was the expression of skill in his work that the paramedic found so rewarding:

– *What does it feel like when a job has gone well?*

It's like when you see a sports team and they're not obviously communicating with each other, but things are happening without instruction. Its effortless. They're operating on a different plane.

I'm going to cannulate. I reach for a drug. It's handed to me before I even ask.

And the absence of skill that made e-commerce warehouse work a '*mentally excruciating exercise*':

The stock is brought to you on these towers.

You climb to the top of a small ladder.

You take the item from the tower.

You scan the item and place it on a shelf behind you.

You press the screen to confirm that you've put the item on the shelf.

That's it.

The final component of a good task is trust. A good task is one that you are trusted to do. From trust come freedom and autonomy, things that matter so much that they can make even the most difficult working conditions – long hours, low pay, exhaustion – bearable. This is what the delivery rider, himself working long tiring hours for low pay, found:

> . . . if you're on the bike and you're doing your orders quickly, you don't have too much pressure from the company.
>
> You feel a freedom on the bike.
>
> You are not strapped to a desk.
>
> That's the best thing.

We come to know the importance of things by their loss. The Job Centre work coach had his autonomy taken away. He once ran sessions for jobseekers as he saw fit. Years later, his interactions with jobseekers had been reduced to ten-minute appointments ('*It takes ten minutes to copy their travel tickets, to fill in the reimbursement paperwork, and to set up a payment on the system*'). The loss of freedom made him miserable.

> In the years gone by, when I was a job leader, I felt like I was making a difference to people's lives. Going back to the days of the New Deal, I was left to get on with it. '*Here's the guidance, read it, get on with it.*' Now, I feel like a box ticker.

Lesson four: Pride is an everyday kind of thing

Taking pride in our work is one of those abstractions that we know to be important but which we struggle to define, like love or economic growth. There's an element of imagination to it. The interviewees who were most proud of their work were the ones who performed an act of mental substitution: in their mind, they replaced their real client either for someone they loved – most often, their family – or for themselves.

Even if the car you're working on is a shithole, that could be someone's mum in there. Think about it like that.

I was drawn to something where my son could say, 'My dad does outdoor education and he's involved with all these great things for kids.'

I don't want people to feel like how I've been treated in the past. I love the purity of being kind and respectful to one another. If I could pass that on to someone else, then I've done my job as a human being.

From this imagined substitution, the benefits multiply. Employees give their work purpose; they are not just working for the company or the client, they are creating something so good that they'd be happy to use it and they'd be happy for their family to use it, too. And this greater sense of purpose leads to better work. A car panel repaired with more care and less filler. A drunken punter treated with more respect. That better work then carries a higher satisfaction of its own: *he looked at the work and the work looked good.*

There are parts of the economy that are less well suited to the imaginative act inherent in this form of pride. It is easy for a builder to build an extension for a client as if he were building it for himself, but other construction workers might struggle to do the same when building a warehouse. It is easy for an immigration lawyer to work as hard for their client as they would for a relative, but it is less easy for a corporate lawyer restructuring a company's debt to do the same. The greater the abstraction in one's work – the further away it is from your life or your family's lives – the more difficult it is to feel proud in this way.

There's a certain smallness and domesticity to this kind of pride. In fact, there's a certain smallness and a domesticity to be found in all four of the lessons given here. The portrait they give of a happy and meaningful working life is one of well-adjusted ordinariness; each of us in our small corner, buffeted by events outside of our control, caring about work (but not too much), and getting on with satisfying tasks for eight hours a day – no worlds to win, no universes to master. It's an approach to thinking about work that takes Philip Larkin's 'Born Yesterday' as career advice:

> In fact, may you be dull –
> If that is what a skilled,
> Vigilant, flexible,
> Unemphasized, enthralled
> Catching of happiness is called.[15]

This is a hopeful idea. If a mundane and small working life is often a happy one, then meaningful work is within reach of most of us. It

15 Philip Larkin, 'Born Yesterday', *The Less Deceived* (East Yorkshire: Marvell Press, 1955).

isn't something reserved exclusively for the winners of society's meritocratic games. Instead, it is far more common than that: all you need is satisfying tasks (clear in outcome, un-rushed, and marked by skill and autonomy), nice people, enough money to get by, and then almost any job – whatever its perceived status – can be enjoyable and rewarding. In this way, many of the interviewees found happiness at work in all sorts of surprising places. Consider, for example, the soldier who left the army and began working in a fast-food restaurant:

> I was really embarrassed, because it's one of the threats they use in the army, 'You can leave if you want, but you're going to end up flipping burgers', like it was the worst thing in the world . . . When I was working there, I used to pull my hat down over my head hoping nobody I knew would come in and see me. It was horrible for about a month but then I realized that I enjoyed it, that I had some transferrable skills, and that I was treated better by the fast-food chain than I was by the army.

We shouldn't forget, however, that the hopeful and the naive often walk hand in hand. And when we idealize the ordinary in our working lives, we risk ignoring the world as it is; we close our eyes to the economic realities that demand working lives that are far from small and ordinary.

Consider the vast infrastructure that needs to be built in the coming decades. Railways, sewers, new systems for generating and distributing power. These projects require people to work on a grand scale; it requires, for example, the site manager that I interviewed, who turned away from a career in domestic construction, and who now exhausts himself trying to tame the '*massive, complex machine*' of the commercial construction site.

There is infrastructure to be built and there are also taxes to be paid. Over half of government receipts come from national insurance contributions and income tax. Over 60 per cent of income tax is paid by the top 10 per cent of earners. Our national finances are built upon the taxation of a chronically ambitious minority: the lawyers and bankers who think nothing of copying the eighty-hour weeks of their peers in New York (as the lawyer said, '*The last email is typically sent at 2.30 a.m.*') or the entrepreneurs who are consumed by the companies they create. You cannot ask these people to holster their ambitions in order to pursue a career of ordinary contentment: to do so would be an act of national fiscal irresponsibility.

At the other end of the economy, among those whose lives are precarious, holding out the '*enthralled catching of happiness*' as an ideal of working life is similarly naive. Consider the call centre worker stuck in her job ('*I feel like I'm already bad at this job, so when I look at other jobs from time to time, I talk myself out of applying*'). Consider the man who worked as a carer during the day and as a delivery rider at night ('*Feeling tired is the worst thing about the job*'). Both are trapped by circumstance. For them, well-adjusted contentment is out of reach. Long hours, difficult work, and worries about money sour whatever satisfaction work might have carried in their lives.

For many of us, then, reality demands that the ordinary working life gives way to the extraordinary. This gets us to the problem that runs through so many of the preceding interviews: the things that tend to make us happy at work – the pride, the lack of abstraction, the immediate and satisfying tasks, the autonomy, the smallness ('*I don't want to be on a million pounds a year. I don't want to be any higher than I am*') – seem to cower before the demands of the modern economy, with its tendency towards complexity and speed and scale.

It's a dilemma with no ready answer. A problem of the Earl Wiener type. What would he have said if he were still alive? He would, I imagine, have referred us to another of his laws. This time to the 25th law. It is as good an answer as any:

Law 25: Some problems have no solution. If you encounter one of these, you can always convene a committee . . .

Acknowledgements

You will, of course, have noticed that most of the words in this book are not my own. They are the words of dozens of open-minded strangers, people who were kind enough to sit down with me, often for several hours, to share the story of their working lives. I am deeply grateful to them for that act of generosity. It is a generosity that is not to be underestimated; after all, I'm not sure how I would have responded to someone approaching me in the street (or, indeed, online) to ask for two hours of my time to talk about work. In agreeing to speak to me, these people trusted me with stories about their lives. I can only hope that I have repaid that trust by putting their spoken words down onto the page with art and clarity.

I would also like to extend my apologies and gratitude to the thirty or so people whom I interviewed but whose stories do not appear in the book. Leaving these interviews out was difficult. They were as insightful and enjoyable to read as any. However, the need to shorten the book won the day.

I am grateful to my agent, James Gill, and to his assistant, Amber Garvey, for their help. In 2022, I sent Jim a speculative email containing the proposal for *Is This Working?*. The email mentioned Studs Terkel. What a stroke of luck it was that Jim not only opened this email, but that he was also a fan of Studs. Jim understood immediately what I was trying to do with this book and ever since has been a constant source of counsel and guidance.

I am fortunate to be published by Picador. I am indebted to the team there: to Laila Kazzuz, John Sugar, Andy Cook, Rosie Shackles, and in particular to my editor, George Morley. I am grateful, first, for the fact that George and the team took a chance on *Is This Working?*, and, second, for everything that they have done since agreeing to publish the book. I am especially grateful to George and Rosie for their hard work, patience, and always-perceptive editing,

A heartfelt thank you to everyone who has helped with this book over the past few years: thank you to Jonny for telling me how the publishing industry works; thank you to Bea, who came up with the title in Brockwell Park; thank you to Alice and Jeremy for their constant support of our young family (and for lending me a nook in which to work); thank you to my parents, John and Rebecca, for all their love and practical help (from fielding a grandchild to reading drafts), for handing down their precious interests in history and literature to all of us Colenutt children, and for being so phlegmatic when I said that I was running away from a career at the Bar to travel around the country interviewing people.

Finally, to my wife, Annie, and to my daughter, Iris, my love and gratitude is indescribable. I'm glad that we exist.